Maintain and Repair Your Notebook, Palmtop, or Pen Computer

Maintain and Repair Your Notebook, Palmtop, or Pen Computer

Stephen J. Bigelow

Windcrest®/McGraw-Hill

New York San Francisco Washington, D.C. Auckland Bogotá
Caracas Lisbon London Madrid Mexico City Milan
Montreal New Delhi San Juan Singapore
Sydney Tokyo Toronto

FIRST EDITION
FIRST PRINTING

© 1994 by **TAB Books**.
Published by Windcrest Books, an imprint of McGraw-Hill, Inc.
The name "Windcrest" is a registered trademark of McGraw-Hill, Inc.

Library of Congress Cataloging-in-Publication Data
Bigelow, Stephen J.
   Maintain and repair your notebook, palmtop or pen computer / by
Stephen Bigelow.
     p. cm.
   Includes index.
   ISBN 0-8306-4454-7   ISBN 0-8306-44555-5 (pbk.)
   1. Microcomputers—Maintenance and repair. 2. Macintosh PowerBook
notebook computers—Maintenance and repair. 3. Pen-based computers-
-Maintenance and repair. 4. HP95LX (Computer)—Maintenance and
repair. I. Title.
TK7887.B54   1993   93-28420
621.39'16—dc20   CIP

Acquisitions editor: Roland S. Phelps
Editorial team: Alan H. Danis, Editor
              Susan Wahlman, Managing Editor
              Joanne M. Slike, Executive Editor
              Joann Woy, Indexer
Production team: Katherine G. Brown, Director
                Rhonda E. Baker, Coding
                Jana L. Fisher, Coding
                Lisa M. Mellott, Coding
                Brenda M. Plasterer, Coding
                Tina M. Sourbier, Coding
                Rose McFarland, Layout
                Linda L. King, Proofreading
                N. Nadine McFarland, Quality Control
Design team: Jaclyn J. Boone, Designer
            Brian Allison, Associate Designer
Cover design: Holberg Design, York, Pa.
Computer photograph: ©Jim Cornfield/Westlight   WU1
Marble photograph:© M. Angelo/Westlight   4428

This book is dedicated to my wonderful wife, Kathleen. Without her loving encouragement and support, this book would still have been possible, but not nearly worth the effort.

Dedication

Contents

Acknowledgments

It is simply impossible to prepare a state-of-the-art troubleshooting-and-repair text such as this one without the encouragement, cooperation, and support of a great many talented and generous individuals. I would like to thank the following individuals and organizations for their gracious contributions to this book.

Ms. Kristi Bolin, Seagate Technology, Inc.

Ms. Randi Braunwalder, Hewlett-Packard Co. (Boise Division)

Ms. Mindy Chanaud, Temerlin McClain (for Texas Instruments)

Ms. Terri DiMarco, J2 Marketing Services (for Seiko Instruments)

Mr. Gregg Elmore, B+K Precision (a division of Maxtec International)

Mr. William J. Goffi, Maxell Corp.

Ms. Sharon Gregory, SunDisk Corp.

Ms. Traci Hayes, Hill and Knowlton (for Toshiba America Information Systems, Inc.)

Ms. Jennifer B. Hennigan, AMP, Inc.

Ms. Gina M. Lugo, AST Research, Inc.

Ms. Fran McGehee, Tandy Corporation/Radio Shack

Mr. Jim Miller, MiniStor Peripherals Corp.

Mr. Tom Parrish, Integral Peripherals, Inc.

Ms. Annette M. Petagna, MicroTouch Systems, Inc.

Mr. Dino Pomponio, Panasonic

Ms. Barbara Rowland, Quantum Corp.

Ms. Amy Rupley, Logitech, Inc.

Ms. Betsy Taub, Fujitsu Microelectronics, Inc.

Mr. Chris Temple, GRiD Systems, Inc.

Mr. Ray Vincenzo, Dorf & Stanton (for Sharp Electronics)

Ms. Faith Wall, Microsoft Corp.

Ms. Darleen Walters, Hewlett-Packard Co. (Corvallis Division)

Mr. Bill Wittmann, Fujitsu Personal Systems, Inc.

Mr. Dan Zemaitis, Suncom, Inc.

Special thanks to my acquisitions editor, Roland S. Phelps; executive editor, Joanne Slike; managing editor, Susan Wahlman; and the entire staff at TAB/McGraw-Hill for their outstanding advice and limitless patience. Thank you also for the use of the Tandy 1500HD and Sharp OZ-8200 organizer that were dissected for this book.

Finally, thanks to my friends and colleagues at the Millipore Corporation, Chet, George, Dave, and Brian. Your interest and encouragement made a big difference—thanks a lot!

AMP™	AMP, Inc.
AST™	AST Research, Inc.
Fujitsu™	Fujitsu Microelectronics, Inc.
PoquetPC™ PoquetPAD™	Fujitsu Personal Systems, Inc.
PenPoint™	GO Corp.
GRiD™ GRiDPAD™ PALMPAD™	GRiD Systems Corp.
HP™ Kitty Hawk Personal Storage Module™	Hewlett-Packard Co.
Integral™	Integral Peripherals, Inc.
Intel™ 8088™ 80286™ 80386™ 80486™ x286™ x386™ x486™	Intel Corp.
IBM™ PC/AT™ PC/XT™ PS/2™	International Business Machines, Inc.
Logitech™ Trackman Portable™	Logitech, Inc.
Lotus 1-2-3™	Lotus Development Corp.
Maxell™	Maxell Corp.
Maxtor™	Maxtor Corp.
Ball Point Mouse™ MS™ MS-DOS™ Microsoft™ Windows™ Windows for Pen Computing™	Microsoft Corp.
MicroTouch® QuickPoint® TouchPen® UnMouse®	MicroTouch Systems, Inc.
MiniStor™ PORTables Series™	MiniStor Peripherals Corp.
Tri-State™	National Semiconductor Corp.
ProDrive™ Quantum™	Quantum Corp.
Seagate™	Seagate Technology, Inc.

Seiko™	Seiko Instruments
Suncom™ Crystal Mouse™ ErgoStick™ ICONtroller™	Suncom, Inc.
SunDisk™ SDP™	SunDisk Corp.
Tandy™	Tandy Corp.
Texas Instruments™ TI™ TravelMate™	Texas Instruments, Inc.
Toshiba™ Satellite™	Toshiba America Information Systems, Inc.

Preface

Stop for a moment and consider your notebook, laptop, palmtop, or pen computer. Is it working properly right now? Is the display crisp and clear? Is its floppy drive, hard drive, or memory card working reliably? Is the keyboard or mouse as responsive as you would like it to be?

The chances are that your answer to such questions is "yes." My experience has been that most small computers (notebooks, palmtops, and pen computers) perform well through years of normal use regardless of their particular technologies or options. Like most other machines, however, your small computer is going to have problems sooner or later. When your system finally does need service, will you know what to do or what to look for? You can save a great deal of time and money by tackling your own repairs.

If the word *troubleshooting* sends a chill down your spine, or the thought of disassembling that small computer on your workbench makes your head spin, don't panic! This book carefully explains how notebooks, palmtops, and pen computers work and what their components are. You see each major subassembly in detail along with its major problems and solutions. You even learn a series of preventive maintenance procedures that can keep your system running longer.

Small-computer repair is not as difficult as you might think. After you read this book and familiarize yourself with your particular computer, just roll up your sleeves, open your toolbox, and keep this book handy for quick reference. It won't be long before you can maintain and repair your own notebook, palmtop, or pen computer.

Introduction

Troubleshooting has always been a bizarre pursuit—an activity that falls somewhere between art and science, often requiring a healthy mixture of both. I've done a lot of computer troubleshooting, and the advice I give to novice troubleshooters is always the same: troubleshooting is a three-legged stool. That is, it requires three important elements to achieve a successful repair: (1) the right tools (and test equipment) for the job; (2) the right replacement parts; and (3) the right technical information. If any of these three elements are weak or missing, your repair will probably be hindered—maybe even impossible.

Unfortunately, it's not always easy to establish each of these three legs. After all, tools and test equipment might be expensive (especially when compared to the price of the unit you're going to fix), specialized parts might sometimes be difficult to obtain, and information may be scarce or nonexistent.

That's why I prepared this book. With the startling advances in notebook computer systems and the rapid acceptance of palmtops and pen computers, it seems only natural to provide a book for small-computer users and electronics enthusiasts that can help you make better repairs in less time. The book shows you what tools and equipment you need, how to use them, and where to go for many replacement parts. It provides not only information about how and why your small computer works, but also presents a comprehensive set of troubleshooting techniques that you can put to work right away. This book is intended to maximize your troubleshooting success and to help you make the most of your resources. If you need more comprehensive technical information and procedures, refer to my book *Troubleshooting and Repairing Notebook, Palmtop, and Pen Computers: A Technician's Guide* (Windcrest #4427).

I am interested in your success! I've made every effort to ensure a thorough and thoughtful guide. Please feel free to share your personal troubleshooting experiences or test equipment techniques with me, send me questions about parts and vendors, and let me know what you want to see in future editions. You can contact me by mail at:

Stephen J. Bigelow
Dynamic Learning Systems
P.O. Box 805
Marlboro, MA 01752

or you can fax me at (508) 366-9487.

If you decide to send a fax, be sure to include your full name, address, and telephone number where you can be reached or faxed. Although I can't provide full-time telephone support, I'll answer every message by mail or fax.

Hope to hear from you!

1 Introduction to small computers

If you've followed the evolution of personal computers at all, you witnessed the incredible advances in desktop computer capabilities. Processing speed and performance, memory, mass-storage systems, graphics, and computer communications all have progressed radically.

In the past few years, however, the empire of desktop computers has been invaded by a powerful new generation of portable computer systems. Laptop and notebook computers now commonly offer the same capabilities and processing power of the latest desktop systems (FIG. 1-1). The ongoing wave of pocket-sized (or *palmtop*) and pen-based computers provide performance that is at least equivalent to the IBM XT of the early 1980s—but in light, convenient, hand-held packages.

This aggressive new generation of personal computers has been phenomenally successful because it allows you to do something rarely possible (or practical) with desktop systems—bring computing power "on-the-road." Such mobility is accomplished by using advanced integrated circuits (ICs) that combine many complex functions on the same device. Highly efficient liquid crystal displays (LCDs), low-power mass-storage systems, and innovative new input devices operate for many hours on batteries. The result is light weight, high reliability, and long operating life. Given the incredibly competitive nature of the

1-1
Two Tandy notebook computers.

Tandy Corp./Radio Shack

personal computer industry, prices have quickly fallen into a range affordable to many users.

Whether you are a desktop computer veteran or an absolute computer novice, this book is designed to provide the information you need to understand the new world of laptops, notebooks, palmtops, and pen computers. You will also learn the tools and techniques that you need to maintain these systems.

Before you get started, you should know that this book groups laptops, notebooks, palmtops, and pen computers under the general category of *small computer*. Whenever you see the term *small computer*, it could be referring to any notebook, palmtop, or pen system.

Comparing the small computers

Each class of small computer enjoys its own particular set of physical and performance attributes. Before you jump into the technical aspects of small computers, you might want to understand a bit about each computer class and the way in which it differs from the others.

Notebook systems

Laptop and notebook computers are the largest and most powerful of the small computers (FIG. 1-2). They are physically larger, with dimensions typically 27.94 cm (11") wide, 21.59 cm (8.5") deep, and 5.08 cm (2") high. They use a classic clamshell design that allows the display panel to be swung open from the computer body. These computers were dubbed *notebooks* because early designers wanted to give users a common, nonthreatening frame of reference that users could readily identify. After all, how comfortable would you be going out to buy a "clamshell" computer?

Tandy Corp./Radio Shack

1-2
A Tandy 3800HD computer.

Some older notebooks used plasma displays to provide bright, sharp images; however, plasma technology requires an unusually large amount of power to operate properly—too much power for batteries. Plasma displays are still in use today, but almost all small computers have an LCD option or version. LCDs require only a few watts of power to operate and are manufactured in color or black-and-white versions.

Notebook displays supply reasonably wide viewing areas with diagonal screen sizes from 20.32 cm (8") to 25.40 cm (10"). Current LCD displays can achieve resolutions of 640×480 pixels (VGA) or higher—even in color.

Notebook keyboards are almost full-size, QWERTY-style devices that are identical to your desktop computer's keyboard, with the exception of the function keys, which might be half-size keys. They are usually located in a horizontal line above the other keys.

Notebook computers generally supply enough room for both magnetic hard drives and 8.89 cm (3.5") floppy drives. Floppy drives have changed very little from their original design. Regular double-density diskettes hold about 700K, and high-density diskettes hold 1.44Mb. While hard drives are considered standard equipment for notebook computers, the particular size (or storage capacity) of the hard drive is optional. Of all the developments in computer design, hard drives have undergone some of the most impressive advances—they now can pack 200Mb of information into a surprisingly small package. Hard drives of 60Mb to 80Mb are now quite inexpensive.

Instead of conventional magnetic storage media, some notebook computers use solid-state memory cards to hold programs and data. *Storage cards* are not much larger than everyday credit cards, yet their storage capacity easily exceeds that of floppy disks. Advanced storage cards provide mass-storage capabilities, some holding more than 40Mb.

Storage cards can be inserted and removed from a small computer as easily as a floppy disk, yet storage-card drives are much smaller and contain no mechanical or moving parts (except for a connector and perhaps a lever to eject the card). Storage cards are small and reliable—ideal for small computers, where simplicity, light weight, and low power consumption are important.

Notebook computers make use of the most advanced, high-performance integrated circuits available. The array of complex functions that must be performed throughout a small computer are handled by a remarkably few (but powerful) ICs—many designed exclusively for use as part of a computer processing *chip set*. Notebooks utilize the latest microprocessors, such as Intel's x386 and x486, or Advanced Micro Devices' (AMD) Am386SL. Most processors in notebook applications operate between 20 and 33 MHz.

Very little discrete (or glue) logic is found in small computers in comparison to older desktop systems. IC manufacturers have largely integrated any glue logic right into their more powerful processing components. The widespread use of logic gate arrays and customized ASICs also helped to reduce the chip count in small-computer systems. The few discrete logic ICs that are still found are primarily interface components such as high-speed bus buffers, data converters, power handling, and communication ICs.

Memory ICs, while purely logic devices, are considered in a class by themselves due to the sheer volume of memory needed to handle today's demanding software. Notebook computers can hold just as much memory as full-featured desktop systems. It is not unusual to find notebooks packed with 4Mb, 8Mb, or 16Mb of fast dynamic RAM. Like hard drives, memory is standard equipment for every computer system, but you are left to choose the right amount of memory for your application. Notebooks with 2Mb or 4Mb are common. The addition of extended memory is usually as simple as plugging in a new memory card or module.

The comprehensive use of low-power ICs, memory, and mass-storage systems, combined with innovative power conservation techniques have extended the working battery life in notebooks from 2 hours to more than 4 hours. The newest notebooks will soon approach 6 hours of operation per charge. Even the batteries are improving. Advances in nickel-cadmium (NiCd) batteries, along with the large-scale introduction of nickel-metal hydride (NiMH) batteries promise to continue extending battery life.

Of course, the size and power found in notebook-class computers does not come without a weight penalty. Notebooks are typically between 2.27 and 3.63 kg (5 and 8 lbs), with up to .68 kg (1.5 lbs) of the weight being taken up by the batteries. The flat-panel display, hard drive, and floppy drive make up large portions of the remaining weight. Notebook manufacturers are currently working to reduce weight in every possible area while still maintaining and improving features and performance.

Palmtop computers represent the smallest and lightest computing systems currently in commercial use (FIG. 1-3). Palmtops are characteristically small, with typical dimensions less than 20.32 cm (8") wide, about 10.16 cm (4") deep, and roughly 2.54 cm (1") high. Like notebooks, palmtops employ a clamshell design that allows the flat panel display to be swung open from the body of the unit. Such svelte dimensions are intended to allow palmtops to travel in shirt pockets or briefcases. Aside from their clamshell package design, however, palmtops and notebooks offer very different performance characteristics.

Palmtop systems

1-3
An HP95LX palmtop computer.

You should understand that two distinctly different design mentalities are involved in palmtop computer design. Some palmtops have originally started out as pocket organizers—the designers then just added functions and options to try to tackle more serious jobs. The result is often a very small machine with little memory (64K to 128K) using a low-performance (and often proprietary) processor and operating system that offer little or no DOS compatibility. On the positive side, most of these low-end computers do provide tools to transfer files to and from desktop or notebook systems. Such communications capabilities allow even the simplest palmtop to at least supplement a desktop or notebook system.

The other popular palmtop approach is to redesign a desktop or notebook computer in a palmtop package and incorporate as much DOS compatibility as possible right from the beginning. Such top-down designs from Hewlett-Packard, Fujitsu, and Zeos have produced palmtops with substantial memory and flexibility.

As you might expect, the incredibly small palmtop form factor (another way of saying "overall size") makes it currently impossible to incorporate all the capabilities found in other small-computer classes. One of the most noticeable simplifications is in the palmtop's flat panel display. Palmtops use relatively low-resolution graphic displays with diagonal sizes ranging from a scant 6.86 cm (2.7") up to a respectable 17.02 cm (6.7"). Without high-resolution graphics ability, palmtops can run few DOS application programs except for text-based programs like spreadsheets and word processors. Fortunately, simple LCDs consume very little power and require only simple controller ICs for proper operation.

With available space at an absolute premium, palmtops have generally abandoned floppy drives and hard drives in favor of solid-state memory and mass-storage cards. The use of solid-state storage cards also results in significant power and weight savings for palmtop systems. Many palmtops use the popular interface supported by the Personal Computer Memory Card Industry Association (PCMCIA), but a few manufacturers retain their own proprietary data storage modules. The first magnetic hard drive system to find use in palmtops is probably the Kitty Hawk hard drive manufactured by Hewlett-Packard for its HP 95LX series palmtops. The Kitty Hawk is just a little over 2.54 cm (1") wide, and at 28 g (1 oz), the drive can hold 20Mb. The Kitty Hawk draws almost no power when it is idle (not actually reading or writing). As the smallest hard drive in production today, the Kitty Hawk and its successors will undoubtedly find use in the next generation of palmtop and pen-based designs. A few palmtops provide support for external 8.89 cm (3.5") floppy drives.

It is said that too much of a good thing is not necessarily good. This is especially true for palmtop keyboards. Palmtops cram up to 92 keys in an area of only a few square centimeters. With so many keys confined to such a small area, touch typing becomes virtually impossible, even when the keyboard is arranged in standard QWERTY fashion: two-finger typing is considered the norm. Palmtop keyboards also provide a number of special function keys that seem unfamiliar if you are experienced with desktop or notebook keyboards.

Palmtops use an arrangement of highly integrated IC chip sets and ASICs to support their operations. While many organizer-based palmtops use proprietary microprocessors and chip sets, the DOS-oriented palmtops use readily available microprocessors such as the Intel 8088, its CMOS cousin the 80C88, or the NEC V20 or V30.

Memory capacity is largely dependent on the particular type of palmtop computer being used. As a general rule, organizer-based palmtops offer only limited amounts of memory; 64K is typical, but units with 128K of memory can be found. DOS-oriented palmtops offer much more base memory; usually 512K that is expandable to 1Mb or more. Substantial memory allows more sophisticated application programs to be executed.

As a result of the palmtop's relative simplicity and small size, its power requirements are usually far less demanding than notebook or pen-based systems. Extremely thin, organizer-based palmtops are run from two or three lithium coin cells similar to the type used in hand-held calculators. Larger, DOS-oriented palmtops typically demand more power, so two or three AA batteries are used. Such light battery requirements add very little weight to palmtops that weigh from .26 kg (9 oz) to .54 kg (19 oz) for the very largest models.

As of this writing, all but the largest palmtops lack the sophistication and computing power to compete with notebook or pen-based systems. For the most part, palmtops are used to supplement desktop or notebook systems by providing mobility for well-established application programs such as Lotus 1-2-3 or Microsoft Word. As palmtops continue to mature, their complexity and capabilities will almost certainly increase.

Computers have traditionally been controlled by keyboards. Users type commands and data directly on the keyboard, or press a key in response to a menu choice. Although keyboard control is a reliable and well-established type of user interface, it is not intuitive. Key locations and typing skills must be learned (and even then are highly prone to errors). Pointing devices such as mice and joysticks have become popular, but still lack the intuitive control that would be handy for many applications.

Pen-based systems

Pen computers (FIG. 1-4), sometimes called *pentops*, are intended to provide a new level of intuitive, "plain-language" control using a digitized pen input. Users can literally write or tap on predetermined touch-sensitive areas of the display to input text or commands. While the concept of pen computers has been around for years, the combination of complex writing interpretation software, powerful processing components to run the software at a reasonable speed, and reliable pen/stylus digitizers have only recently become available. The pen interface might redefine the ways in which humans and computers interact.

1-4
A GRiDPADSL pen-based computer.

GRiD Systems Corp.

Pen computers are slightly smaller than notebook computers, at a width of 22.86 cm (9"), a depth of 15.75 cm (6.2"), and roughly a height of 5.08 cm (2"). While these dimensions make pentops too large to fit in your palm, they are certainly small and light enough to carry easily. Pen computers fit readily into your briefcase.

Instead of using an electromechanical keyboard array, input to a pen computer is accomplished by moving a pen (or *stylus*) in physical contact with a sensitive, high-resolution digitizing layer (digitizer). The digitizer is virtually clear, and is typically mounted as an overlay directly in front of the pentop's flat-panel display. Once the stylus contacts the digitizer, the computer calculates the point of contact and responds appropriately. If you are running a program that uses an icon-driven graphic user interface (GUI), such as Microsoft's Windows, you touch the pen to the desired icon. This action is identical to clicking on the icon with a mouse or trackball. If you are using the pen to write or draw, pen movements on the digitizer are interpreted and shown in real time on the display. This feedback creates the illusion that your pen is actually leaving marks on the display. The marks that appear are commonly referred to as the *ink*. There are currently three major digitizer technologies: resistive, electrostatic (capacitive), and electromagnetic (RF). These techniques are detailed in chapter 8. For keyboard enthusiasts, most pen computers also support an external input for full-sized PC/XT or PC/AT-style keyboards.

Pentops rely on high-resolution graphic LCDs for their displays. At this time, color graphics adaptor (CGA) modes are common for inexpensive pen computers. CGA can handle 640×200 pixel resolution. Larger, more sophisticated pen-computer displays offer resolutions up to 640×480 pixels. Pen computers use respectable display sizes—some models offer VGA-compatible displays that are 25.4 cm (10") diagonal.

Storage-card drives require almost no space for interface electronics, and virtually no mechanical parts except for the card connector itself, and perhaps a card ejector lever. Like palmtops, pen computers are ideal candidates for solid-state memory and mass-storage cards. Mechanical simplicity reduces a pentop's weight, cost, and power requirements, while increasing its overall long-term reliability. Solid-state memory cards have largely replaced magnetic floppy disks for storing programs and data. Mass-storage cards are used to provide large volumes (20Mb, 40Mb, or more) of storage. Both types of cards contain no moving parts or magnetic media and can be transported directly between computers with compatible drive interfaces. To compete with the great expense of mass-storage cards, some pen computers incorporate small hard drives in 4.57 cm (1.8") or 3.30 cm (1.3") form factors.

The complexity of pen-computer processors and support logic is impressive. Although the performance of many pentops is comparable to an accelerated (turbo) PC/XT computer, the entire computer can be implemented using only a handful of highly integrated circuits. As with palmtops, lower performance can be advantageous since slower processing usually results in lower power consumption—thus longer battery life. At least two popular pen computers use versions of the V20 (8088-based, 10 MHz) microprocessor manufactured by NEC. High-performance pen systems can use variations of Intel's x386 processor.

In general, the high-performance systems also offer high-resolution VGA-compatible LCDs, fine pen sensitivity at more than 250 points per inch, and high-capacity hard drives of 60Mb or larger. Such high-performance pen computers are competing at almost the same level as many notebook systems. It is also interesting to note that the advanced pentops are just about as large as many notebooks. Typical pen-computer dimensions run 23.62 cm (9.3") deep, 29.21 cm (11.5") wide, and 3.81 cm (1.5") high. Virtually all varieties of pen computer are designed to operate in the DOS environment for running Windows or direct DOS applications.

Memory capacity is usually respectable for even the simplest pen computer. As a minimum, a pen computer offers 640K of RAM to handle many classic DOS applications, but many pentops provide 1 or 2Mb of extended/expanded RAM for advanced applications. Some pentop models provide 4Mb of RAM, which can be expanded to 20Mb.

Pen computers offer a wide range of battery life depending on the performance level and options of the particular system. Some pen systems work on two AA batteries for up to 48 hours, while more demanding systems get only 8 hours. The high-performance pen computers obtain rechargeable battery life in the range of 4 to 5 hours, which is compatible with many state-of-the-art notebooks. Pen computers range in weight from .454 kg (1 lb) for simple systems up to 1.36 kg (3 lbs) for high-performance systems.

Now that you have an overview of the various small-computer systems, the next section of this chapter introduces you to basic computer concepts and architectures common to all computers.

Computer concepts

Many times, we tend to focus so tightly on one particular type of computer or application that we forget that every make, model, and size of computer available today evolved from the same ancestry, using the same technologies. In the face of today's complexity and confusion about computers and their abilities, it is a good idea to step back and review some elementary computer concepts and considerations. If you already have a good knowledge of computer basics, feel free to skip this section. For those of you whose computer background is a bit weak, the following material might give you a better appreciation of today's computers and a better understanding of the materials presented in this book. Let's start at the beginning.

Logic primer

In any review of computer technology, it is important for you to understand how a computer perceives information and data and to know how that information is represented with electronic circuits. This section explains computer logic fundamentals.

The elementary premise of computer logic is that a condition or signal is either TRUE or FALSE. Signals can also be considered as either ON or OFF, or YES or NO. There is nothing new about this concept—it's been around for thousands of years. But only in the past 40 years or so has this kind of logic been applied to electronic systems. Since computer logic works only with two conditions, it is generally known as *binary logic*, or *binary*.

For an electronic circuit to deal with binary logic, a direct relationship must exist between logic states and electrical states. As a general rule, a binary TRUE or ON usually indicates the presence of a voltage, while a binary FALSE or OFF indicates the absence of a voltage. Integrated circuits perform logical operations based on the voltage levels existing on each signal line. The relationship between logic conditions and voltage conditions becomes very important later in this book when you must make electrical logic measurements for troubleshooting.

You are all familiar with the decimal number system, which consists of ten characters (0 through 9). Each character (or *digit*) represents a discrete quantity. By combining numbers, we can represent virtually any quantity. The same is true for binary logic.

The binary logic system is a number system with two characters, 0 and 1. A TRUE condition is considered as a logic 1 and a FALSE condition is considered as a logic 0. Binary digits can also be combined to represent almost any quantity. Where a decimal digit can be 0 through 9, however, a binary digit (also called a *bit*) can only be 0 or 1.

In the decimal system, one digit can express 10 levels (or magnitudes), 0 through 9. When the quantity to be expressed exceeds those 10 levels, the number carries over into a higher place, equal to 10 raised to the power of the place, as shown in FIG. 1-5.

Decimal

10^4	10^3	10^2	10^1	10^0
10,000s	1,000s	100s	10s	1s

```
9 ×  100 = 900
3 ×   10 =  30
1 ×    1 =   1
         -----
          931  decimal value
```

Binary

1-5
Comparison of decimal and binary number systems.

2^7	2^6	2^5	2^4	2^3	2^2	2^1	2^0
127ths	64ths	32nds	16ths	8ths	4ths	2s	1s
		1	0	1	1	0	1

```
1 × 32 = 32
0 × 16 =  0
1 ×  8 =  8
1 ×  4 =  4
0 ×  2 =  0
1 ×  1 =  1
       ----
        45  decimal value
```

For example, 931 has a 9 in the hundreds place, a 3 in the tens place, and a 1 in the ones place. You have done this automatically since grammar school.

Since the binary system uses two digits instead of ten, you see in FIG. 1-5 that each place value in the binary system is much less than the same place in a decimal system. This is because each place value is raised to the power of 2 instead of the power of 10. The binary number 101101 has a 1 in the 32nds place, the 8ths place, the 4ths place, and the 1s place. Therefore, as shown in the chart in FIG. 1-5, the binary number 101101 is equal to the decimal number 45. Four bits can express 2^4 or 16 quantities, 0 to 15; 8 bits can express 2^8 or 256 quantities, 0 to 255.

Hexadecimal numbers

The *hexadecimal* number system uses 16 digits—the characters 0 to 9, and the letters A, B, C, D, E, and F (to represent the quantities 10 to 15). The methods used to form binary and decimal numbers are also used to form hexadecimal (hex) numbers, but each place position is now base 16 instead of base 2 or base 10. For example, the decimal numbers 0 to 15 are represented equal to 0000 to 1111 in binary, and 0 to F in hexadecimal. The decimal number 16 is 0001 0000 in binary and 10 in hex. Do not confuse a hex 10, binary 10 and decimal 10—each number is in a different number system and represents a different quantity. TABLE 1-1 shows the relationship between decimal, binary, and hexadecimal numbers.

Table 1-1
Relationship between decimal, binary, and hexadecimal numbers.

Decimal	Binary	Hexadecimal
0	0	0
1	1	1
2	10	2
3	11	3
4	100	4
5	101	5
6	110	6
7	111	7
8	1000	8
9	1001	9
10	1010	A
11	1011	B
12	1100	C
13	1101	D
14	1110	E
15	1111	F

There is a direct relationship between hex and binary numbers. From TABLE 1-1, the hex number 2FB can be replaced by the binary number 0010 1111 1011. Use the binary-to-decimal translation shown in FIG. 1-5 to convert the binary number into its decimal equivalent, 763.

What is a computer?

In the broadest sense, a *digital computer* is a device that receives (or *inputs*), stores, manipulates, and sends (or *outputs*) data—nothing more. Every computer ever built is based on this concept. To fulfill this definition, every computer must contain the four major functional elements illustrated in FIG. 1-6: a central processing unit (CPU, microprocessor, or μP), memory, input device(s), and output device(s). While a modern, full-featured computer might contain many functions, each one can generally be categorized as one of these four elements. Let's examine each element.

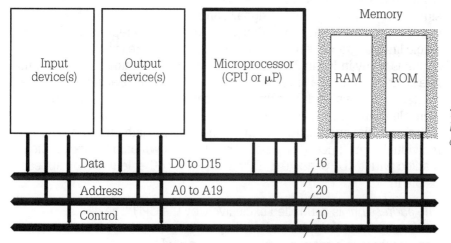

1-6
Diagram of a simple computer system.

Bus width nomenclature

The central processing unit

A CPU is capable of only three operations on data: arithmetic, logic, and control—that's it. Arithmetic operations allow a CPU to add, subtract, multiply, and divide. Logical operations let a CPU make comparisons and decisions about data. Control operations let a CPU move and access data within the computer's system. A typical microprocessor such as Intel's x286 is actually capable of over 100 individual operations that each fall into one of the three categories. A more sophisticated CPU like Intel's x486 offers more than 200 unique and powerful operations, but each of those operations are arithmetic, logic, or control operations. With such a seemingly limited scope of capabilities, you might wonder why a CPU is so important to a computer.

In truth, the power of a CPU is not in its range of abilities, but in its flexibility—the ability of a CPU to perform its operations in any order as instructed. The instructions that direct a microprocessor's operations are a *program*. Programs are stored in memory outside of the CPU. The CPU gets its instructions and data from the program in memory and executes each arithmetic, logic, or control operation that corresponds to the program instruction.

Thus, by altering the instructions or data in a program, one CPU can perform an entirely different set of operations. This adaptability caused the CPU to be considered the "brain" of the digital computer. Today's computers utilize an arsenal of powerful ICs to control items such as hard drives, keyboards, and flat-panel displays, but the instructions that make all those parts work together are still executed by the CPU.

Notice that the microprocessor receives three major sets of electronic signals: data signals, address signals, and control signals. Each set of signals is referred to as a *bus*. Bus paths are typically represented as bold, single lines or graphic arrows, but it is important to realize that a bus contains many individual signal wires. You may sometimes see each bus line is intersected by a small slash and a number. The slash confirms the existence of a bus, and the number indicates the number of individual signal lines in the bus. For example, the *data bus* of FIG. 1-6 is marked with a slash and the number 16, which means that the data bus uses 16 individual signal lines. Every signal line has its own unique label, typically marked with a "D" prefix (e.g., D00 to D15), but other letters may appear before it.

The *address bus* is controlled exclusively by the CPU. The digital information placed on the address bus defines the precise location in the system where information is placed or accessed by the CPU. Microprocessors can usually address more than 16 million locations.

The data bus carries digital information to or from the unique locations specified by the address bus. The information on a data bus might be an instruction needed by the CPU, the result of a calculation or comparison, the destination of a program or subroutine jump, or other functions. The microprocessor uses the data bus to input or output data. This two-way capability makes the bus *bidirectional*.

The *control bus* carries a variety of CPU signals to direct the system. For example, one control signal defines whether the CPU is reading or writing on the data bus. If the read/write (R/W) control line indicates a READ, the CPU inputs the contents of its data bus from the location specified by the address bus. If a WRITE is directed by the R/W line, the CPU outputs data to the address specified by the address bus. The exact number and function of each control signal depend on the particular microprocessor being used.

Digital memory is as important as the CPU is to computers. In fact, a CPU will not work without memory to store data and program instructions. Memory is attached to the three main computer busses (address, data, and control), so the CPU generally has direct access to the memory. In the world of computer systems, there are two general categories of memory: *temporary memory* and *permanent memory*. Every computer contains both temporary and permanent memory, and both memory types play vital roles in a computer's operation.

Memory

Temporary memory is referred to as random access memory (RAM), which can be used to store application programs loaded from a hard drive or floppy drive. RAM also holds data that changes quickly or regularly, such as the calculation results or the contents of a word processor program. RAM is generally considered to be *volatile* memory because its contents are retained only as long as power is supplied to the memory. If the power is turned off, the RAM contents are lost. To guard against loss of memory during accidental power failure, some computers use small batteries to back up RAM contents when the power is removed. Solid-state memory cards use batteries extensively to maintain the card's RAM when the card is removed from the system.

Understand that there are several different types of RAM, each with its own characteristics. Static RAM (SRAM) is the earliest and most straightforward type of temporary memory. Unfortunately, SRAMs suffer from limited storage capacity and speed restrictions. Dynamic RAM (DRAM) overcomes the speed and capacity limits of earlier SRAMs, but a DRAM's contents must be refreshed routinely during computer operation. Refreshing requires extra control circuitry; therefore, battery backup methods are not well suited to DRAMs.

Permanent memory, or read-only memory (ROM), is used to hold program instructions or data just like RAM; however, ROM contents can only be read. Once a ROM is programmed, its contents cannot be changed. The advantage of ROM is that it is *nonvolatile* in that its contents remain intact when the computer power is off. Battery backup is not necessary to maintain ROM contents. Your computer uses ROM to hold the basic input/output system (BIOS), which instructs the computer how to initialize, self-test, and prepare to load its disk operating system. Small computers, such as pentops and palmtops, will even provide DOS on the ROM in the computer instead of letting the system load it from a hard drive, floppy drive, or storage card. As with RAM, there are several different types of ROM that you should be familiar with. Each ROM type is optimized for particular uses.

Classic ROM (also called *mask-ROM*) is the simplest and oldest form of ROM. Each piece of digital information is built into the ROM during manufacturing. The original information to be contained in the ROM is specified by the company purchasing the ROMs. Once a ROM is manufactured, its contents can never be changed. This lack of flexibility makes program development difficult with classic ROM devices. The expense and time required to obtain manufactured ROMs can be justified only with a high-volume purchase of devices containing well-proven information.

The natural solution to mask-ROM limitations is to make the devices programmable by the IC user instead of the IC manufacturer. *Programmable ROMs* (PROMs) make it possible for software companies to purchase blank PROMs and to program the PROMs as desired. However, once a PROM is programmed, its contents cannot be changed. PROMs are also referred to as *one-time-programmable ROMs* (OTP ROMs).

Erasable PROMs (EPROMs) can also be programmed by the IC user instead of the IC manufacturer, but its contents can be erased by exposing the IC to short-wavelength ultraviolet (UV) light for a certain period of time. Light is admitted through a small quartz window in the IC case cover. A typical EPROM can be erased and reprogrammed many times before it fails. Thus, EPROMs are reusable, and they are often used for new program development—if the software must be changed, simply erase the EPROM and reprogram it with new information.

Electrically erasable PROMs (EEPROMs) are an advancement over EPROMs because ultraviolet light is not needed to erase the contents. Instead, a brief, high-energy electrical pulse is applied at a control pin after one of the EEPROM's addresses is selected. New data can then be written to that address. This kind of flexible operation literally allows an EEPROM to be reprogrammed while it is installed in a working circuit. Unfortunately, the time required to erase and rewrite each address is far too great to make EEPROMs any real competition for RAM storage.

Input devices   Although a CPU and memory technically constitute a working computer, it would have very little practical value since it would have absolutely no interaction with the outside world. In order to be useful, a computer must carry data to or from the outside world. For our purposes, we can consider the outside world of a computer to be any component or mechanism beyond the CPU and memory.

Input devices are a huge category of circuits and electromechanical devices that provide digital data to the microprocessor. The CPU uses input data to adapt to changes in the outside world. A keyboard is perhaps the most common of all input devices. When you press a key, a numerical code is generated by the keyboard and sent to the CPU, which recognizes that a key has been pressed, and uses the numerical code for further processing. Data can be input on demand from other devices such as floppy drives, hard drives, solid-state storage cards, and serial communication ports.

Even when a computer reads and processes data from input devices, it is not complete until the results of the computer's operations are sent to the outside world in a coherent, meaningful form. As with input devices, the outside world is considered to be any component or mechanism beyond the CPU and memory.

Output devices

For the purposes of this chapter, an output device is a component or electromechanical element to which the microprocessor can send data. Computer monitors and flat-panel displays are typical output devices. A microprocessor outputs numerical codes representing commands, text, and graphics to a video controller IC. The video controller processes these numerical codes and stores the information to be displayed in video RAM. Video RAM is a relatively small amount of memory belonging to the display device—it is not part of the CPU's core memory. The video controller steps through the contents of its video RAM and directs the operation of the display device independent of the CPU. Of course, the CPU also delivers data to many other devices such as floppy drives, hard drives, solid-state storage cards, and serial communication ports, as well as other key ICs within the computer.

Now that you know the basic elements required to form a working computer system, it's time to put some of those concepts to work and see how a real computer is achieved. The Tandy 1500HD laptop computer is shown in the block diagram of FIG. 1-7. While it might look intimidating at first glance, you see that it follows all of the principles discussed so far. This part of the chapter introduces each of the laptop's elements, and presents some of the system's major features. Each of the system's features is covered in more detail in this book.

A practical model

The system's main microprocessor is IC1, a version of NEC's V20: a 10 MHz, 8088-compatible CPU. Notice that there are three sets of signals: the address bus (AD0 to AD7 and A8 to A19), the data bus (AD0 to AD7), and control signals. You might wonder why AD0 through AD7 handle data as well as part of the address. These signal lines are *multiplexed*. For a part of each processing cycle, the lines carry the lower 8 bits of the 20-

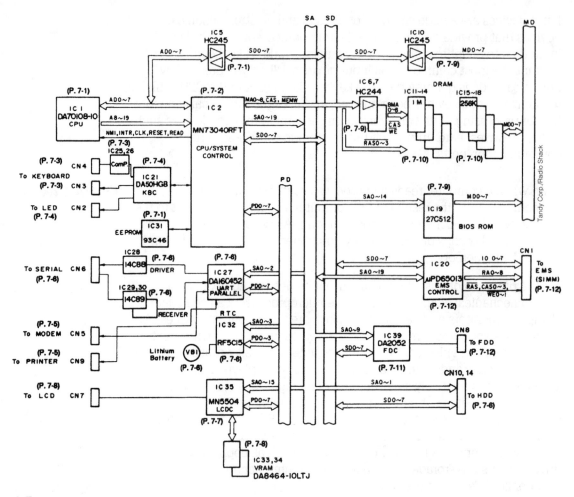

1-7 *Diagram of a practical computer system.*

bit address bus. For another part of the same cycle, the lines carry the 8 data bits (thus the signal prefix "AD" instead of just "D"). The microprocessor communicates directly with the system controller, IC2, and has direct access to the system data bus through IC5.

The system controller is an advanced ASIC designed to handle most of the bull-work involved in the computer's operation. A system controller replaces dozens of discrete-logic ICs by providing key functions in a single, efficient package. IC2 has control of the system address bus (SA0 to SA19) and the system data bus (SD0 to SD7). The controller also supports an auxiliary (or peripheral) data bus (PD0 to PD7), which is used to transfer information to the communication port controller (IC27), a real-time clock circuit (IC32), and the LCD controller (IC35). Finally, the system controller provides timing and refresh signals to maintain the computer's core memory (DRAM ICs IC11 to IC18).

The keyboard's switch-matrix row and column signals are connected through connectors CN3 and CN4 to the keyboard controller (KBC) IC21. A keyboard controller constantly scans the row and column lines of the keyboard matrix. When you press a key, the KBC generates a numerical code that corresponds to the pressed key. This key code is processed by the system controller (IC2) and made available to the CPU.

A small EEPROM (IC31) is available to the system controller. The EEPROM is used to hold the system's configuration settings. Since IC31 is electrically erasable, the system controller can update any necessary configuration settings. Once a configuration is changed, though, the EEPROM retains its data even when the power is turned off.

Computer communication is handled by the UART/parallel communication controller (IC27), a highly integrated device that handles an RS232 serial port at CN6, a modem port at CN5, and a Centronics-type parallel printer port at CN9. Serial driver IC28 converts digital information from IC27 into bipolar serial data levels (*bipolar* means both positive and negative voltages). Serial receivers IC29 and IC30 perform just the opposite function by translating bipolar serial data levels into logic levels compatible with IC27. The controller is addressed over the system address bus by the system controller. Data traveling in and out of the communication controller is carried on the peripheral data bus, which is also managed by the system controller.

The real-time controller (RTC) IC32 is basically the system calendar. It is responsible for tracking time in hours, minutes, and seconds, as well as the date in years, months, days, and day-of-week. The RTC also supplies a fast clock signal that the computer uses for measuring precise time delays. The RTC is addressed over the system address bus and is written to or read from over the peripheral data bus, as directed by the system controller. A lithium battery is used exclusively to maintain the RTC's operation when computer power is off.

A flat-panel display (in this case a 640×200 pixel LCD) is operated by LCD controller (LCDC) IC35 in conjunction with a small amount of memory (video RAM IC33 and IC34) used to hold video information. When character or graphic data must be sent to the display, the system controller addresses the appropriate location in the LCDC through the system address bus and writes the necessary data to the LCDC over the peripheral data bus. In turn, the LCDC stores its display information in video RAM. When the display is updated (every few milliseconds), the

LCDC reads through the contents of its VRAM data and delivers that pixel data to the LCD for display.

Connectors CN10 and CN14 provide system addresses and system data to an optional hard-drive module. The hard drive in this particular system incorporates all necessary controller and interface circuitry in the drive package. On the other hand, floppy disk controller (FDC) IC39 does reside on the system board, where it has direct access to the system address and system data busses. The system controller directs the FDC's operations by addressing the FDC for READ or WRITE operations. The FDC reads or writes data to the driver IC on the floppy disk mechanism. The FDC also provides the floppy disk/driver IC with all of the logic signals necessary to control motor operation, disk tracking, disk side selection, etc.

In addition to the core memory provided on the system board, many small computers make provisions to add extra (extended) memory to the computer. Early desktop computers sometimes provided for extra memory by supplying empty IC sockets on the motherboard, or allowing for an add-on board. However, empty sockets force you to disassemble the computer and install ICs—often a miserable experience for even skilled computer users. Fortunately, most small computers incorporate memory ICs on a module that can be plugged into the computer from the outside. Single, in-line memory modules (SIMMs) are a very popular design for laptops and notebook systems, but palmtop and pen systems are too small for such modules. Instead, small computers are beginning to use solid-state DRAM cards that plug into the computer with other solid-state memory cards.

Regardless of what form your extended memory takes, it must still be interfaced to the computer's system busses. This interface is accomplished by a controller IC—in this case, an extended memory system (EMS) controller IC20. When extended memory is accessed, the system controller addresses IC20 through the system address bus. Data and commands are then written to the EMS controller. It is then the EMS controller that accesses the appropriate place in extended memory. For FIG. 1-7, a SIMM can be plugged into connector CN1.

As with almost all small computers, the basic input/output system (BIOS) is contained in ROM. BIOS is essentially a set of small programs that initialize and test the computer. BIOS also provides the routines needed to tell the computer how to handle its background functions, such as reading the keyboard, operating its communication ports, handling its floppy and hard drives, writing to the display, and other functions. BIOS causes the computer to begin loading DOS. The computer's RAM is used to hold DOS once it is loaded, as well as any application programs to be run. All major memory is addressed through the system address bus, but data is handled along a separate memory data bus (MD0 to MD7).

Now that you've reviewed the elements of a practical computer system, you might wonder why a computer would create so many data busses. The answer has to do with processing efficiency. The system controller is designed specifically for that particular computer, so it can literally control several areas of the computer simultaneously. Even then, the system controller only has to send high-level commands or data to a selection of highly integrated controllers, each of which is responsible for directing the low-level functions needed to make the computer work.

For example, the CPU does not cause pixels to be displayed on a flat-panel display. If a letter is to be displayed, the CPU directs the system controller to write a character to the LCDC. Once the character is written, it is up to the LCDC to interpret the character and generate the pixel patterns needed to form the desired image. The flat-panel display provides the row and column driver circuitry to actually illuminate the desired pixels.

Another example is the keyboard interface. It is the keyboard controller that determines just what key or key combination has been pressed. The system controller does not have to discern what key row and column is active, or whether a Shift, Caps Lock, or Ctrl key is being depressed. The system controller receives only a number code.

2 Components

Before you tackle any sort of computer repair, it is important that you understand components that you will encounter (FIG. 2-1). You must know what each component looks like, what purpose it serves, and how it is marked and rated. Fundamental component knowledge lets you understand just what you are looking at when your small computer is finally apart, and lets you easily find your way around its circuitry. Component knowledge also lets you spot obvious defects, such as burns or cracks. The components described here include both conventional (*through-hole*) components, and surface-mount devices.

This chapter is not intended to provide a detailed background in electronics theory—that is impossible to accomplish in a single book chapter. Instead, this chapter provides you with the essential characteristics and principles associated with common components used in small computers. If you have questions, or need more information, feel free to contact the author directly or refer to any of the many fine books available on electronics theory.

Passive components

Passive components are those components that store or dissipate a circuit's energy in some controlled fashion. Resistors, capacitors, and inductors are passive components. The term *passive* is used to indicate that such parts serve little practical purpose by themselves—you could not build a computer using only resistors, capacitors, and inductors.

2-1
A Toshiba Satellite T1800.

Passive components are used to set up circuit conditions for semiconductor-based parts such as diodes, transistors, and, primarily, integrated circuits.

All resistors serve a single purpose—to dissipate power in a controlled fashion. Resistors appear in many circuits, but are almost always used for voltage division, current limiting, and similar functions. Resistors dissipate power by presenting a resistance to current flow. Wasted energy is shed as heat by the resistors. In small-computer circuits, however, so little energy is wasted by resistors that virtually no temperature increase is detectable. In high-energy circuits, such as power supplies or amplifiers, resistors can shed substantial amounts of heat. The basic unit of resistance is the *ohm*, represented by the Greek symbol omega (Ω). Resistance is also presented in thousands of ohms, or kilohms (kΩ), and in millions of ohms, or megohms (MΩ).

Figure 2-2 shows a carbon-composition resistor. Two metal leads are inserted into a molded body containing a packed carbon filling. Since it is much harder for current to pass through the carbon than through the leads, the carbon filling provides resistance to the current flow. By varying the composition of the carbon filling, the resistance value can be altered anywhere from 0.1 Ω to 20 MΩ. Carbon resistors are the oldest type of

Resistors

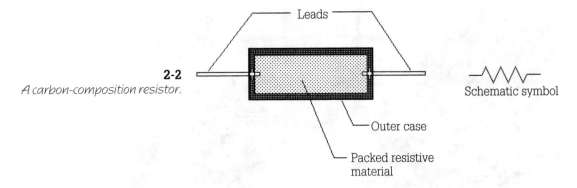

2-2
A carbon-composition resistor.

Leads

Outer case

Packed resistive material

Schematic symbol

resistors. Unfortunately, carbon resistors suffer from relatively poor tolerance (±10% or worse) and they are larger than newer resistor types.

Carbon-film resistors, as shown in FIG. 2-3, have mostly replaced carbon-composition resistors in most circuits that require through-hole resistors. In place of the carbon filling, a very precise layer of carbon film is applied to a thin ceramic tube. The thickness of the carbon film determines the resistance—thicker coatings yield lower resistance levels, and vice versa. Metal leads are attached to caps at both ends, and the entire finished assembly is dipped in epoxy or ceramic. Carbon-film resistors are generally more accurate than carbon-composition resistors because the manufacturing process is more precise.

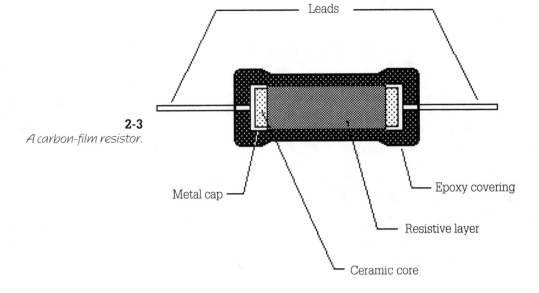

2-3
A carbon-film resistor.

Leads

Metal cap

Epoxy covering

Resistive layer

Ceramic core

A surface-mount (SMT) resistor is shown in FIG. 2-4. As with carbon-film resistors, SMT resistors are formed by depositing a layer of carbon film on a thin ceramic substrate and attaching metal tabs on both ends. SMT resistors are soldered directly to the top or bottom of a printed circuit (PC) board instead of using leads to penetrate the PC board. SMT resistors are incredibly small devices (only a few square millimeters in area), yet they offer very tight tolerances. Such small resistors are used extensively in small computers.

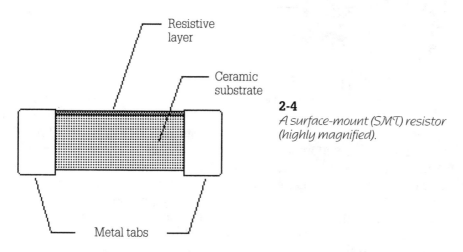

Resistive layer

Ceramic substrate

Metal tabs

2-4
A surface-mount (SMT) resistor (highly magnified).

Adjustable resistors, known as *potentiometers, pots,* or *rheostats,* are usually employed to adjust volume, contrast, or some other circuit operating parameter. The potentiometer shown in FIG. 2-5, consists of a moveable metal wiper resting on a layer of resistive film. Although the total resistance of the film is fixed, the resistance between either end and the wiper blade varies as the wiper is moved. There are two typical types of adjustable resistors: knob-type, where the wiper is turned clockwise or counterclockwise using a rotating metal shaft; or slide-type, where the wiper is moved back and forth in a straight line.

In addition to value and tolerance, resistors are also rated in terms of power handling capacity. Power is normally measured in watts (W), and is dependent on the amount of current (I) and voltage (V) applied to the resistor as given by the expression, $P = I \times V$. Resistors are typically manufactured in $\frac{1}{16}$ W, $\frac{1}{8}$ W, $\frac{1}{4}$ W, $\frac{1}{2}$ W, 1 W, 2 W, and 5 W sizes to handle a wide variety of power conditions. Size is directly related to power dissipation ability, so larger resistors generally handle larger amounts of power than smaller resistors of the same value.

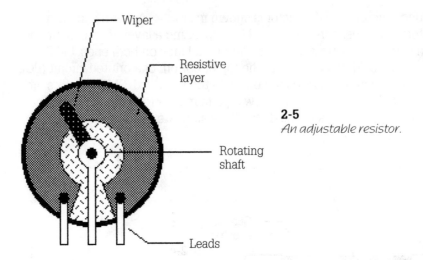

Wiper

Resistive
layer

2-5
An adjustable resistor.

Rotating
shaft

Leads

As long as power dissipation is kept below its rating, a resistor should hold its value and perform indefinitely. However, when a resistor's power rating is exceeded, it does not dissipate heat fast enough to maintain a stable temperature. Ultimately, the resistor overheats and burns out, forming an open circuit. A burned-out resistor might appear slightly discolored, or burned and cracked, depending on the severity and duration of its overheating. Extreme overheating can also burn a PC board. Replace any faulty resistors that you find.

Potentiometer failures usually take the form of intermittent connections between the wiper blade and the resistive film. Remember that the film wears away as the wiper moves back and forth across it. Over time, enough film might wear away at certain points so that the wiper does not make good contact at those points. This can result in erratic or intermittent operation. With small computers, it is rarely necessary to continually adjust contrast or brightness once optimum levels are found, so it is unlikely for adjustable resistors to wear out in small computers; however, dust and debris might collect and cause intermittent operation when an adjustment is needed. Try cleaning an intermittent potentiometer with a high-quality electronic contact cleaner, if possible, or any intermittent potentiometers or rheostats.

Reading resistors Every resistor is marked with its proper value. Marking allows resistors to be identified on sight and compared to schematics or part layout drawings. Now that you know what resistors look like, you should know how to recognize their values without having to rely on test equipment. There are three ways to mark resistors: explicit marking, color coding, and numerical marking. It is important to understand all three types of marking because many circuits use resistors with a mix of marking schemes.

Explicit marking is just as the name implies—the actual resistance is written on the resistor. Large ceramic resistors often use explicit marking. Their long, rectangular bodies are usually large enough to hold clearly printed characters.

Color coding has long been popular for marking carbon resistors because they are too small for explicit markings. The 12 resistor code colors are shown in TABLE 2-1. The first ten colors (black through white) are used as value and multiplier colors, and silver and gold serve as tolerance indicators.

Table 2-1
Standard resistor color code.

Color	Value	Multiplier	
Black	0	1	
Brown	1	10	
Red	2	100	
Orange	3	1000	
Yellow	4	10,000	
Green	5	100,000	
Blue	6	1,000,000	
Violet	7	. . .	
Gray	8	. . .	
White	9	. . .	
Silver	. . .	. . .	10% tolerance
Gold	. . .	. . .	5% tolerance

The color code uses a series of up to five colored bands as illustrated in FIG. 2-6. Band number 1 is always located closest to the edge of the resistor. Bands 1 and 2 are the value bands, and band 3 is the multiplier band. A fourth band (if present), will be silver or gold to indicate the resistor's tolerance. On rare occasions, you may encounter a fifth band, which indicates the reliability of a resistor (and is used only for military and aerospace-grade resistors).

As an example, suppose the resistor of FIG. 2-6 had three bands, colored brown, black, and red. TABLE 2-1 shows that brown = 1, black = 0, and red = 100 (because it is in the multiplier band). The resistance is [band 1][band 2] × [band 3], or 10 × 100, or 1000 Ω, or 1 kΩ. If the first three color

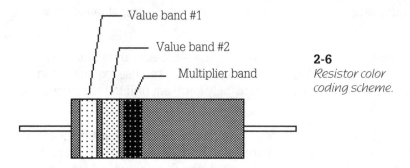

Value band #1

Value band #2

Multiplier band

2-6
Resistor color coding scheme.

bands were red, red, orange; since red = 2 and orange = 1000, the resistance is 22 × 1000, or 22,000 Ω, or 22 KΩ.

A fourth band, if found, shows the resistor's tolerance. A gold band represents an excellent tolerance of ±5% of rated value. A silver band represents a fair tolerance of ±10%, and no tolerance band indicates a poor tolerance of ±20%. A faulty resistor should be replaced with resistor of equal or smaller tolerance whenever possible.

Color-coded resistors have rapidly been giving way to an assortment of SMT resistors, which are far too small for clear color coding. Instead, a three digit numerical code is used. Each digit corresponds to the first three bands of the color code, as shown in FIG. 2-7.

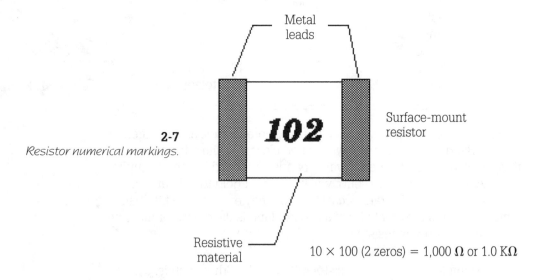

Metal leads

Surface-mount resistor

2-7
Resistor numerical markings.

Resistive material

10 × 100 (2 zeros) = 1,000 Ω or 1.0 KΩ

The first two numbers are value digits, and the third number is the multiplier, which indicates how many zeros should be added to the value. For instance, 102 denotes a value of 10 with 2 zeros added on to make the number 1000, or 1 kΩ. Likewise, a marking of 331 would be read as 330 Ω.

Capacitors

Capacitors are simply energy storage devices that store energy in the form of an electrical charge. By themselves, capacitors have little practical use, but the capacitor principle has important applications when combined with other components in filters, resonant or timing circuits, and power supplies. Capacitance is measured in farads (F). In actual practice, a farad is a very large amount of capacitance, so most capacitors are measured in μF (microfarads, or millionths of a farad) and pF (picofarads, or millionths of a millionth of a farad).

A capacitor is little more than two conductive plates separated by an insulator (a *dielectric*) as shown in FIG. 2-8. The amount of capacitance provided by this type of assembly depends on the area of each plate, the dielectric material that separates them, and the distance between them (the thickness of the dielectric). Larger capacitance values can be created by rolling up a plate/dielectric assembly and housing it in a cylinder.

2-8
Cutaway view of a simple plate capacitor.

Plate

Dielectric material

Outer case

Plate

Plate

Top view

Leads

Side view

When voltage is applied to a capacitor, electrons flow into it until it is fully charged. At that point, current stops flowing (even though voltage may still be applied), and the voltage across the capacitor will equal its applied voltage. If the applied voltage is removed, the capacitor will tend to retain the charge of electrons on its plates. Just how long it does this depends on the specific materials used to construct the capacitor as well as its overall size. Internal resistance through the dielectric material eventually bleeds off any charge. For the purposes of this book, all you really need to remember is that capacitors store an electrical charge.

There are usually two types of capacitors that you should be familiar with, *fixed* and *electrolytic*. Various capacitor types and shapes are shown in FIG. 2-9. Fixed capacitors are nonpolarized devices that can be inserted into a circuit regardless of lead orientation. Many fixed capacitors are assembled as small wafers or disks with aluminum foil conductive plates and dielectrics such as paper, mica, and various ceramic materials. The complete assembly is coated with a hard plastic, epoxy, or ceramic housing to keep out humidity. Larger capacitors might be assembled into large, hermetically sealed canisters. Fixed capacitors are also designed in surface-mount form.

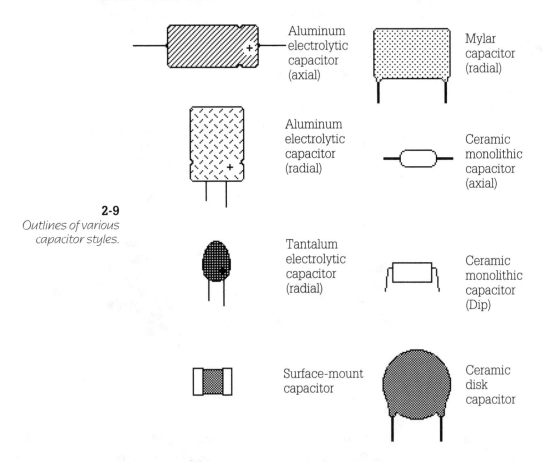

2-9
Outlines of various capacitor styles.

Electrolytic capacitors are polarized components and must be inserted into a circuit in the proper orientation with respect to the applied voltage. Tantalum capacitors are often found in a dipped (or teardrop) shape or as small canisters. Aluminum electrolytic capacitors are usually used in general-purpose applications requiring polarized devices. The difference between fixed and electrolytic capacitors is primarily in their materials, but the principles and purpose of capacitance remain the same.

Capacitors are often designated as *axial* or *radial* devices. This simply refers to the capacitor's particular lead configuration. When both leads emerge from the same end of the capacitor, the device is said to be radial. If the leads emerge from either side, the capacitor is known as axial.

Surface-mount (SMT) capacitors are usually fixed ceramic devices that use a dielectric core capped by electrodes on the ends. If an electrolytic capacitor is needed, an SMT tantalum device is usually used. Although the construction of an SMT tantalum capacitor differs substantially from a ceramic SMT capacitor, they both appear very similar to the unaided eye. All polarized capacitors are marked with some type of polarity indicator.

Like resistors, most capacitors tend to be rugged and reliable. Since they only store energy (they don't dissipate it), it is virtually impossible to burn them out. Capacitors can be damaged or destroyed by exceeding their working voltage (WV) rating, or by reversing the orientation of a polarized device in a circuit. This can occur if a failure elsewhere in a circuit causes excessive energy to be applied across a capacitor, or if you install a new electrolytic capacitor incorrectly.

Like resistors, all capacitors carry markings to identify their values. Once you understand the markings, you will be able to determine capacitor values on sight. Capacitors are also marked in three ways: color coding, explicit marking, and numerical codes.

Reading capacitors

Color-coded capacitors use a color marking scheme very similar to resistor color codes. The first few colors represent a value, while a third color indicates a multiplier. Today, color coding is rarely used in capacitor manufacturing, so this book does not discuss the subject. Color coding has largely been replaced by explicit markings and numerical codes, but you should be aware that older capacitors might carry a color code.

Explicit marking is used with capacitors that are physically large enough to carry their printed value. Large, ceramic disk, mylar, and electrolytic capacitors have plenty of surface area to hold readable markings. Note that all polarized capacitors, regardless of size, must show which of their two leads are positive or negative. Be certain to pay close attention to polarizer markings whenever you are testing or replacing capacitors.

Small, nonpolarized capacitors and many sizes of SMT capacitors use numerical coding schemes. Numerical coding results in smaller, simpler markings that are relatively easy to read. The pattern of numerical marking is very similar to that of numerically coded resistors. A series of three digits is used: the first two digits indicate a value, and the third digit is a multiplier. Unfortunately, a capacitor's multiplier digit can be used to shift a decimal point to the left or the right. The direction of the shift depends on the overall size of the capacitor. Figure 2-10 illustrates both a left and a right shift.

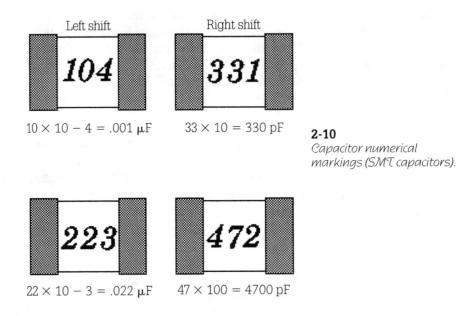

Left shift

104

$10 \times 10 - 4 = .001 \ \mu F$

Right shift

331

$33 \times 10 = 330 \ pF$

2-10
Capacitor numerical markings (SMT capacitors).

223

$22 \times 10 - 3 = .022 \ \mu F$

472

$47 \times 100 = 4700 \ pF$

Large capacitors tend to have larger amounts of capacitance (in the μF range), so the multiplier digit shifts the decimal point to the left. For the ceramic capacitor marked 104, the first two digits are the value (significant) digits, and the third digit moves the decimal point that number of places to the left. The ceramic capacitor would then be read 10 $\times 10^{-4} = .001 \ \mu F$. A marking of 223 would be read $22 \times 10^{-3} = .022 \ \mu F$.

Very small capacitors—especially SMT capacitors—tend to offer extremely small values of capacitance (in the picofarad range), so the decimal point is shifted to the right by a multiplier. An SMT capacitor marked 331 would be $33 \times 10^1 = 330 \ pF$. A marking of 472 would be 47 $\times 10^2 = 4700 \ pF$.

The question of which way to shift the decimal point is very perplexing because it largely depends on the overall size of the capacitor and the conventions of its manufacturer. To ensure that your estimates are correct, check your estimates with a capacitance meter.

Inductors are also energy storage devices. However, unlike capacitors, inductors store energy in the form of a magnetic field. Before the introduction of integrated circuits, inductors served a key role with capacitors in the formation of filters and resonant (tuned) circuits. While advances in solid-state electronics have made inductors virtually obsolete in traditional applications, they remain invaluable for high-energy circuits such as power supplies. Inductors are used in transformers, motors, and relays. The unit of inductance is the henry (H), but smaller inductors are found in the millihenry (mH) or microhenry (µH) range.

An inductor is little more than a simple length of wire. Basic electric principles state that a magnetic field is produced when current is passed through a conductor. However, the inductance generated by a single strand of wire is rarely large enough to be useful. To establish useful levels of inductance, a conductor is wrapped in the shape of a coil, as shown in FIG. 2-11. Coiling the inductor concentrates the magnetic field, forming magnetic poles. To concentrate the magnetic field even further, the coil is around a permeable core, which is any material that can be magnetized, such as iron or steel.

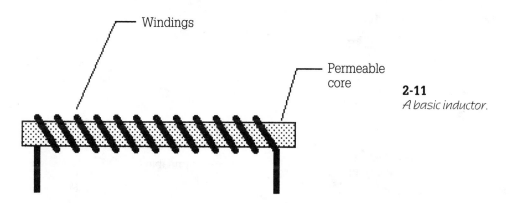

Windings

Permeable core

2-11
A basic inductor.

Coils are available in many shapes and sizes, a few of which are shown in FIG. 2-12. The particular size and shape depends on the amount of energy that must be stored and the desired magnetic characteristics. Small computers use larger coils in their power supplies or alternating current (ac) adaptors. Small coils are also available in SMT or leaded packages.

A transformer is a combination of all working in tandem. As FIG. 2-13 illustrates, it is composed of three important elements: a primary (input) winding, a secondary (output) winding, and a permeable core structure. Transformers are used to alter (transform) ac voltage and current levels in

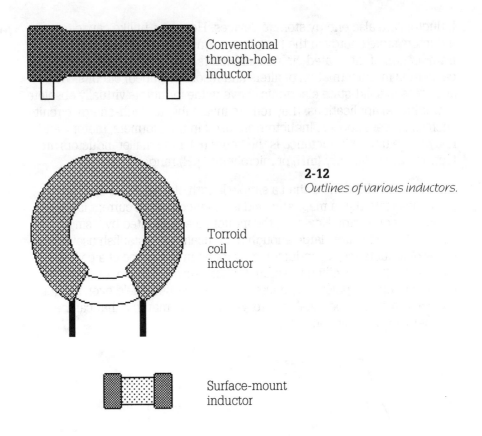

Conventional
through-hole
inductor

Torroid
coil
inductor

2-12
Outlines of various inductors.

Surface-mount
inductor

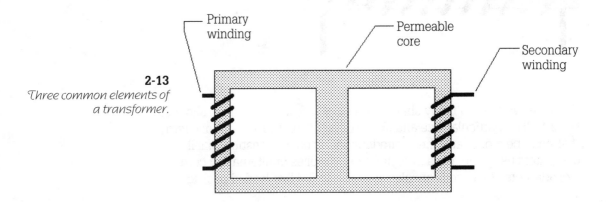

Primary
winding

Permeable
core

Secondary
winding

2-13
*Three common elements of
a transformer.*

a circuit and to isolate one circuit from another. An ac signal is applied to
the primary winding. Since the magnitude of this input signal is
constantly changing, the magnetic field it generates constantly fluctuates
as well. When this fluctuating magnetic field intersects the secondary

coil, an ac signal is created (induced) in the coil. This principle is known as *magnetic coupling*. The secondary ac signal duplicates the primary signal. Primary and secondary windings are often wound around the same core structure, providing efficient magnetic coupling from the primary coil to the secondary coil.

The actual amount of voltage and current induced on a secondary coil depends on the ratio of the number of primary windings to the number of secondary windings. This relationship is known as the *turns ratio*. If the secondary coil contains more windings than the primary coil, then the voltage induced across the secondary coil will be greater than the primary voltage. For example, if the transformer has 1000 primary windings and 2000 secondary windings, the turns ratio is 1000÷2000 = ½. With 10 V applied to the primary, the secondary voltage is approximately 10÷½ = 20 V. This arrangement is known as a *step-up transformer*. If the situation were reversed, with 2000 primary windings and 1000 secondary windings, turns ratio would then be 2000÷1000 = 2. Therefore, if 30 V is applied to the primary, the secondary voltage would be 30÷2 = 15 V. This is known as a *step-down transformer*.

Current in a transformer is stepped opposite to the proportion of voltage steps. If voltage is stepped down by the factor of a turns ratio, the corresponding current is stepped up by the same factor. This relationship ensures that power out of a transformer is about equal to the power applied to the transformer.

Since inductors are energy storage devices, they should not dissipate any power by themselves. However, the wire resistance in each coil, combined with magnetic losses in the core, allows some power to be lost as heat. Heat buildup is the leading cause of inductor failure. Long-term exposure to heat can eventually break down the tough enamel insulation on the windings and cause a short circuit, which lowers the coil's overall resistance, which draws even more current. Breakdown accelerates until the coil is destroyed.

Fuses

Circuits must be protected from overloads. A faulty power supply or bad circuit component can force excess current into a circuit or component, leading to the component's destruction and a more expensive, time-consuming repair. Fuses are used to disconnect power to a circuit whenever the current flow exceeds safe operating limits.

A typical fuse is little more than a strand of fine wire mounted between two metal caps, as shown in FIG. 2-14. The fuse is inserted in series with the circuit to be protected. While the circuit is in operation, the current in the circuit passes through the fuse. As long as the current remains below

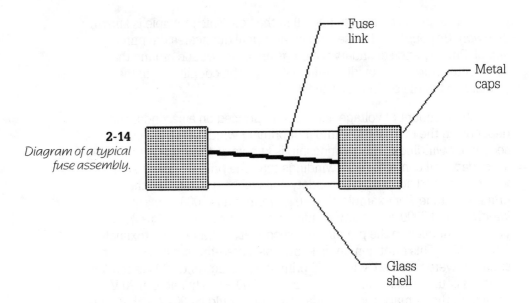

2-14
Diagram of a typical fuse assembly.

Fuse link

Metal caps

Glass shell

the fuse's rated value, the circuit will continue to operate. If a component or power supply failure increases the current above the fuse's rated value, the wire in the fuse burns out, creating an open circuit, which stops all current flow in the circuit.

Fuses come in many shapes and sizes, as shown in FIG. 2-15. Which fuse is used depends on the circuit being protected and the space available. You are probably familiar with the cartridge-type fuses illustrated in FIG. 2-15, but few small computers use these large devices. Instead, a new generation of microfuses or picofuses are being used in small computers, most of which are mounted directly onto a PC board just like any other component. Some fuses are available in surface-mount (SMT) styles to minimize the amount of mounting area required.

A burned-out fuse must be replaced before the circuit can be operated again. Cartridge fuse replacement is easy because you remove the fuse from its holder and replace it. Small fuses, however, are often soldered into the circuit. These fixed fuses require you to expose the circuit, desolder the old fuse, and solder a new fuse in its place. Use extreme caution whenever replacing fixed fuses. If the fixed fuse fails as soon as the power is applied to the circuit, that is an indication that an additional or more serious problem is present. Check all other components and power sources before repowering the circuit again.

Never defeat a fuse by replacing it with a regular wire or some other device. Without a fuse, a circuit or power supply might be destroyed or extensively damaged and might also create a fire hazard.

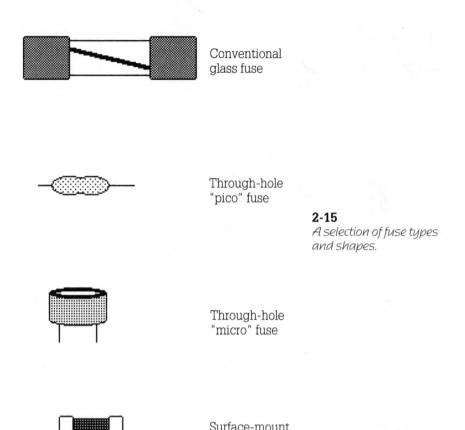

Conventional
glass fuse

Through-hole
"pico" fuse

2-15
*A selection of fuse types
and shapes.*

Through-hole
"micro" fuse

Surface-mount
fuse

Active components

Diodes, transistors, and integrated circuits form a much broader and more exciting group of active components. These components are called *active* because each part, instead of being passive, uses a circuit's energy to accomplish specific, practical functions. The next section provides an overview of common active components, and shows you what functions the parts perform.

Diodes

A classic diode is a two-terminal semiconductor device that allows current to flow in one direction but not in the reverse direction. This one-way property is known as *rectification*. As you see in chapter 5, rectification is absolutely essential to the basic operation of every power supply and battery charging circuit.

Diodes are available in a wide array of case styles, as shown in FIG. 2-16. The size and materials used in a diode depend on the amount of current to be carried. Glass-cased diodes, usually made with silicon, are generally used for low-power (small-signal) applications. Plastic or ceramic cased diodes are typically used for low or medium power applications like

Anode   Cathode

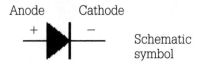

Schematic
symbol

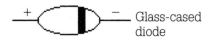

+ ⬜ −   Plastic-cased
diode

2-16
Typical diode outlines.

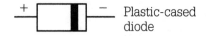

Glass-cased
diode

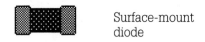

Surface-mount
diode

power supplies, circuit isolation, or inductive flyback protection. Diodes
are also available in SMT packages. A diode has two terminals—the
anode is the positive terminal and the cathode is the negative terminal.
Note that a diode's cathode is always marked with a solid stripe or bar.

Whenever you deal with rectifier diodes (regardless of the case size or
style), you should be concerned with two major diode specifications:
forward current (I_f) and peak inverse voltage (PIV). Choose replacement
diodes with I_f and PIV values that closely match the defective diode.
When a silicon diode is forward biased as shown in FIG. 2-17, the diode
develops a constant voltage drop of about 0.6 Vdc. The remainder of the
applied voltage will drop across the current limiting resistor. Since a diode
dissipates power, it is important to choose a current limiting resistor that
restricts forward current to a safe level; otherwise, the diode may be
destroyed by excess heat.

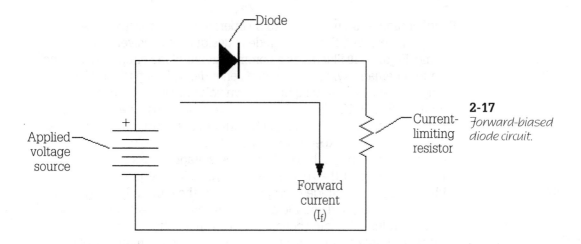

2-17
Forward-biased diode circuit.

A reverse-biased diode, such as the one shown in FIG. 2-18, acts almost like an open switch—no current flows in the circuit. This also demonstrates the essential principle of rectification: diode current flows in one direction only. Whatever voltage is applied across the diode appears across it. Even if the reverse voltage level were increased, the diode would not conduct. However, there are limits to the reverse voltage that a diode can take, that limit being the PIV. If reverse voltage exceeds PIV, the diode junction can rupture and fail as either an open or short circuit. Typical PIV ratings can easily exceed 200 V.

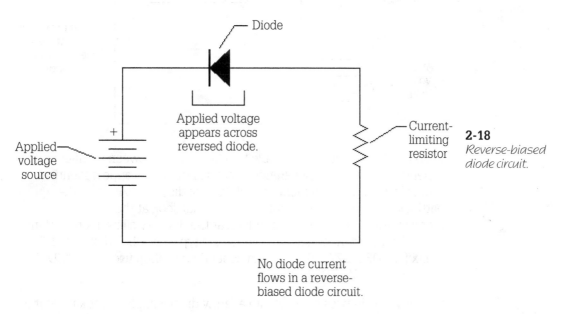

2-18
Reverse-biased diode circuit.

Rectifier diodes are not meant to be operated in the reverse-biased condition; however, the zener diode is designed exclusively for reverse biasing. Figure 2-19 illustrates a common zener diode circuit. Notice the unique schematic symbol used for a zener diode. When the applied voltage is below the zener's breakdown voltage (typical zener diodes operate at 5, 6, 9, 12, 15, or 24 Vdc), the voltage across the zener diode is equal to the applied voltage and no current flows through the diode. As the applied voltage exceeds the zener's breakdown voltage, current begins to flow through the diode and the voltage across the zener remains clamped at the zener's level (i.e., 5, 6, 9, 12 Vdc, etc.). Any additional applied voltage is dropped across the current limiting resistor. As long as the applied voltage exceeds the zener's breakdown voltage, the zener voltage remains constant. This zener action makes zener diodes perfect as simple regulators, and is the basis for most methods of linear voltage regulation. Chapter 5 discusses regulation in much more detail.

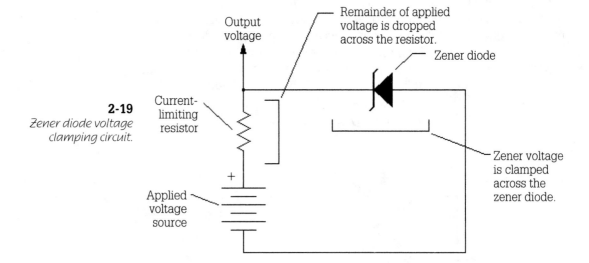

2-19
Zener diode voltage clamping circuit.

Output voltage

Remainder of applied voltage is dropped across the resistor.

Zener diode

Current-limiting resistor

Zener voltage is clamped across the zener diode.

Applied voltage source

Keep in mind that it is impossible to differentiate between rectifier and zener diodes by their appearance because both types appear identical. The only ways you can identify each type of diode is to look up the particular device in a cross-reference manual, look at the part's representation in a schematic, or look at the device's silk screen marking on the PC board. Rectifier-type diodes are typically labeled with a "D" prefix (i.e., D32, D27, D3, etc.), and zener diodes often use "Z" or "ZD" prefixes (i.e., ZD5, ZD201, etc.).

Similarly, it is impossible to locate a faulty diode simply by looking at it unless the diode was destroyed by a sudden, severe overload. Such overloads are virtually nonexistent in small computers, so you must use test instruments to test the diode. Test instruments are discussed in the next chapter.

During the operation of all semiconductor devices, electrons must bridge a semiconductor junction. By modifying the construction of a junction and encapsulating it with a diffuse plastic housing, electrons moving across a junction liberate photons of visible (or infrared) light. This is the basic principle behind light-emitting diodes (LEDs). An LED is shown in FIG. 2-20. Notice that an LED is little more than a diode—the wavy arrows

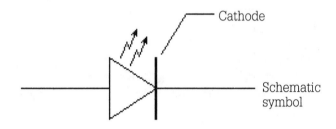

Cathode

Schematic symbol

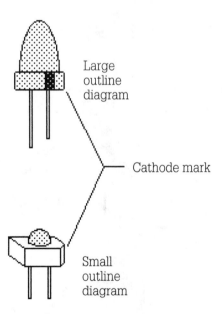

Large outline diagram

Cathode mark

Small outline diagram

2-20
An LED schematic and outline diagrams.

indicate that light is moving away from the device. Altering the chemical composition of an LED's materials alters the wavelength of the emitted light, producing yellow, orange, red, green, blue, and infrared LEDs. Like ordinary diodes, LEDs are intended to be forward biased, but LED voltage drops are higher (0.8 to 3.5 Vdc), and LEDs often require 10 to 35 mA of current to generate the optimum amount of light.

There are two other diode-based devices that you should be familiar with, the silicon-controlled rectifier (SCR) and the triac. You might encounter either of these elements in your small computer's power supply or battery charging circuit. An SCR is shown in FIG. 2-21. Notice that SCRs are three-terminal devices. In addition to an anode and a cathode, a *gate terminal* is added to control the SCR. An ordinary diode turns on whenever it is forward biased. An SCR must also be forward biased as well as triggered by applying a positive voltage (trigger signal) to the gate. Once triggered, an SCR continues to conduct as long as current is flowing through the SCR. Removing the gate voltage does not stop the SCR from conducting once it has started. If current stops after the gate voltage is removed, the SCR has to be re-triggered. Since SCRs are three-terminal devices, they

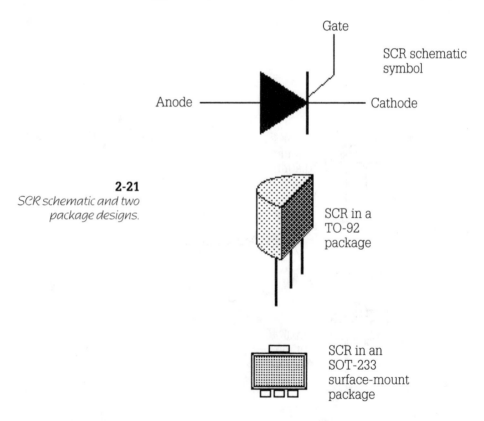

Gate

SCR schematic symbol

Anode ——————— Cathode

2-21
SCR schematic and two package designs.

SCR in a TO-92 package

SCR in an SOT-233 surface-mount package

are often packaged in a fashion very similar to transistors. Most low- or medium-power SCRs are even packaged in SMT packages.

A triac behaves very much like an SCR, but can be triggered to conduct current in either direction instead of just one direction, as in the SCR. Figure 2-22 shows a typical triac. Notice that a triac is given two anodes because it conducts in both directions. A triac conducts once it is triggered by a voltage on its gate lead. The trigger voltage must be the same polarity as the voltage across the triac. For example, if there is a positive voltage from A1 to A2, the trigger voltage must be positive. If there is a negative voltage from A1 to A2, the trigger voltage must be negative. Once triggered, a triac conducts until current stops flowing.

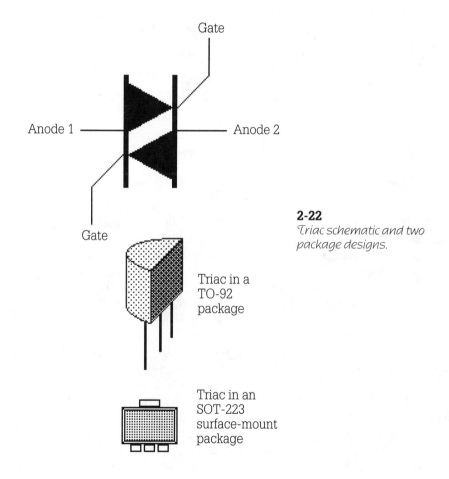

2-22
Triac schematic and two package designs.

Triac in a
TO-92
package

Triac in an
SOT-223
surface-mount
package

After the current stops, the triac must be triggered again before it conducts again.

Diode markings All diodes carry two very important markings as shown in FIG. 2-23—the part number and the cathode marking. The cathode marking indicates the negative diode lead. Since diodes are polarized devices, it is critical that you know which lead is which. Otherwise, an incorrectly replaced diode might cause a circuit malfunction.

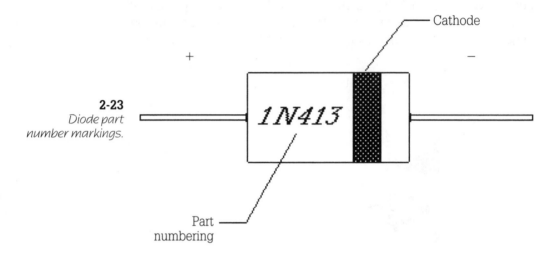

2-23
Diode part number markings.

Unlike passive components, diode part numbers do not contain information on a diode's performance specifications or limits. Instead, the part number is an index, or reference number, which allows you to look up the specification in a manufacturer's or cross-reference data book. Classic diode part numbers begin with the prefix "1N," followed by anywhere from one to four digits. The "1N" prefix is used by the Joint Electron Devices Engineering Council (JEDEC) in the United States to denote devices with one semiconductor junction (diodes). Classic Japanese diode part numbers begin with the prefix "1SS," where "SS" means "small signal."

Of course, you'll probably find diodes with many unique and arcane markings. Fortunately, there are many clues to guide you. Your first clue is the white (or gray) cathode band—at least you can identify the part as a diode. The second identifier is the silk screen lettering on the PC board. Diodes are usually assigned "D" or "ZD" numbering prefixes to denote a rectifier-type or zener diode. Once you feel confident that you identified a diode, use a cross-reference index to look up the suspect part's replacement or equivalent. The specifications you find for the equivalent part in a cross-reference manual will closely (if not exactly) match those for the original part. There are many semiconductor cross-references available.

A transistor is a three-terminal semiconductor device whose output signal is directly controlled by its input signal. Using passive components, a transistor can be configured to perform as an amplifier or as a switch. Unfortunately, there is not enough room in this book to discuss the theory and characteristics of transistors, but you should know the most important concepts of transistors and understand their various uses.

Transistors

There are two major transistor types: bipolar and field-effect transistors (FET). Bipolar transistors are common, inexpensive, general-purpose devices that can be made to handle amplification and switching tasks with equal ease. The three leads of a bipolar transistor are the *base*, *emitter*, and *collector*. In most applications, the base serves as the transistor's input—that is, where the input signal is applied. The emitter is typically tied to ground (usually through one or more values of resistance), and the collector provides the output signal. The transistor can also be configured with the input signal on the collector, the base grounded, and the output on the emitter.

There are two types of bipolar transistors—NPN and PNP. For an NPN transistor, the base voltage is positive with respect to the emitter. As the base voltage increases, the transistor turns on and current flows from the collector to the emitter. As base voltage increases further, the transistor continues to turn on and allows more current into the collector until the transistor finally saturates. A saturated transistor cannot be turned on any further. A PNP transistor requires a negative base voltage with respect to the emitter in order to cause the transistor to turn on and conduct current. As base voltage becomes more negative, the transistor conducts more current until it saturates. By far, NPN transistors are more commonly used in small computers.

A simple, low-power bipolar transistor amplifier circuit schematic is shown in FIG. 2-24. Resistors are used to determine the desired voltage and current conditions that the transistor needs in order to function as a linear amplifier. Initial voltage and current setup is known as *biasing* the transistor. The term *linear* indicates that the output signal is a multiple of the input signal. Capacitors at the input and output prevent dc voltages from entering the amplifier and offsetting its bias levels. Therefore, only ac signals are allowed to pass.

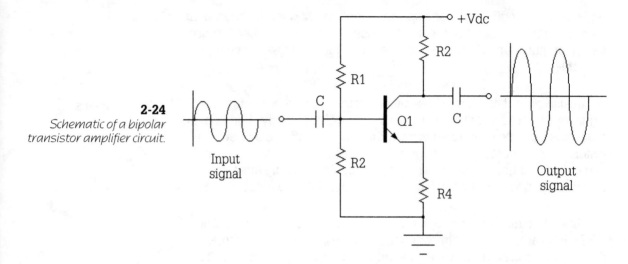

2-24
Schematic of a bipolar transistor amplifier circuit.

When a bipolar transistor is used in a switching circuit (driver circuit), the arrangement is often somewhat simpler, as shown in FIG. 2-25. Unlike a transistor amplifier, whose output signal varies in direct proportion to its input, a switching circuit is either on or off—very much like a mechanical switch. Small computers make extensive use of switching circuits in order to operate LEDs or piezoelectric buzzers. Each pixel in an LCD (whether black and white or color) is driven by a matrix of transistor switching circuits. The typical computer switching circuit uses a digital signal from an integrated circuit (IC) as the control signal. When the control signal is at a logic 0, the transistor (and its load) remains off. When a logic 1 signal is supplied to the driver, the transistor turns on fully (saturates). Current flows through the load, into the collector, through the transistor to the emitter, then to ground. A base resistor is added to limit current into the base from the signal source. An additional resistor might need to be placed in the collector circuit to limit the current if the load is too large.

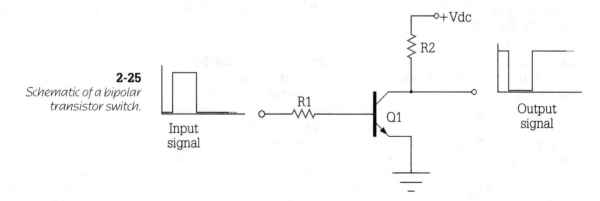

2-25
Schematic of a bipolar transistor switch.

Phototransistors are a unique variation of bipolar transistors. Instead of an electrical signal being used to control the transistor, photons of light provide the base signal. Light enters the phototransistor through a clear quartz or plastic window on the transistor's body. Light striking the transistor's base liberates electrons that become base current. With increasing light entering phototransistor the base current increases, and vice versa. While phototransistors can be operated as linear amplifiers, they are most often found in switching circuits that detect the absence or presence of light.

Although phototransistors can detect light from a wide variety of sources, it is normal to use an LED to supply a known, constant light source. When a phototransistor and LED are matched together in this way, an *optocoupler* is formed, as shown in FIG. 2-26. Notice the new schematic symbol for a phototransistor. The wavy lines indicate that light is entering at the base. Optocouplers are used in floppy drives to detect the presence or absence of a disk's write-protect notch, or to detect if the drive door is closed. Disk drives are covered in detail in chapter 7. Optocouplers can be fabricated on integrated circuits to provide circuit isolation.

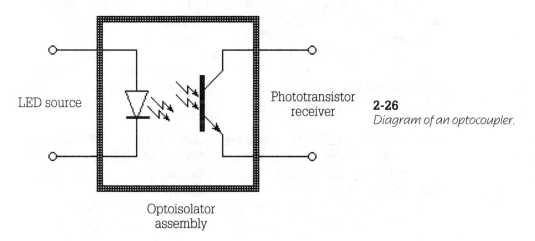

LED source   Phototransistor receiver   **2-26**
Diagram of an optocoupler.

Optoisolator assembly

Field-effect transistors (FETs) are constructed in a radically different fashion than bipolar transistors. Although FETs make use of the same basic materials, FETs can operate as either amplifiers or switches, but require biasing components of much higher values to set the proper operating conditions. FETs are either n-channel or p-channel devices as shown in FIG. 2-27. The difference in transistor type depends on the materials used to construct the FET. An FET has three terminals: a *source*, a *gate*, and a *drain*. These terminals correspond to the emitter, base, and collector of a bipolar transistor. The gate is typically used for the

N-channel FET

Drain

P-channel FET

Drain

Gate

Gate

Source

Source

2-27
*Schematic symbols for
field-effect transistors
(FETs).*

input or control signal. The source is normally tied to ground (sometimes through one or more values of resistance), and the drain supplies the output signal.

When no voltage is applied to an FET's gate, current flows freely from the drain to the source. Any necessary current limiting is provided by inserting a resistor in series with the drain or source circuit. By adjusting the gate control voltage, current flow in the drain and source can be controlled. For an n-channel FET, the control voltage must be negative. As the gate voltage is made more negative, channel current is restricted further until it is cut off entirely. For a p-channel FET, a positive control voltage is needed. Higher positive gate voltages restrict channel current further until the channel is cut off.

A variation of the FET is the Metal-Oxide Semiconductor FET (MOSFET). It is unlikely that you will ever encounter discrete MOSFET devices in your small computer, but many sophisticated digital integrated circuits make extensive use of MOSFETs. One of the few undesirable characteristics of FETs and MOSFETs is their sensitivity to damage by electrostatic discharge (ESD). You will learn about ESD in chapter 4.

There are a variety of electrical specifications that describe the performance and characteristics of particular transistors. When you discover that a transistor must be replaced, it is always wise to use an exact replacement. That way, you are assured that the replacement part will behave as expected. Under some circumstances, however, an exact replacement part might take too long to obtain, or not be available. You can then use cross-reference data to locate substitute parts with specifications similar to the original part. Keep in mind that substituting

parts with a different part—even when specifications are very similar—
might have an unforeseeable effect on the circuit. Do not attempt to use
"close" replacement parts unless you have a keen understanding of
transistor principles and specifications.

Transistors are available in a wide variety of case styles and sizes
depending on the amount of power to be handled. Figure 2-28 illustrates
five popular case styles. Low-power, general-purpose devices are often
packaged in the small, plastic TO-92 cases. The TO-18 metal case is also
used for low-power devices, but the TO-18 shown houses a

TO-92 case
(low power)

TO-18 case
(low-power)
phototransistor
opening shown

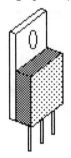

TO-220 case
(medium to
high power)

SOT-223
surface-mount
package

2-28
Various transistor package styles.

SOT-143
surface-mount
package

phototransistor. Note the quartz window on the case top that allows light to enter the device. For regular transistor applications, the TO-18 "top hat" case is all metal.

Medium-power transistors use the larger plastic TO-128 or TO-220 cases. The TO-128 has a thin metal heat sink molded into the top of the device. TO-220 cases use a large metal mounting flange/heat sink located directly behind the plastic case. The flange provides mechanical strength as well as a secure thermal path for an external heat sink. The all-metal TO-3 case is used for high-power transistors. Two mounting holes are provided to bolt the device to a chassis or external heat sink. As a general rule, case size is proportional to the power capacity of the transistor.

Transistors are also manufactured in surface-mount cases. Two typical SMT small-outline transistor (SOT) case styles are shown in FIG. 2-28. Due to their small size, SMT transistors cannot dissipate very much power, but are ideal for small, low-power systems such as notebook, palmtop, or pen computers.

As shown in FIG. 2-29, a transistor's part number is an index or reference number that allows you to look up the part's equivalent components or specifications in a data book or cross-reference manual. The number itself contains no useful information about the part's performance characteristics or limits. Classic bipolar transistor part numbers begin with the prefix "2N," followed by up to five digits. The 2N is used by JEDEC in the United States to denote devices with two semiconductor junctions. Classic Japanese transistor part numbers begin with any of four prefixes: 2SA (high-frequency PNP transistor), 2SB (low-frequency

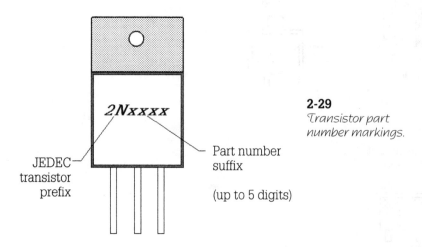

2-29
*Transistor part
number markings.*

2Nxxxx

JEDEC
transistor
prefix

Part number
suffix

(up to 5 digits)

PNP transistor), 2SC (high-frequency NPN transistor), and 2SD (low-frequency NPN transistor). JEDEC uses a 3N prefix to denote FETs or Junction FETs (JFETs). The prefixes 2SJ (p-channel JFET), 2SK (n-channel JFET), and 3SK (n- or p-channel MOSFETs) have been used in Japan.

You will also encounter a great many transistors with arcane or nonstandard markings. In almost all cases, you can identify replacement transistors and look up performance specifications using manufacturers' data or a cross-reference guide. Although the specifications found in a cross-reference guide are for replacement parts, they will generally match the original part's specifications very closely.

As with diodes, transistors rarely show any outward signs of failure unless they have melted or shattered from extreme overload. You generally must use test equipment to identify faulty transistors. Testing can be accomplished by measuring the device while the circuit is running, or removing the device from the circuit and measuring its characteristics out of the circuit.

Integrated circuits (ICs) are by far the most diverse and powerful group of electronic components that you will ever deal with. They have rapidly become the fundamental building blocks of modern electronic circuits. Amplifiers, memories, microprocessors, digital logic arrays, oscillators, timers, regulators, and a myriad of other complex functions are all manufactured as ICs. Circuits that only a decade ago would have required an entire PC board in a desktop computer are now being fabricated entirely on a single IC. Although you can often approximate the complexity (and importance) of an integrated circuit from the number of pins that it has, it is virtually impossible to predict precisely what an IC does just by looking at it. You will need a schematic of the circuit or the manufacturer's data for a particular IC in order to determine its function.

Integrated circuits

Every integrated circuit, whether analog or digital, is composed largely of microscopic transistors, diodes, capacitors, and resistors fabricated onto an IC die. Many capacitors and inductors cannot be fabricated on ICs, so conventional parts are attached to an IC through one or more external leads. Your small computer is almost entirely a digital system; that is, most of the ICs are designed to work with binary signals. The microprocessor, memory, and most of the controller ICs in a small computer are digital logic components. Other ICs, however, are intended to work with analog signal levels. Serial communication ICs, display driver ICs, and disk driver ICs are only some of the analog devices that you will find in a small computer.

A *logic gate* is a circuit that produces a binary result based on one or more binary inputs. A single integrated circuit can hold as few as one logic gate or thousands of logic gates depending on the complexity of the particular IC. There are eight basic types of logic gates: AND, OR, NAND, NOR, INVERTER, BUFFER, XOR (eXclusive OR), and XNOR (eXclusive NOR). Each gate uses its own particular logic symbol as shown in FIG. 2-30. Beside each symbol is the truth table for the particular gate. A truth table illustrates the gate's output for every possible combination of inputs. For the sake of simplicity, no more than two inputs are shown, but individual gates can have four, eight, or more inputs.

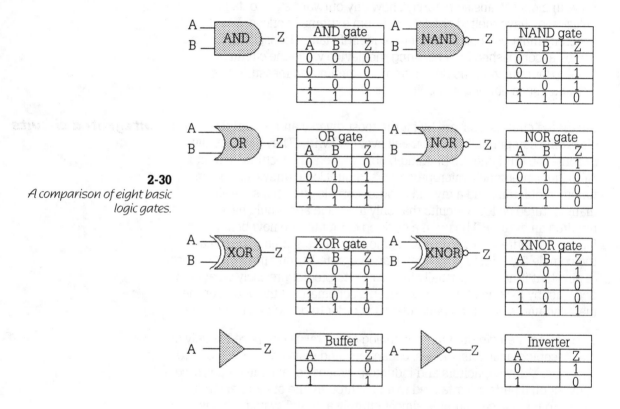

2-30
A comparison of eight basic logic gates.

AND gate

A	B	Z
0	0	0
0	1	0
1	0	0
1	1	1

NAND gate

A	B	Z
0	0	1
0	1	1
1	0	1
1	1	0

OR gate

A	B	Z
0	0	0
0	1	1
1	0	1
1	1	1

NOR gate

A	B	Z
0	0	1
0	1	0
1	0	0
1	1	0

XOR gate

A	B	Z
0	0	0
0	1	1
1	0	1
1	1	0

XNOR gate

A	B	Z
0	0	1
0	1	0
1	0	0
1	1	1

Buffer

A	Z
0	0
1	1

Inverter

A	Z
0	1
1	0

Flip-flops are slightly more involved than general-purpose gates, but are such flexible logic building blocks that they are usually considered to be logic gates. In the simplest sense, flip-flops are memory devices because they can "remember" the various logic states in a circuit. Flip-flops are also ideal for working with logical sequences. You often find flip-flops used around counter-timer circuits. There are three classic variations of flip-flops, as shown in FIG. 2-31: the D flip-flop, the SR flip-flop, and the JK flip-flop. Each flip-flop is shown with its corresponding truth table.

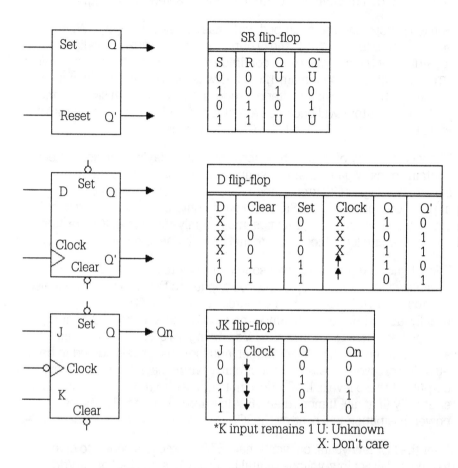

SR flip-flop			
S	R	Q	Q'
0	0	U	U
1	0	1	0
0	1	0	1
1	1	U	U

D flip-flop					
D	Clear	Set	Clock	Q	Q'
X	1	0	X	1	0
X	0	1	X	0	1
X	0	0	X	1	1
1	1	1	↑	1	0
0	1	1	↑	0	1

JK flip-flop			
J	Clock	Q	Qn
0	↓	0	0
0	↓	1	0
1	↓	0	1
1	↓	1	0

*K input remains 1 U: Unknown
X: Don't care

2-31
A comparison of basic flip-flops.

The SR flip-flop is rarely used alone in digital designs because it is *asynchronous*; that is, outputs change as soon as inputs change. Small computers rely on *synchronous* circuits, so unexpected or untimed changes in device outputs cannot be tolerated. The D- and JK-type flip-flops utilize a clock (CLK) input along with data input. As a result, inputs can change at will, but the outputs only change when prompted by a synchronizing clock pulse. D flip-flops are often used to help manage the flow of data along data busses—one flip-flop is used for each data bit.

As you look over the symbols in FIG. 2-30 and FIG. 2-31, notice that some of the inputs have a "bubble" at the device, which indicates negative logic.

In conventional Boolean logic, a TRUE signal indicates an ON condition, or the presence of a voltage. In negative logic, a TRUE signal is OFF, and a voltage is absent. This concept is extremely important in troubleshooting so that you do not confuse a correct signal for an erroneous signal.

Some flip-flops are also equipped with master override inputs. When the set override becomes TRUE, the Q output becomes TRUE immediately regardless of the input or clock condition. If the Q output was TRUE before SET is activated, it will remain TRUE. If Q was FALSE, it will immediately become TRUE. The other master override is RESET. When RESET becomes TRUE, the Q output will become FALSE immediately. Keep in mind that SET and RESET can never be made TRUE simultaneously.

The vast majority of logic components used in today's small computers contain so many gates that it is simply impossible to show them all on a schematic diagram. Current microprocessors, gate arrays, and application-specific ICs (ASICs) can each contain thousands of gates. To simplify schematics and drawings, most highly-integrated ICs are shown only as generic logic blocks interconnected to one another.

Every logic IC requires a power source in order to operate. At least one positive voltage source (V_{CC}) must be applied to the IC. The IC must also be grounded with respect to the source voltage. An IC's ground pin is usually labeled V_{SS} or GND. Since the days of the first logic ICs, supply voltage has been a standard of +5 Vdc. Using a +5 Vdc source, logic 1s are interpreted as +2.4 Vdc or higher, and logic 0s are considered to be +0.8 Vdc or lower. The transistor circuitry within each logic gate provides outputs at these levels. If +5 Vdc is not supplied to the IC, it will function erratically (if at all). If more than +6 Vdc is forced into the IC, excess power dissipation will destroy the IC.

Over the last few years, conventional +5 Vdc logic has begun to give way to a new class of low-voltage digital logic devices. Instead of +5 Vdc being supplied as V_{CC}, +3.0 to +3.3 Vdc is used. Logic 1s and logic 0s remain unchanged. There are advantages to low-voltage logic that have appealed to small-computer designers. Less voltage results in lower power dissipation for each IC—power consumption is reduced, and battery life is significantly improved. You receive more operating time from each battery charge. Also, lower voltage results in less stress on each transistor, so ICs can continue to pack more functions and features into new devices without fear of overheating the devices. Your new notebook or palmtop is probably using at least some low-voltage components right now. Chapter 3 shows you how to measure conventional and low-voltage logic signals. Low-voltage logic will be mentioned throughout the remainder of this book.

Integrated circuits are manufactured in a staggering array of package styles. Older package styles, such as the Dual In-line Package (DIP) and Single In-line Package (SIP), are intended for printed circuits using conventional through-hole assembly. Through-hole assembly requires that a component be inserted with its leads protruding through the PC board. The leads are soldered into place where they protrude. However, the push to pack ever more powerful ICs onto smaller PC boards has given rise to an overwhelming number of surface-mount IC package styles. Figure 2-32 shows a small sampling of typical package styles.

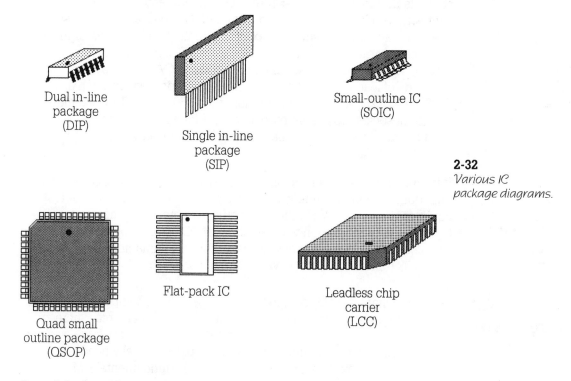

Dual in-line
package
(DIP)

Single in-line
package
(SIP)

Small-outline IC
(SOIC)

Quad small
outline package
(QSOP)

Flat-pack IC

Leadless chip
carrier
(LCC)

2-32
*Various IC
package diagrams.*

One of the key advantages of surface-mount packages is that components can be soldered onto both sides of a PC board, thus almost doubling the amount of available PC board area. The Small Outline IC (SOIC) design appears very similar to a DIP, but the SOIC is significantly smaller and its flat (or gull-wing shaped) pins are tightly spaced. Very Small Outline Package (VSOP) and the Quad Small Outline Package (QSOP) are designed to package complex ICs into extremely small packages with leads on two or four sides. Quad packages are also square (instead of rectangular) with pins on all four sides. Small Outline J-lead (SOJ) packages replace regular gull-wing leads with leads that are bent down and under the device in a "J" shape.

Flat packs tend to be large, square ICs used primarily for more sophisticated functions, such as microprocessors and specialized controllers. A Quad Flat Pack (QFP) and a Thin Quad Flat Pack (TQFP) offer as many as 100 pins (25 pins per side). TQFPs are handy in extremely tight spaces where regular QFPs might interfere with other assemblies. Chip carriers are either leaded (with leads) or unleaded (without leads). Leadless Chip Carriers (LCCs) simply provide exposed contacts that require a chip carrier socket to guarantee proper connections. Plastic Leaded Chip Carrier (PLCC) packages offer J-shaped pins that can either be surface mounted directly to a PC board, or inserted into a chip carrier socket. The Pin Grid Array (PGA) is the most sophisticated packaging scheme in use today. PGAs can provide hundreds of leads on an IC. Sophisticated microprocessors, such as Intel's x486, are packaged in PGAs with more than 150 pins. PGAs also require the use of sockets to ensure proper contact for all pins. Extreme care must be taken to prevent damage to pins when inserting and extracting PGAs.

It is rare for any type of IC to show outward signs of failure, so it is very important for you to carefully check suspect ICs using appropriate test equipment and data while the IC is actually operating in the system. Gather all the information you can about an IC before replacing it, because IC replacement is always risky. You risk damaging the PC board during IC removal, and the new IC during installation.

EM components

Electromechanical (EM) components are specialized components that use electrical energy to produce and deliver mechanical force. There are few EM components in your small computer because of the large size and relatively high power requirements that EM parts typically need. However, you should be familiar with two of the fundamental EM components that you may encounter: motors and relays.

Motors

Motors are an absolutely essential part of every floppy drive and hard drive ever produced. Both types of drives are used to store digital information that is held on small disks coated with layers of magnetic material. A motor is required to spin these disks. A floppy disk must spin at 300 rpm, while a hard drive must spin at 3600 rpm. A floppy drive also requires another motor to move the read/write heads to various recording tracks along the disk's radius. Chapter 7 deals with drive systems in detail. For now, you should concentrate on the motors themselves.

All motors convert electrical energy into rotating mechanical force. In turn, that force is distributed to the proper mechanism (e.g., head-positioning mechanics or disk spindle). A dc motor is typically used to spin disks at a constant speed. Figure 2-33 shows the schematic symbol for a dc motor. Direct current is applied to a powerful coil (armature) wrapped around a motor shaft that is free to turn. The armature is mounted within an array of opposing permanent magnets (field poles). When dc is applied, a magnetic field is produced in the armature. The armature's induced field opposes the fields of the permanent magnets. It is this force of opposition that causes the armature to turn. The motor speed is adjusted by varying the voltage and current to the armature.

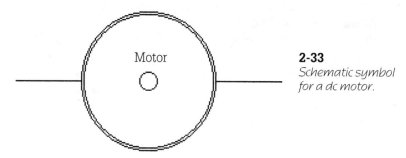

2-33
Schematic symbol for a dc motor.

While dc motors are good for maintaining a constant speed, they are poor for precise positioning applications. A *stepping motor* (stepper) is used to handle positioning. A stepper is constructed quite differently than a dc motor. Steppers use a series of permanent magnets built into a rotating shaft (rotor), while sets of individual coils are positioned about the stationary frame (stator). By powering sets of coils in sequence, the rotor is made to turn at known increments. Each driver signal is a square wave, so the rotor jumps, or steps, quite accurately and remains fixed in its new position for as long as its driver signals maintain their conditions. For example, a typical stepper can achieve a resolution of 1.8 degrees per step. That means the motor must make 200 steps to complete one full revolution. Figure 2-34 shows a schematic symbol for a stepping motor.

Stepping motors are ideal for precise positioning. Since the motor moves in known angular steps, the rotor shaft can be rotated to any position simply by applying the appropriate number of electrical driving pulses. Suppose your motor had to turn 180 degrees. If each motor step equals 1.8 degrees, control circuitry would need to produce 100 pulses to turn

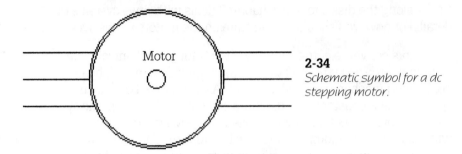

Motor

2-34
*Schematic symbol for a dc
stepping motor.*

the rotor exactly the prescribed amount. In floppy drives, the motor's
rotation is converted into linear motion for read/write head positioning.

Relays   A relay is simply a mechanical switch that is activated by the
electromagnetic force generated by an energized coil. A typical relay
diagram is shown in FIG. 2-35. The switch itself (the contact set) may be
either normally open (N.O.) or normally closed (N.C.) while the coil is de-
energized. When activated, the coil's magnetic field causes normally open
contacts to close, or normally closed contacts to open. Contacts are held
in their actuated positions as long as the coil remains energized. If the
coil is turned off, the contacts return to their normally open or normally
closed states. Keep in mind that a coil can drive more than one set of
contacts.

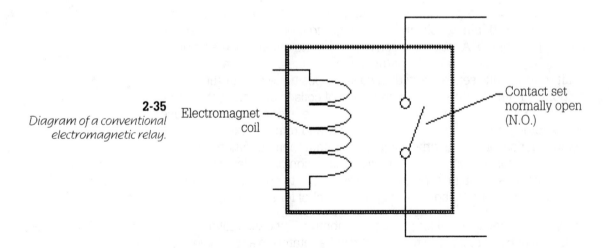

2-35
*Diagram of a conventional
electromagnetic relay.*

Electromagnet
coil

Contact set
normally open
(N.O.)

Your small computer might use a relay in its modem circuit to connect to
the telephone line, but relays are not always easy to recognize on sight.
Most relays used in electronic circuits are housed in small, rectangular
containers of metal or plastic. Low-power relays can be fabricated into

oversized DIP-style or surface-mount IC packages and soldered right onto a PC board just like any other IC. Unless the relay's internal diagram is printed on its outer package, you will need a circuit schematic or relay manufacturer's data to determine which of the relay's pins connect the coil, and which pins connect the contacts.

3

Tools & test instruments

You need a selection of basic tools and test equipment before you tackle a small-computer repair (FIG. 3-1). Test equipment is used to measure important circuit parameters such as voltage, current, resistance, capacitance, and semiconductor junction conditions. Additional test equipment lets you follow logic conditions and view complex waveforms at critical points in the circuit. This chapter introduces the background and testing methods for multimeters, component checkers, logic probes, and simple oscilloscopes.

3-1
An AST 386/25 MHz notebook computer.

If you don't have a well-stocked toolbox, now is a good time to consider things you need. Before beginning a repair, gather up a set of small hand tools and some inexpensive materials. Never underestimate the value of having the proper tools—they sometimes make or break your repair efforts.

Hand tools are basically used to disassemble and reassemble your small computer's housings and enclosures. You don't have to stock top-quality tools, but you should have the proper size and shape tools to do the job. Since notebook, palmtop, and pen computers are extremely small and tightly packaged, select tools that are small and thin wherever possible.

Screwdrivers should be the first item on your list. Most small-computer assemblies are held together with small or medium Phillips-head screws as shown in FIG. 3-2. Once you remove the outer housings, you will probably find that most of the other internal parts are also held down with Phillips screws. Consider obtaining one or two small and one medium Phillips screwdrivers. You will very rarely need a large screwdriver. Each screwdriver should be about 10.16 cm (4") to 15.24 cm (6") long with a wide handle for a good grip. Jeweler's screwdrivers are recommended for palmtop and pen computers. Round out your selection of screwdrivers by adding one small and one medium regular (flat blade) screwdriver. You won't use them as often as Phillips screwdrivers, but regular screwdrivers do come in handy.

Regular   Phillips   Allen   Spline   Torx

3-2
Major screw-head patterns.

You should be aware of three special screw heads. Allen screws use a hexagonal (six-sided) hole instead of regular or Phillips slots. Torx and spline screws use specially shaped holes that accept only the corresponding size and shape of driver. It is a good idea to keep a set of small hex keys on hand, but you rarely find special screw heads in today's small computers. Torx and spline screws are almost never found.

Wrenches are used to hold hexagonal bolt heads or nuts. There are not many instances where you need to remove nuts and bolts, but keep an inexpensive set of small, electronics-grade, open-ended wrenches. If you prefer, you can use a small adjustable wrench instead.

Needlenose pliers are valuable additions to your toolbox. Not as bulky and awkward as ordinary mechanic's pliers, needlenose pliers can be used to grip or bend both mechanical and electronic parts. Needlenose pliers can also be used as heat sinks during desoldering or soldering operations, discussed in more detail in chapter 4. Obtain both a short nose and long nose set of needlenose pliers. Short-nose pliers make great heat sinks, and allow you to grasp parts securely. Long-nose pliers are excellent for picking up and grasping parts lost in the tight confines of a small computer. All needlenose pliers should be small, good-quality, electronics-grade tools.

Diagonal cutters are also an important part of your tool collection. Cutters are used to cut wire and component leads when working with a small computer's electronics. You really need only one set of cutters, but the cutters should be small, good-quality, electronics-grade tools. Cutters should also have a low profile and a small cutting head to fit in tight spaces. Never use cutters to cut plastic, metal, or PC board material.

Add a pair of tweezers to your tool kit. The tweezers should be small, long, and made from antistatic plastic material. Metal tweezers should be avoided wherever possible to prevent accidental short circuits (as well as shocks) if they come into contact with operating circuitry. Metal tweezers can also conduct potentially damaging static charges into sensitive ICs.

Soldering tools You need a good, general-purpose soldering iron to repair your small computer's circuitry. A 20 to 25 W soldering iron with a fine tip is usually best. You can obtain a decent soldering iron from any local electronics store. Most soldering irons are powered directly by ac and are just fine for general touch-ups and heavier work. However, you should consider a dc-powered or gas-fueled iron for desoldering delicate, static-sensitive ICs. No matter what iron you buy, make sure it is recommended as "static-safe."

The iron absolutely must have its own metal stand! Never, under any circumstances, allow a soldering iron to rest unattended on a counter or table top: the potential for nasty burns or fire is simply too great. Keep a wet sponge handy to periodically wipe the iron's tip. Invest in a roll of electronics-grade rosin-core solder.

Desoldering tools are necessary for removing faulty components and wires. Once the solder joint is heated with a soldering iron, a desoldering tool can remove the molten solder, allowing you to easily remove the component or wire. A solder vacuum uses a small, spring-loaded plunger mounted in a narrow cylinder. When triggered, the plunger recoils and generates a vacuum that draws up any molten solder in the vicinity. Solder wick is little more than a fine copper braid. By heating the braid against a solder joint, the braid removes the molten solder by capillary action. These conventional desoldering tools are most effective on through-hole components.

SMT components can also be desoldered with conventional desoldering tools, but more efficient techniques for desoldering SMT parts exist. Specially shaped desoldering tips can ease SMT desoldering by heating all of the component's leads simultaneously. Powered vacuum pumps can also be used to remove molten solder much more thoroughly than spring-loaded versions.

A hand-held, battery-powered vacuum cleaner is helpful in routine maintenance operations. Periodically removing dust and debris from your keyboard can help prevent intermittent key operation. Brush or vacuum any dust that may be accumulating in your computer's vent holes. Clear vent holes will help keep your small computer running cooler.

Miscellany

Most small-computer systems use surface-mounted ICs, so you rarely need IC inserters and extractors. The exception to this rule is for Plastic Lead Chip Carriers (PLCC). Once a PLCC has been inserted into its holder, there is virtually no way to remove it without using a special PLCC extraction tool. Figure 3-3 shows the tool and several sizes of PLCC sockets. Insert the extractor tool's tips into the slots at either set of opposing corners on a PLCC socket. Squeeze the extractor gently to push the tips under the IC, then wiggle the IC to pull it free. Once an IC is free, be certain to keep it on an antistatic mat, or on a piece of antistatic foam.

3-3
PLCC removal tool and PLCC sockets.

Keep a supply of antistatic materials in your tool kit to help prevent accidental damage to your expensive electronics. An antistatic wrist strap connects your body to ground in order to remove any static charge buildup from your body. Whenever working with PC boards and ICs, use antistatic foam to hold ICs and antistatic bags to hold PC boards. Avoid styrofoam and other plastics because they hold static charges. You might also want to invest in an antistatic mat, which rolls out onto a desk or workbench and connects to ground much like a wrist strap. An antistatic mat allows you to place delicate PC boards and chassis on your workbench while you work with them.

Keep an assortment of solid and stranded hookup wire in your toolbox. Wire should be between 18 to 24 AWG (gauge), preferably above 20 AWG. Heat shrink tubing is another handy material for your repairs. Tubing can be cut to length as needed, then positioned and shrunk to insulate wire splices and long component leads. You can buy a special heat gun to shrink the tubing, but an ordinary hair blow drier usually works just as well. When heating tubing, be certain to direct hot air away from ICs and PC boards.

Multimeters

A multimeter is by far the handiest and most versatile piece of test equipment that you'll ever use (FIG. 3-4). If you don't already own a good multimeter, now would be a good time to consider purchasing one. Even the most basic digital multimeters are capable of measuring resistance, ac and dc voltage, and ac and dc current. For under $150, you can buy a digital multimeter that includes handy features, such as a capacitance checker, a frequency meter, an extended current measuring range, a continuity buzzer, and even a diode and transistor checker. These are features that will aid you not only in small-computer repairs, but in many other types of electronic repairs as well. Digital multimeters are easier to read, more tolerant of operator error, and more precise then analog multimeters. Digital multimeters are assumed to be used throughout this book.

3-4
A full-featured digital multimeter.

B+K Precision

For most multimeters, there are only three things to consider during setup and use. First, turn the meter on. Unlike analog multimeters, digital multimeters require power to operate LCDs and LEDs. Make sure that you turn meter power off when you are finished testing. Power awareness helps to conserve battery life. Second, set the meter to the desired function or mode, such as frequency, voltage, capacitance, or resistance, that is appropriate for your measurement.

Finally, select the meter's range for its selected function. Ideally, you should choose the range that is nearest to (but above) the level you expect to measure. For example, suppose you are measuring a 9 Vdc battery. Set your meter to the dc voltage function, then set the range as close to (but greater than) 9 Vdc as possible. If the voltage ranges are 0.2 Vdc, 2 Vdc, 20 Vdc, and 200 Vdc, select the 20 Vdc range.

If you are unsure about which range to use, start by choosing the highest possible range. Once you take some measurements and get a better idea of the actual reading, you can adjust the meter's range "on the fly" to achieve a more precise reading. If your reading exceeds the meter's current range, an overrange warning is displayed until you increase the meter's range above the measured value. Some digital multimeters automatically select the appropriate range setting when a signal is applied.

It is usually a good idea to check the integrity of your test leads (probes) from time to time. Since test leads undergo a serious amount of tugging and general abuse, you should confirm that the probes are working as expected. There are few experiences more frustrating than to replace parts that your meter indicated were faulty only to discover that the meter leads were bad.

To check your leads, set your meter to the resistance function and select the lowest scale (such as 0.1 Ω). You will see an overrange condition, which is expected when setting up for resistance measurements. Make sure that both test probes are inserted into the meter properly and touch the probe tips together. The resistance reading should drop to about 0 Ω to indicate that your meter probes are intact. If you do not see roughly 0 Ω, check your probes carefully. After you have proven out your test probes, return the multimeter to its original function and range so that you may continue testing.

You may see other terms related to multimeter testing, such as *static* and *dynamic*. Static tests are usually made on components (either in or out of a circuit) with the power removed. Resistance, capacitance, and semiconductor junction tests are all static tests. Dynamic tests typically examine circuit conditions, so power must be applied to the circuit and all components must be in place. Voltage, current, and frequency are the most common dynamic tests. Now that you have a grasp of multimeter handling, let's look at multimeter test techniques.

Measuring voltage Every signal in your small computer has a certain amount of voltage associated with it. By measuring signal voltages with a multimeter (or other test instrument), you can usually make a determination as to whether or not the signal is correct. Supply voltages that provide power to your circuits can also be measured to ensure that components are receiving enough energy to operate. Voltage tests are the most fundamental and important dynamic tests in electronics.

Multimeters can measure both ac and dc voltages directly. Remember that all voltage measurements are taken in parallel with the desired circuit or component. Never interrupt a circuit and attempt to measure voltage in series with other components. Those readings would be meaningless, and your circuit will probably not even function.

Follow your setup guidelines and configure your meter to measure ac or dc voltage as required. Then select the proper range for the voltages you will be measuring. If you are unsure just what range to use, always start with the largest possible range. An autoranging multimeter sets its own range once a signal is applied. Place your test leads across (in parallel with) the circuit or part under test, as shown in FIG. 3-5, and read the

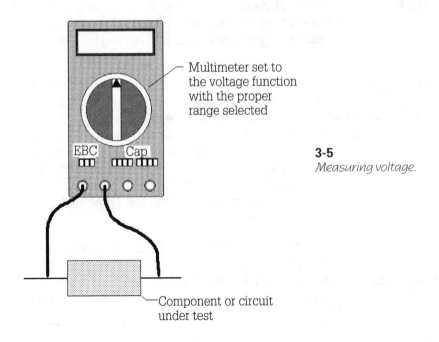

Multimeter set to the voltage function with the proper range selected

3-5
Measuring voltage.

Component or circuit under test

voltage directly from the meter's digital display. All dc voltage readings are polarity-sensitive, so if you read +5 Vdc and reverse the test leads, you will see a reading of –5 Vdc. All ac voltage readings are not polarity-sensitive.

Most general-purpose multimeters allow you to measure ac and dc current in an operating circuit, although there are typically fewer ranges to select. As with voltage measurements, current is a dynamic test, so the circuit or component being tested must be under power. However, current must be measured in series with a circuit or component.

Measuring current

Unfortunately, inserting a meter in series is not always a simple task. In many cases, you must interrupt a circuit at the point you want to measure and connect your test leads across the break. While it might be quite easy to interrupt a circuit, remember that you have to put the circuit back together, so use care when choosing a point to break. Never attempt to measure current in parallel across a component or circuit. Current meters, by their very nature, exhibit a very low resistance across their test leads (often below 0.1 Ω). Placing a current meter in parallel can cause a short circuit across a component, which can damage that component, the circuit under test, or the meter itself.

Set your multimeter to the desired function (dcA or acA) and appropriate range. If you are unsure about the proper range, set the meter to its largest possible range. It is usually necessary to plug your positive test lead into a current input jack on the multimeter. Unless your multimeter is protected by an internal fuse (as most meters are), its internal current measurement circuits can be damaged by excessive current. Make sure that your meter can handle the maximum amount of current you are expecting to measure.

Turn off all power to a circuit before inserting a current meter. This prevents any unpredictable or undesirable circuit operation when you actually interrupt the circuit. If you wish to measure the power supply current feeding a circuit, such as in FIG. 3-6, break the power supply line at any convenient point, insert the meter carefully, then reapply the power. Read the current directly from the meter's display. This procedure can also be used for taking current measurements within a circuit.

Measuring frequency

Some multimeters offer a frequency counter that can read the frequency of a sinusoidal signal. The ranges that are available depend on your particular meter. Simple hand-held meters can often read up to 100 kHz, while benchtop models can handle 10 MHz or more. Frequency measurements are dynamic readings made with circuit power applied.

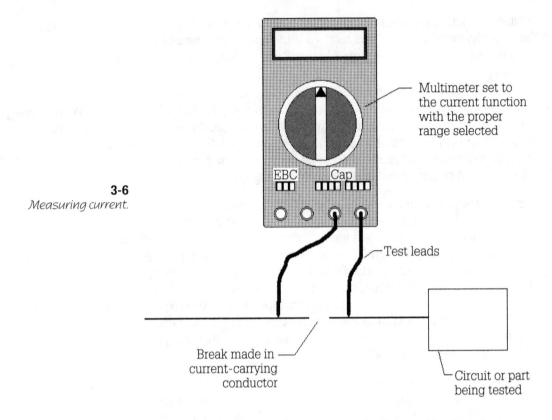

3-6
Measuring current.

Multimeter set to
the current function
with the proper
range selected

EBC   Cap

Test leads

Break made in
current-carrying
conductor

Circuit or part
being tested

Set your multimeter to its frequency counter function and select the
appropriate range. If you are unsure just what range to use, start your
measurements at the highest possible range. Place your test leads in
parallel across the component or circuit to be tested as shown in FIG. 3-7,
and read the frequency directly from the meter's display. An auto-ranging
multimeter will select the proper range when the signal is applied.

Frequency measurements have little practical use in small-computer
repair since most signals you encounter will be square instead of
sinusoidal. Square waves usually yield false readings unless the meter is
designed specifically for square wave readings. A digital frequency
counter and an oscilloscope should be used to measure square waves.

**Measuring
resistance**

Resistance, in ohms, is the most common static measurement that your
multimeter is capable of performing. This is a handy function, not only for
checking resistors but for checking other resistive elements like wires,
solenoids, motors, connectors, and some basic semiconductor
components. Resistance is a static test, so all power to the component or
circuit must be removed. It might be necessary to remove at least one

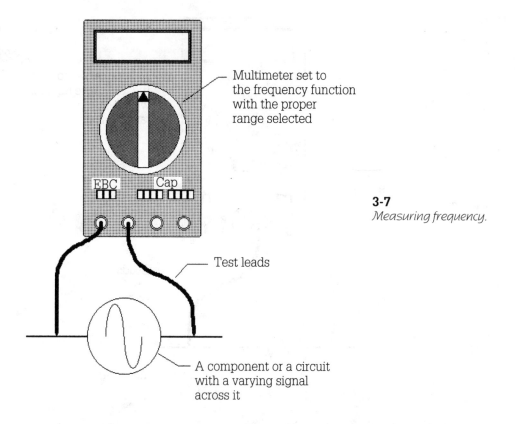

Multimeter set to
the frequency function
with the proper
range selected

3-7
Measuring frequency.

Test leads

A component or a circuit
with a varying signal
across it

EBC   Cap

component lead from its circuit to prevent interconnections with other components from causing false readings. Ordinary resistors, coils, and wires can be checked simply by switching to a resistance function (often marked OHMS, or Ω) and selecting the appropriate range. Auto-ranging multimeters select the proper range after the meter's test leads are connected. Many multimeters can reliably measure resistance up to about 20 MΩ. Place your test leads in parallel across the component as shown in FIG. 3-8, and read resistance directly from the meter's display. If the resistance exceeds the selected range, the display will indicate an overrange (or infinite resistance) condition.

Continuity checks are made to ensure a reliable, low-resistance connection between two points. For example, you could check the continuity of a cable between two connectors to ensure that both ends are connected properly. Set your multimeter to a low resistance scale and place your test leads across both points to measure. Ideally, good continuity should be about 0 Ω. Continuity tests can also be taken to show that a short circuit has not occurred between two points.

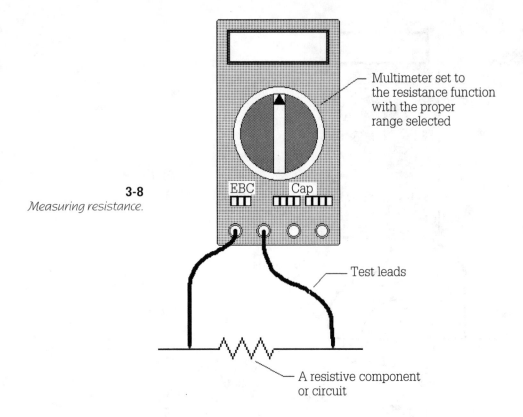

3-8
Measuring resistance.

Multimeter set to
the resistance function
with the proper
range selected

Test leads

A resistive component
or circuit

Measuring There are two methods of checking a capacitor using a multimeter: by
capacitors exact measurement, and by a quality check. The exact measurement test
determines the actual capacitor value. If the reading is close enough to
the value marked on the capacitor, you know the device is good. If not,
you know the device is faulty and should be replaced. Exact
measurement requires your multimeter to be equipped with a built-in
capacitance checker. If your meter does not have a built-in capacitance
checker, you can measure a capacitor directly on any other type of special
component checker, such as the ones shown in FIG. 3-9 and FIG. 3-10. You
could also use your multimeter to perform a simple quality check of a
suspect capacitor.

Capacitor checkers, whether built into your multimeter or part of a standalone component checker, are extremely simple to use. Turn off all circuit
power. Set the function to measure capacitors, select the range of
capacitance to be measured, then place your test probes in parallel across
the capacitor to be measured. You should remove at least one of the
capacitor's leads from the circuit being tested in order to prevent the
interconnections of other components from affecting the capacitance

3-9
*A general-purpose
multimeter and
component checker.*

3-10
*A specialized, hand-held
component checker.*

reading. In some cases, it may be easier to remove the suspect part entirely before measuring it. Some meters provide test slots that let you insert the component directly into the meter. Once in place, you can read the capacitor's value directly from the meter display.

If your multimeter is not equipped with an internal capacitor checker, you can use the resistance ranges of your ohmmeter to approximate a capacitor's quality. This type of check, as we describe it, provides a "quick-and-dirty" judgment of whether the capacitor is good or bad. The principle behind this type of check is simple: all ohmmeter ranges use an internal battery to supply current to the component under test. When that current is applied to a working capacitor, as shown in FIG. 3-11, it will cause the capacitor to charge. Charge accumulates as the ohmmeter is left connected. When first connected, the uncharged capacitor draws a

3-11
Measuring the quality of a capacitor using the ohmmeter function of a multimeter.

Multimeter set to the resistance function with a medium to high range selected

Resistance (Ω) ∞

Open
Small value
Medium value
Large value

Shorted

φ

time (t)

Resistance readings versus time

EBC Cap

Test leads

+

Capacitor

healthy amount of current—this reads as low resistance. As the capacitor charges, its rate of charge slows down and less and less current is drawn as time goes on—this results in a gradually increasing resistance level. Ideally, a fully charged capacitor stops drawing current, which results in an overrange or infinite resistance display. When a capacitor behaves in this way, it is probably good.

Understand that you are not actually measuring resistance OR capacitance here, but only the profile of a capacitor's charging characteristic. If the capacitor is extremely small (in the picofarad range), or is open, it will not accept any substantial charge, so the multimeter will read infinity almost immediately. If a capacitor is partially (or totally) short circuited, it will not hold a charge, so you may read 0 Ω, or the resistance might climb to some value below infinity and remain there. In either case, the capacitor is probably defective. If you doubt your readings, check several other capacitors of the same value and compare readings. Be sure to make this test on a moderate- to high-resistance scale. A low-resistance scale might overrange too quickly to achieve a clear reading.

Diode checks Many multimeters provide a special diode resistance scale used to check the static resistance of common diode junctions. Since working diodes conduct current only in one direction, the diode check lets you determine whether a diode is open or short circuited. Remember that diode checking is a static test, so power must be removed from the part under test. Before making measurements, be certain that at least one of the diode's leads has been removed from the circuit. Isolating the diode prevents interconnections with other circuit components from causing false readings.

Select the diode option from your multimeter's resistance functions. You generally do not have to bother with a range setting while in the diode mode. Connect your test leads in parallel with the diode in the forward-bias direction as shown in FIG. 3-12. A working silicon diode should exhibit a static resistance between about 450 Ω and 700 Ω, which will read directly on the meter's display. Reverse the orientation of your test probes to reverse-bias the diode as in FIG. 3-13. Since a working diode will not conduct at all in the reverse direction, you should read infinite resistance.

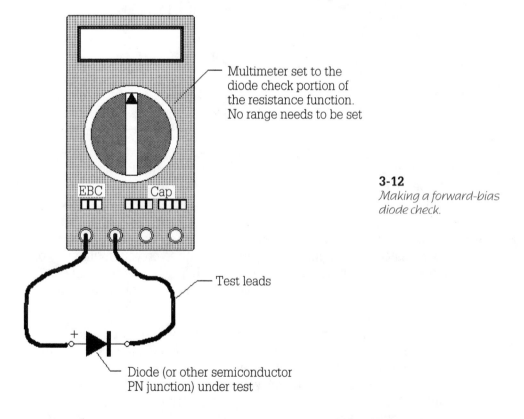

Multimeter set to the diode check portion of the resistance function. No range needs to be set

3-12
Making a forward-bias diode check.

Test leads

Diode (or other semiconductor PN junction) under test

A short-circuited diode will exhibit a very low resistance in the forward and reverse-biased directions. This indicates a shorted semiconductor junction. An open-circuited diode will exhibit very high resistance

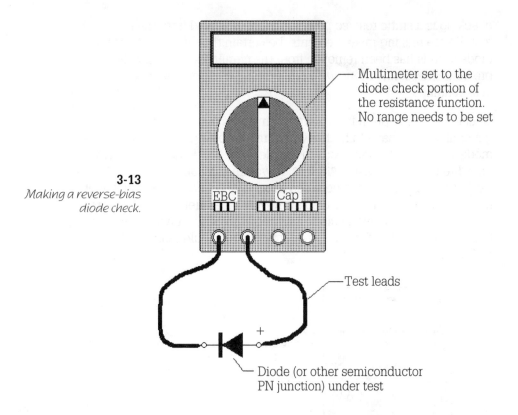

Multimeter set to the
diode check portion of
the resistance function.
No range needs to be set

EBC   Cap

3-13
*Making a reverse-bias
diode check.*

Test leads

+

Diode (or other semiconductor
PN junction) under test

(usually infinity) in both its forward and reverse-biased directions. An open or shorted diode must be replaced. If you feel unsure how to interpret your measurements, test several other comparable diodes and compare readings.

Transistor checks Transistors are slightly more sophisticated semiconductor devices that can be tested using a transistor checking function on your multimeter or component checker. Transistor junctions can also be checked using a multimeter's diode function. The following procedures show you both methods of transistor checking.

Some multimeters feature a built-in transistor checker that measures a transistor's gain (called *beta* or hfe) directly. By comparing measured gain to the gain value specified in the manufacturer's data (or measurements taken from other identical parts), you can easily determine whether the transistor is operating properly. Multimeters with a transistor checker generally offer a test fixture right on the meter's face. The fixture consists of two, three-hole sockets—one for NPN devices, and one for PNP devices. If your meter offers a transistor checker, insert the transistor into the test fixture on the meter's face.

Since all bipolar transistors are three-terminal devices (emitter, base, and collector), they must be inserted into the meter in their proper lead orientation before you can achieve a correct reading. Manufacturer's data sheets for a transistor will identify each lead and tell you the approximate gain reading that you should expect to see. Once the transistor is inserted correctly in its socket, you can read gain directly from the meter's display.

Set the meter to its transistor checker function. You should not be concerned about selecting a range when checking transistors. Insert the transistor into its test fixture. An unusually low reading (or 0) suggests a short-circuited transistor, while a high (or infinite) reading indicates an open-circuited transistor. In either case, the transistor is probably defective and should be replaced. If you are uncertain of your readings, test several other identical transistors and compare your readings.

If your particular multimeter or parts tester offers only a diode checker, you can approximate the transistor's condition by measuring its semiconductor junctions individually. Figure 3-14 illustrates the transistor junction test method. Although structurally different from conventional diodes, the base-emitter and base-collector junctions of bipolar transistors behave just like diodes. As a general rule, you should remove the transistor from its circuit to prevent false readings caused by other interconnected components. Junction testing is also handy for all

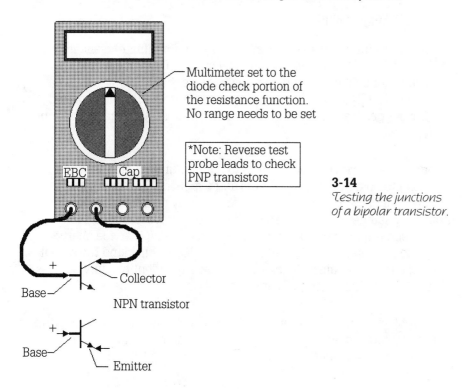

Multimeter set to the diode check portion of the resistance function. No range needs to be set

*Note: Reverse test probe leads to check PNP transistors

3-14
Testing the junctions of a bipolar transistor.

EBC   Cap

Base — Collector

NPN transistor

Base — Emitter

varieties of SMT transistors that do not fit into conventional multimeter test sockets.

Set your multimeter to its diode resistance function. If your suspect transistor is NPN type (manufacturer's data or a corresponding schematic symbol will tell you), place the positive test lead at the transistor's base and the negative test lead on the transistor's emitter. This test lead arrangement should forward-bias the transistor's base-emitter junction and result in a normal amount of diode resistance (450 to 700 Ω). Reverse the test leads across the base-emitter junction. The junction should now be reverse-biased, showing infinite resistance. Repeat this entire procedure for the base-collector junction.

If your suspect transistor is the PNP type, reverse the test leads before using the previous procedure. In other words, a junction that is forward-biased in an NPN transistor will be reverse-biased in a PNP device. To forward-bias the base-emitter junction of a PNP transistor, place the positive test lead on the emitter, and the negative test lead on the base. The same concept holds true for the base-collector junction.

Once both junctions are checked, measure the diode resistance from collector to emitter. You should read infinite resistance in both test lead orientations. Although there should be no connection from collector to emitter while the transistor is unpowered, a short circuit can sometimes develop during a failure.

If any of your junctions read an unusually high (or infinite) resistance in both directions, the junction is probably open. An unusually low resistance (or 0 Ω) in either direction suggests that the junction has a short circuit. Any resistance below infinity between the collector and emitter suggests a damaged transistor. In any case, the transistor should be replaced.

IC checks   There are very few conclusive ways to test integrated circuits without resorting to complex logic analyzers and expensive IC test equipment. ICs are so incredibly diverse that there is simply no universal test that will pinpoint a failure. However, you can make extensive use of IC service charts (sometimes called service checkout charts). IC service charts show the logic (or voltage) level for each pin of an IC. By checking the actual state of each pin against the chart, you can often identify faulty devices. You see more about using IC service charts later in this book.

Logic probes   The problem with multimeters is that they do not relate very well to the fast-changing signals found in digital logic circuits. A multimeter can certainly measure whether a logic voltage is on or off, but if that logic signal changes quickly (such as a clock or bus signal, a dc voltmeter will show only the average signal. Logic probes are little more than extremely simple voltage sensors, but a logic probe precisely and conveniently detects digital logic levels, clock signals, and digital pulses. Some logic probes operate at speeds greater than 50 MHz.

Logic probes are rather simple-looking devices, as shown in FIG. 3-15. Indeed, logic probes are perhaps the simplest and least expensive test instruments that you will ever use, but they provide valuable and reliable information. A logic probe can be powered from its own internal battery or from the circuit under test. Regardless of how the probe is powered, it must be connected into the common (ground) of the circuit being tested to ensure a proper reference level. If the probe is powered from the circuit under test, attach the probe's power lead to a logic supply voltage source in the circuit. Logic probes are capable of working from a wide range of supply voltages (typically 4 to 18 Vdc).

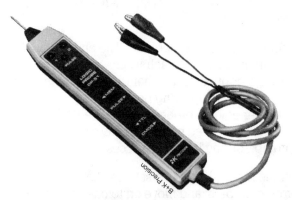

3-15
*A general-purpose
50 MHz logic probe.*

Logic probes use a series of LED indicators to display the measured condition: a logic HIGH (1), a logic LOW (0), or a pulse (clock) signal. Some logic probe models offer a switch that allows the probe to operate with two common logic families, TTL and CMOS. You might sometimes find TTL and CMOS devices in the same circuit, but one family of logic devices will usually dominate.

**Reading the
logic probe**

To use a logic probe, touch its metal tip to the desired IC or component lead. Be certain that the point you wish to measure is, in fact, a logic point because high-voltage signals can damage the logic probe. The logic state is interpreted by a few simple gates within the probe, then displayed on the appropriate LED. TABLE 3-1 illustrates the LED sequences for one particular type of logic probe. By comparing the probe's measurements to the information contained in an IC service chart, you can determine whether or not the suspect IC is behaving properly.

Table 3-1
Typical logic probe LED patterns.

Input signal		HI LED	LO LED	PULSE LED
Logic "1"	TTL or CMOS	ON	OFF	OFF
Logic "0"	TTL or CMOS	OFF	ON	OFF
Bad logic level or open circuit		OFF	OFF	OFF
Square wave	<200 kHz	ON	ON	BLINK
Square wave	>200 kHz	ON/OFF	ON/OFF	BLINK
Narrow "high" pulse		OFF	ON/OFF	BLINK
Narrow "low" pulse		ON/OFF	OFF	BLINK

Logic probes &
service charts

Although the logic probe provides an array of very useful information about the various conditions of digital circuits, that information is difficult to interpret unless you have something to compare your readings with. After all, how do you know if a signal is right or wrong if you don't know what it's supposed to be in the first place? A service chart supplies that reference information for comparison.

TABLE 3-2 shows a simple service chart for a single IC. The chart is similar to those found in service documentation. For each IC pin, you find an average dc voltage reading, a description of whether the pin is an input or output, and logic probe conditions. By supplying both types of readings, you can use either your voltmeter or logic probe to check the IC. Also note that each chart is made under defined circuit conditions (e.g., standing idle at the DOS prompt, during hard drive access, etc.).

When your readings match the levels shown in a service chart, you can assume that the IC is operating properly and move on to check another IC. When you find an IC output that is incorrect, the IC generating the output may well be defective. If you find an IC input that is incorrect, the IC accepting the input could be faulty, but make sure to check the IC(s) providing the questionable signal before changing the suspect IC. Remember that troubleshooting is an analysis of cause and effect relationships—in order to correct the effect, you must correct the cause.

So what happens when you do not have a service chart with which to compare your readings? There is no simple answer to this question, but you usually have three options. First, you could take a proactive roll in troubleshooting and develop your own service charts. This requires you to disassemble your machine before it fails and make a complete set of measurements, which you would keep tucked away until you need them. The second approach is to use common sense in conjunction with a

Table 3-2
Sample service chart.

Integrated Circuit Service Chart				
IC Part Number: SN7400			IC Number: U29	
IC Function: QUAD, 2-INPUT NAND GATE				

IC Pin	Logic Cond.	Voltage	I/O	Descriptions and Notes
1	0	0.3 V	I	GATE 1
2	1	3.8 V	I	
3	1	4.2 V	O	
4	0	0.2 V	I	GATE 2
5	0	0.2 V	I	
6	1	4.6 V	O	
7		0 V		GROUND
8	PULSE	2.16 V	O	GATE 3
9	PULSE	2.3 V	I	
10	1	4.3 V	I	
11	0	0.1 V	O	GATE 4
12	1	4.2 V	I	
13	1	4.4 V	I	
14		+5 V		+ Vcc

schematic or service data. Does a particular reading make sense? For example, if you see pulse activity on every data bus line but one, chances are an IC is freezing the suspect data line. Experience will teach you which signal readings are right and which are wrong. Finally, you could forego troubleshooting to the component level altogether and simply replace to the module or subsystem level (i.e., replace power supplies, LCD assemblies, motherboards, etc.).

Reading low-voltage logic

For years, digital logic ICs have been powered by a +5 Vdc supply voltage. If you have any experience at all with digital logic, you probably recognize the +5 Vdc standard. However, the +5 Vdc standard is quickly being replaced by a new, low-voltage standard, +3.3 Vdc. A lower supply voltage means that ICs will draw significantly less power (meaning fewer battery changes or longer charge life) and run cooler. With ICs running at 3 volts, what happens to logic signal levels?

Fortunately, the family of new 3 volt ICs still operate within the accepted conventions of 5 volt logic levels. For example, a 5 volt logic IC provides a minimum logic 1 output of +2.4 Vdc, and a maximum logic 0 output of +0.4 Vdc, while accepting a minimum logic 1 input of +2.0 Vdc and a maximum logic 0 input of +0.8 Vdc. The new 3 volt logic tends to "ride the rails" by providing a logic 1 at about +3.0 Vdc and a logic 0 of roughly 0 Vdc, yet it accepts a minimum logic 1 input of +2.0 Vdc and a maximum logic 0 input of +0.8 Vdc.

As you might see, the two logic families use compatible logic levels. The only problem arises when a logic 1 from a 5 volt gate (which can be as high as +4.9 Vdc) drives a 3 volt logic input. When an input voltage exceeds a supply voltage in this way, the low-voltage logic can be damaged. Low-voltage logic designers are investing a great deal of effort to overcome this voltage incompatibility problem. The relationship of logic levels to voltage levels is illustrated graphically in FIG. 3-16.

3-16
A graphic comparison of +5 volt and low-voltage logic levels.

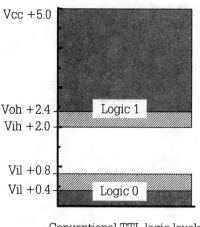

Conventional TTL logic levels

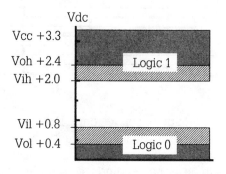

Low-voltage TTL logic levels

As far as your troubleshooting effort is concerned, be aware that your small computer probably utilizes at least a few (but possibly all) low-voltage logic components. Since the logic levels are at least compatible in principle, your logic probe should be able to provide the correct readings as long as it is being powered and grounded correctly.

Oscilloscopes

Oscilloscopes offer a tremendous advantage over multimeters and logic probes. Instead of reading signals in terms of numbers or lighted indicators, an oscilloscope will show voltage versus time on a graphical display. Not only can you observe ac and dc voltages, but oscilloscopes enable you to watch any other unusual signals that occur in real time. If you have used an oscilloscope (or seen one used), then you probably know just how useful they can be. Oscilloscopes, such as the one shown in FIG. 3-17, might appear somewhat overwhelming at first, but many of their operations work the same way regardless of what model you use.

3-17
Photo of a 60 MHz analog oscilloscope.

Controls

In spite of the wide variations in features and complexity, most controls are common to all oscilloscopes. Controls fall into four categories: horizontal (time base) control, vertical (voltage sensitivity) control, housekeeping controls, and optional (enhanced) controls.

Housekeeping controls handle such mundane functions as oscilloscope power, trace intensity, graticule intensity, trace magnification, horizontal trace offset, vertical trace offset, and the trace finder. Generally speaking, any control that affects the trace itself (not the way trace information is being displayed) is called a housekeeping control.

Since an oscilloscope displays voltage versus time, adjusting either the voltage sensitivity or the time-base settings alters the display's appearance. Horizontal controls manipulate the left-to-right time appearance (sweep) of the voltage signal. Your oscilloscope's master time base is adjusted using the TIME/DIV knob or buttons. This sets the rate at which voltage signals are swept onto the screen. As a general rule, smaller TIME/DIV settings allow shorter events to be displayed more clearly, and vice versa. Remaining horizontal controls include a horizontal display mode selector, sweep trigger selector and sensitivity, trigger coupling selection, and trigger source selection. Your particular oscilloscope may offer even more controls.

An adjustment to the oscilloscope's voltage sensitivity will also alter the display. Vertical controls affect the deflection (up-to-down appearance) of your signal. An oscilloscope's vertical sensitivity is controlled with the VOLTS/DIV knob or buttons. When the VOLTS/DIV setting is made smaller (voltage sensitivity is increased), signals will appear larger vertically. A larger VOLTS/DIV setting decreases voltage sensitivity, so voltage signals will appear smaller vertically. Other vertical controls include coupling selection, vertical mode selection, and a display inverter switch.

Your oscilloscope might have any number of optional controls, depending on its cost and complexity, but cursor and storage controls are two of the most common. Some digital oscilloscopes offer horizontal and vertical on-screen cursors to aid in the evaluation of waveforms. Panel controls allow each cursor to be moved around the screen. The relative distance between the cursors is then calculated and converted to a corresponding voltage, time, or frequency value and displayed on the screen in appropriate units. Storage oscilloscopes allow a screen display to be held right on the screen, or saved in digital memory within the oscilloscope.

Oscilloscope specifications

There are important specifications that you should be familiar with when choosing and using an oscilloscope. The first is called *bandwidth*. Bandwidth represents the absolute range of frequencies that an oscilloscope can work with. Bandwidth does not mean that all signals within that frequency range will be displayed clearly. Bandwidth is usually rated from dc to some maximum frequency. For example, a relatively inexpensive oscilloscope may cover dc to 20 MHz, while a top-of-the-line model may work up to 200 MHz or more. Broad bandwidth is very expensive, more so than any other feature.

The vertical deflection (or vertical sensitivity) is another important specification. It is listed as the minimum to maximum VOLTS/DIV settings that are offered, and the number of steps that are available within that range. A typical model may provide vertical sensitivity from 5 mV/DIV to 5 V/DIV broken down into 10 steps.

A time base (or sweep range) specification represents the minimum to maximum time base rates that an oscilloscope can produce, and the number of TIME/DIV increments available within that range. A range of 0.1 μs/DIV to 0.2 sec/DIV in 20 steps is not unusual. You will typically find a greater number of time base increments than sensitivity increments.

There is a maximum voltage input that an oscilloscope is capable of handling. If the maximum input voltage level is exceeded, the oscilloscope's input amplifier may be damaged. A maximum voltage input of 400 V (dc or peak ac) is common for most basic models, but more sophisticated models can accept input voltages better than 1000 V. An oscilloscope's input will present a load to whatever circuit or component across which it is placed. This is called *input impedance*, and is usually expressed as a combined value of resistance and capacitance. To guarantee proper operation over the model's entire bandwidth, select a probe with load characteristics similar to those of the oscilloscope. Most oscilloscopes have an input impedance of 1 MΩ with anywhere from 10 to 50 pF of capacitance.

The accuracy of an oscilloscope represents the vertical and horizontal accuracy presented in the CRT display. Oscilloscopes are usually not as accurate as multimeters. Typical oscilloscopes can provide ±3% accuracy, so a 1-V measurement may be displayed between 0.97 V to 1.03 V (not considering human errors in reading the CRT's graticule). However, since the strength of an oscilloscope is its ability to graphically display complex and quickly changing signals, ±3% accuracy is often more than adequate.

Oscilloscope start-up procedure

Before you begin taking measurements, a clear, stable trace must be obtained (if not already visible). If a trace is not already visible, make sure that any CRT screen storage modes are turned off, and that trace intensity is turned up to at least 50%. Set the trace triggering to its automatic mode and adjust the horizontal and vertical offset controls to the center of their ranges. Be sure to select an internal trigger source from the channel your probe is plugged in to, then adjust the trigger level until a stable trace is displayed. Vary your vertical offset if necessary to center the trace in the CRT.

If a trace is not yet visible, use the beam finder to reveal the beam's location. A beam finder simply compresses the vertical and horizontal ranges and forces a trace onto the display. This gives you a rough idea of the trace's relative position. Once you are able to finally move the trace into position, adjust your focus and intensity controls to obtain a crisp, sharp trace. Keep the intensity at a moderately low level to improve display accuracy and preserve the CRT phosphors.

Your oscilloscope should be calibrated to its probe before use. A typical oscilloscope probe is shown in FIG. 3-18. Calibration is a quick and straightforward operation that requires only a low-amplitude, low-frequency square wave. Many models have a built-in calibration-signal generator (usually a 1 kHz, 300 mV square wave with a duty cycle of 50%). Attach your probe to the desired input jack and place the probe tip across the calibration signal. Adjust your horizontal (TIME/DIV) and vertical (VOLTS/DIV) controls so that one or two complete cycles are clearly shown on the CRT.

3-18
Photo of a typical oscilloscope probe assembly.

Observe the visual characteristics of the test signal as shown in FIG. 3-19. If the square wave's corners are rounded, there may not be enough probe capacitance (sometimes denoted with the label "Cprobe"). Spiked square wave corners suggest too much capacitance in the probe. Either way, the scope and probe are not matched properly. You must adjust the probe capacitance to establish a good electrical match; otherwise, signal distortion will result during your measurements. Slowly adjust the variable capacitance of your probe until the corners shown on the calibration signal are as square as possible. If you are not able to achieve a clean square wave, try a different probe.

Voltage measurements   The first step in any voltage measurement is to set your normal trace (baseline) where you want it. Normally, the baseline is placed along the center of the graticule during start-up, but it can be placed anywhere along the CRT so long as the trace is visible. To establish a baseline, switch your input coupling control to its ground position. Grounding the input disconnects any existing input signal and ensures a zero reading. Adjust the vertical offset control to shift the baseline wherever

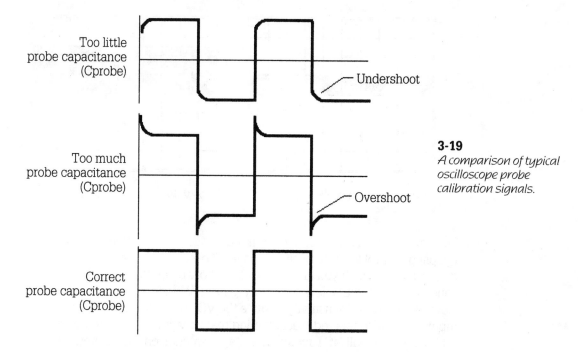

Too little probe capacitance (Cprobe)

— Undershoot

Too much probe capacitance (Cprobe)

— Overshoot

Correct probe capacitance (Cprobe)

3-19
A comparison of typical oscilloscope probe calibration signals.

you want the zero reading to be (usually in the display center). If you have no particular preference, simply center the trace in the CRT.

To measure dc, set your input coupling switch to its dc position and adjust the VOLTS/DIV control to provide the desired sensitivity. If you are unsure just which sensitivity is appropriate, start with a very low sensitivity (a large VOLTS/DIV setting), then carefully increase sensitivity (reduce the VOLTS/DIV setting) after your input signal is connected. This procedure prevents a trace from simply jumping off the screen when an unknown signal is first applied. If your signal does happen to leave the visible portion of the display, you could reduce the sensitivity (increase the VOLTS/DIV setting) to make the trace visible again.

For example, suppose you were measuring a +5 Vdc power supply output. If VOLTS/DIV is set to 5 VOLTS/DIV, each major vertical division of the CRT display represents 5 Vdc, so your +5 Vdc signal should appear 1 full division above the baseline (5 VOLTS/DIV × 1 DIV = 5 Vdc), as shown in FIG. 3-20. At a VOLTS/DIV setting of 2 VOLTS/DIV, the same +5 Vdc signal would now appear 2.5 divisions above your baseline (2 VOLTS/DIV × 2.5 DIV = 5 Vdc). If your input signal is a negative voltage, the trace would appear below the baseline, but it would be read the same way.

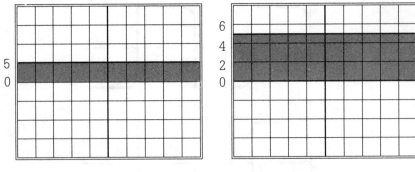

3-20
Measuring dc voltages with an oscilloscope.

5 volts/division scale   2 volts/division scale

You can read ac signals directly from the oscilloscope. Switch your input coupling control to its ac position and set a baseline just as you would for dc measurements. If you are unsure about how to set the vertical sensitivity, start with a low sensitivity (a large VOLTS/DIV setting), then slowly increase the sensitivity (reduce the VOLTS/DIV setting) once your input signal is connected. Keep in mind that ac voltage measurements on an oscilloscope will NOT match ac voltage readings on a multimeter. An oscilloscope displays instantaneous peak values for a waveform, while ac voltmeters measure in terms of root mean square (RMS) values. To convert a peak voltage reading to RMS, divide the peak reading by 1.414. Another limitation of multimeters is that they can only measure sinusoidal ac signals. Square, triangle, or other unusual waveforms will be interpreted as an average value by a multimeter.

When measuring an ac signal, you might have to adjust the oscilloscope's trigger level control to obtain a stable (still) trace. As FIG. 3-21 illustrates, signal voltages can be measured directly from the display. For example,

3-21
Measuring ac voltages with an oscilloscope.

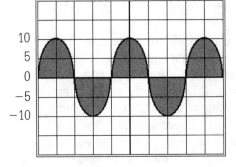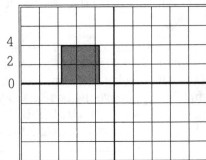

the sinusoidal waveform of FIG. 3-21 varies from −10 to +10 volts. If oscilloscope sensitivity is set to 5 VOLTS/DIV, signal peaks would occur 2 divisions above and 2 divisions below the baseline. Since the oscilloscope provides peak measurements, an ac voltmeter would show the signal as (peak voltage)÷1.414 = 10÷1.414 = 7.07 VRMS.

An oscilloscope is an ideal tool for measuring critical parameters such as pulse width, duty cycle, and frequency. It is the horizontal sensitivity control (TIME/DIV) that comes into play with time and frequency measurements. Before making any measurements, you must first obtain a clear baseline as you would for voltage measurements. When a baseline is established and a signal is finally connected, adjust the TIME/DIV control to display one or two complete signal cycles.

Time & frequency measurements

Typical period measurements are illustrated in FIG. 3-22. With VOLTS/DIV set to 5 ms/DIV, the sinusoidal waveform shown repeats every 2 divisions. This represents a period of 5 ms÷DIV × 2 DIV = 10 ms. Since frequency is simply the reciprocal of time, it can be calculated by inverting the time value. A period of 10 ms represents a frequency of 1÷10 ms = 100 Hz. This also works for square waves and regularly repeating nonsinusoidal waveforms. The square wave shown in FIG. 3-22 repeats every 4 divisions. At a TIME/DIV setting of 1 ms/DIV, its period would be 4 ms. This corresponds to a frequency of 1÷4 ms = 250 Hz.

Instead of measuring the entire period of a pulse cycle, you can read the time between any two points of interest. For the square wave of FIG. 3-22, you could read the pulse width to be 1 ms. You could also read the low portion of the cycle as a duration of 3 ms (added together for a total signal

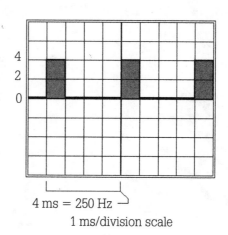

3-22
Measuring time on an oscilloscope.

10 ms = 100 Hz
5 ms/division scale

4 ms = 250 Hz
1 ms/division scale

period of 4 ms). A signal's duty cycle is simply the percentage of a signal's ON time to its total period. For example, a square wave that is ON for 2 ms and OFF for 2 ms would have a duty cycle of (2 ms × 100)÷(2 ms + 2 ms) = 50%. For an ON time of 1 ms and an OFF time of 3 ms, its duty cycle would be (1 ms × 100)÷(1 ms + 3 ms) = 25%, and so on.

4 Service guidelines

Electronic troubleshooting is a strange pursuit—an activity that falls somewhere between art and science. Its success depends not only on the right documentation and test equipment, but on intuition and a thorough, careful approach. This chapter shows you how to evaluate and track down problems in your small computer, locate technical data, and offers a series of service guidelines that can help ease your work.

Regardless of how complex your particular laptop, notebook, palmtop, or pen computer may be, a dependable troubleshooting procedure can be broken down into four basic steps as illustrated in FIG. 4-2:

The troubleshooting process

1. Define your symptoms
2. Identify and isolate the potential source (or location) of the problem
3. Repair or replace the suspected component or assembly
4. Retest the unit thoroughly to be sure that you have solved the problem. If you have not solved the problem, return to step 1.

This is a universal procedure that you can apply to any sort of troubleshooting—not just computer equipment.

Sooner or later, your small computer will break down. In many cases, the cause may be as simple as a loose wire or connector, or as complicated as an IC failure. Before you open your toolbox, though, you should have a

Define your symptoms

4-1
A Texas Instruments TravelMate 3000 WinSX notebook computer.

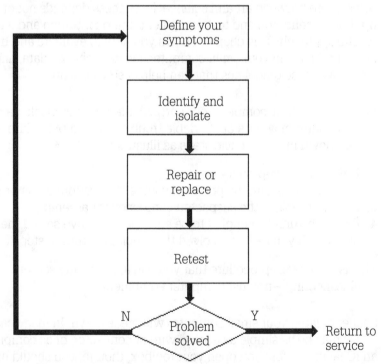

4-2
Flowchart for the universal troubleshooting process.

Define your symptoms

Identify and isolate

Repair or replace

Retest

Problem solved

N

Y

Return to service

good understanding of all the symptoms. It's not enough to simply say, "It's busted!" Think about the symptoms carefully. Ask yourself honestly just what is (or is not) happening. Consider when the problem occurs. Is the keyboard working properly? Is the LCD or plasma display crisp and bright? Does this problem occur only when the computer is tapped or moved? By recognizing and understanding your symptoms, you'll be better able to trace a problem to the appropriate assembly or component.

Take the time to write down as many symptoms as you can—whatever you see or hear (or don't see and hear). This note-taking might seem tedious now, but once you have begun your repair, a written record of symptoms and circumstances will help to keep you focused on the task at hand. It will also help to jog your memory if you must explain the symptoms to someone else at a later date.

Before you try to isolate a problem in a small computer, you must first be sure that it is the equipment itself that is causing the problem. In many circumstances, this will be fairly obvious, but there may be situations that appear ambiguous (e.g., no power, no DOS prompt, etc.). Always remember that your small computer works because of an intimate mingling of hardware and software. A faulty or improperly configured piece of software can cause serious computer errors.

Identify & isolate

When you are confident that the failure lies in your computer's hardware, you can start identifying possible problem areas. Start your search at the subsection level. The troubleshooting procedures in this book guide you through the major sections of today's small computers and aid you in deciding which subsection might be at fault. When you have identified a potential problem area, you can begin the actual repair process, and possibly even track the fault to the component level.

Once you understand what is wrong and where to look, you can begin the repair process that you believe will correct the problem. Small computers are almost entirely electronic devices—there are virtually no mechanical parts except for the keyboard and magnetic drives—so most procedures require the exchange of electronic or electromechanical parts. As a general rule, all procedures should be considered important and should be followed carefully.

Repair or replace

Parts are usually classified as components or subassemblies. A component is the smallest part that you can work with. Components serve many different purposes in a small computer. Resistors, capacitors, transformers, motors, and ICs are just a few examples of components. Components contain no serviceable parts within themselves; therefore, a defective component must be replaced. A subassembly can be made up of many individual components. Unlike components, subassemblies serve a single specific purpose in a small computer (such as a floppy drive), but they can usually be repaired by locating and replacing faulty components. Note that it is always acceptable to replace a defective subassembly with a new one, but complete subassemblies can be more expensive and more difficult to obtain than components.

The mail-order companies listed in appendix A can provide you with general-purpose electronic components and equipment to aid in your repair. Most will send you their complete catalog(s) or product listing(s) at your request. Keep in mind, however, that small computers make extensive use of special integrated circuits and physical assemblies. For special parts, you will often have to deal directly with the manufacturer. Going to the manufacturer is always somewhat of a calculated risk—they might choose to do business only with their affiliated service centers, or just refuse to sell parts to consumers. If you do find a manufacturer willing to sell you parts, you should know the exact code or part number used by that manufacturer (often available right from the manufacturer's technical data, if you have it). Keep in mind that many manufacturers are ill-equipped to deal directly with individual consumers, so be patient and be prepared to make several calls.

During a repair, you may reach a roadblock that requires you to leave your equipment for a day or two (maybe longer). Make it a point to reassemble your system as much as possible before leaving it. Gather any loose parts in plastic bags, seal them shut, and mark them clearly. If you are working with electronic circuits, make sure to use good quality antistatic boxes or bags for storage. Reassembly will prevent a playful pet, curious child, or a well-meaning spouse from accidentally misplacing or discarding parts while the system is on your workbench. This is twice as important if your workspace is in a well-traveled or family area. You also will not forget how to assemble the equipment later on.

Retest When a repair is finally complete, you must re-assemble the small computer carefully before testing it. If the problem remains, re-evaluate the symptoms and narrow the problem to another part of the equipment. If normal operation is restored (or greatly improved), test the computer's various functions. When you can verify that your symptoms have disappeared during actual operation, return the equipment to service.

Do not be discouraged if the equipment still malfunctions. Simply walk away, clear your head, and start again by defining the current symptoms. Never continue with a repair if you are tired or frustrated—tomorrow is another day. Also realize that there might be more than one bad part to deal with. Remember that a small computer is just a collection of assemblies, and each assembly is a collection of parts. Normally, everything works together, but when one part fails, it might cause one or more interconnected parts to fail as well. When repairing components, be prepared to make several repair attempts before the computer is completely repaired.

Information is perhaps your most valuable tool when repairing any electronic equipment. Highly involved electronic troubleshooting generally requires a complete set of schematics and a parts list. Some small-computer manufacturers do sell technical information for their products (or at least their older products). GRiD Systems and Tandy Corporation (Radio Shack) are just two manufacturers that make technical data available to consumers. Contact the customer service department of the manufacturer for specific data prices and availability. Be sure to request a service manual (not an owner's or user's manual).

Notes on technical information

If you do obtain technical information, it is strongly recommended that you have the data on hand before starting any repair. Service manuals often contain important information on custom or application-specific integrated circuits (ASICs) used in the equipment that you will be unable to obtain elsewhere.

As with any type of electronic troubleshooting, there is always a risk of further damage being accidentally caused to equipment during repair. With sophisticated computer electronics, that damage hazard is an *electrostatic discharge* (ESD) that can destroy sensitive electronic parts.

Static electricity

If you've ever walked across a carpet on a cold, dry winter day, you probably got a shock, which is ESD, when you touched a doorknob or any other metal object. Under the right conditions, your body can accumulate static charge potentials that exceed 20,000 V!

When you provide a conductive path for electrons, that built-up charge rushes away from your body at the point closest to the metal object. The result is often a brief, stinging shock, which can be startling and annoying, but is generally harmless to you (and the doorknob). Semiconductor devices, on the other hand, are highly susceptible to physical damage from ESD. If the charge goes from you to the IC (instead of the doorknob), permanent damage can be caused to a good circuit. This section introduces you to static electricity and shows you how to prevent ESD damage during repairs.

Static formation   When two dissimilar materials are rubbed together (such as a carpet and the soles of your shoes), friction causes electrons to move from one material to the other. The excess (or lack) of electrons causes a charge of equal but opposite polarities to develop on each material. Since electrons are not flowing, there is no current, so the charge is *static*. However, the charge exhibits a voltage potential. As materials continue to rub together, the charge increases, sometimes to thousands of volts.

In a human being, static charges are often developed by normal, everyday activities, such as combing your hair. Friction between the comb and your hair causes opposing charges to develop. Sliding across a vinyl car seat, pulling a sweater on or off, or taking clothes out of a dryer are just some of the ways static charges can appear in your body—it is virtually impossible to prevent this from happening. ESD is more pronounced in winter months because dry (low-humidity) air allows a greater accumulation of charge. In the summer, humidity in the air tends to bleed away (or short circuit) most accumulated charges before they reach shock levels that you can feel. Regardless of the season, though, ESD is always present to some degree, and always a danger to sensitive electronics.

Device damage   ESD poses a serious threat to most advanced ICs, which can easily be destroyed by static discharges of just a few hundred volts—well below your ability to feel a shock. Static discharge at sufficient levels can damage bipolar transistors, transistor-transistor logic (TTL) gates, emitter-coupled logic (ECL) gates, operational amplifiers (op-amps), silicon-controlled rectifiers (SCRs), and junction field-effect transistors (JFETs), but certainly the most susceptible components to ESD are those ICs fabricated with metal-oxide semiconductor (MOS) technology. A typical MOS transistor is shown in FIG. 4-3.

MOS devices (PMOS, NMOS, HMOS, CMOS, etc.) have become the cornerstone of high-performance ICs such as memories, high-speed logic and microprocessors, and other advanced components found in today's small computers. Typical MOS ICs can easily contain over 500,000 transistors on a single IC die. Every part of these transistors must constantly be made smaller to keep pace with the demand for ever-higher levels of IC complexity. As each part of the transistor shrinks, however, its inherent breakdown voltage drops, and susceptibility to ESD damage increases.

A typical MOS transistor breakdown is illustrated in FIG. 4-4. Notice the areas of positive and negative semiconductor material that forms its three terminals: the source, the gate, and the drain. The gate is isolated from

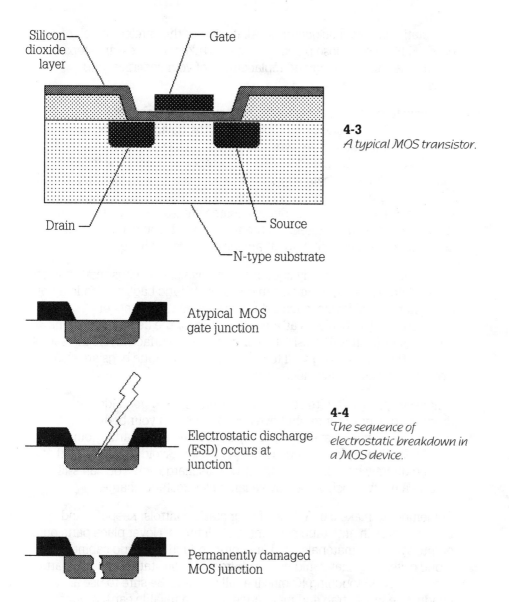

Silicon dioxide layer

Gate

4-3
A typical MOS transistor.

Drain

Source

N-type substrate

Atypical MOS gate junction

Electrostatic discharge (ESD) occurs at junction

4-4
The sequence of electrostatic breakdown in a MOS device.

Permanently damaged MOS junction

the other parts of the transistor by an extremely thin film of silicon dioxide (sometimes called the *oxide layer*). High voltages, like those from ESD, can easily overload the oxide layer, resulting in a puncture (a pin-hole) through the gate. Once this happens, the transistor (and therefore the entire IC) is permanently defective and must be replaced.

Never underestimate the importance of static control during your repairs. Without realizing it, you could destroy a new IC or circuit board before you even have the chance to install it—and you would never even know

Controlling static electricity

that static damage has occurred. All it takes is the careless touch of a charged hand or a loose piece of clothing. Take the necessary steps to ensure the safe handling and replacement of your sensitive (and expensive) electronics.

One way to control static is to keep charges away from boards and ICs to begin with. This is often accomplished by the device's packaging and shipping container. ICs are typically packed in a specially made conductive foam. Carbon granules are compounded into the foam to make it conductive. Foam support helps to resist IC lead bending, absorbs vibrations, and keeps every lead of the IC at the same potential (equipotential bonding). Conductive foam is reusable, so you can insert ICs for safe keeping and remove them as needed. You can purchase conductive foam from just about any electronics retail store.

Circuit boards are normally kept in conductive plastic bags that dissipate static charges before damage can occur. Antistatic bags are made up of different material layers, each exhibiting different amounts of conductivity. The bag acts as a *faraday cage* for the device it contains. Electrons from an ESD dissipate along the bag's surface layers instead of passing through the bag wall to its contents. Antistatic bags are also available through many electronics retail stores.

Whenever you work with sensitive electronics, it's a good idea to dissipate charges that might have accumulated on your body. A conductive fabric wrist strap soundly connected to an earth ground will slowly bleed away any charges from your body. Avoid grabbing hold of a ground directly because, although it will discharge you, you can still receive a nasty shock if you have a large electrostatic charge.

Remember to make careful use of your static controls. Keep ICs and circuit boards in antistatic containers at all times. Never place parts onto or into synthetic materials (such as non-conductive plastic cabinets or fabric coverings) that could hold a charge. Handle static-sensitive parts carefully. Avoid touching IC pins if at all possible. Be sure to use a conductive wrist strap and mat connected to a reliable earth ground.

Electricity hazards

No matter how harmless your small computer might appear, always remember that potential shock hazards can exist. Once the computer's power supply is disassembled, there can be several locations where live ac voltage is exposed and easily accessible. Electronic equipment operates at 120 Vac at 60 Hz. Many European countries use 240 Vac at 50 Hz. When this kind of voltage potential establishes a path through your body, it can cause a flow of current large enough to stop your heart. Since it only takes about 100 mA to trigger a cardiac arrest, and a typical power supply fuse is rated for 1 or 2 A, fuses and circuit breakers will not protect you.

It is your skin's resistance that limits the flow of current through your body. Ohm's law states that for any voltage, current flow increases as resistance drops (and vice versa). Dry skin exhibits a high resistance of several hundred-thousand ohms, while the resistance of moist, cut, or wet skin can drop to only several hundred ohms. This means that even comparatively low voltages can produce a shock if your skin resistance is low enough. Some examples will help to demonstrate this action.

Suppose a worker's hands come across a live 120 Vac circuit. If the worker's skin is dry (say 120 KΩ), an electrical shock of 1 mA (120 V$\div$120,000 Ω) would result. This shock would be harmless—probably a brief, tingling sensation. After a hard day's work, though, perspiration could decrease skin resistance to perhaps 12 KΩ. This would allow a far more substantial shock of 10 mA. At that level, the shock could paralyze the worker and make it difficult or impossible to let go of the "live" conductors. A burn (perhaps serious) could result at the points of contact, but it probably would not be fatal. Consider a worker whose hands or clothing are wet, causing the effective skin resistance to drop to a low value (1.2 KΩ for example). At 120 volts, the resulting shock of 100 mA could be instantly fatal without immediate cardiopulmonary resuscitation (CPR).

Take the following steps to protect yourself from injury:

1. Keep your small-computer's power supply unplugged (not just turned off) as much as possible during disassembly and repair. When you must perform a service procedure that requires power to be applied, plug the supply into an isolation transformer (such as the one shown in FIG. 4-5) just long enough to perform your procedure, then unplug it. This makes the repair safer for you and anyone else that might happen along.
2. When you work on a power supply, try to wear rubber gloves. They will insulate your hands just like the insulation on a wire. You might think that rubber gloves are inconvenient and uncomfortable, but they are far better than the inconvenience and discomfort of an electric shock. Make it a point to wear a long-sleeved shirt with sleeves rolled down and buttoned as this will insulate your forearms.
3. If rubber gloves are absolutely out of the question for one reason or another, remove all metal jewelry and work with one hand behind your back. Metal jewelry is an excellent conductor. If you catch your ring or watchband hook onto a "live" ac line, jewelry can conduct current

directly to your skin. By keeping one hand behind your back, you cannot grasp both ends of a live ac line to complete a strong current path through your heart.

4. Work dry! Do not work with wet hands or clothing. Do not work in wet or damp environments. Make sure that nearby fire extinguishing equipment is suitable for electrical fires.

5. Treat electricity with tremendous respect. Whenever electronic circuitry is exposed (especially power supply circuitry), a shock hazard does exist. Remember, it is the flow of current through your body, not the voltage potential, that can injure you. Insulate yourself as much as possible from any exposed wiring.

4-5
An isolation transformer.

B+K Precision

Soldering

Soldering is the most commonly used method of connecting wires and components within an electrical or electronic circuit. Metal surfaces (in this case, component leads, wires, or printed circuit boards) are heated to a high temperature and joined with a layer of compatible metal in its molten state. When performed correctly with the right materials, soldering forms a lasting, corrosion-proof, intermolecular bond that is mechanically strong and electrically sound. All that is required is the appropriate soldering iron and electronics-grade, 60/40 solder. This section explains the tools and techniques for both regular and surface-mount soldering.

Soldering background

By strict definition, *soldering* is a process of bonding metals together. There are three distinct types of soldering: brazing, silver soldering, and soft soldering. Brazing and silver soldering are used when working with hard or precious metals, but soft soldering is the technique of choice for electronics work. In order to bond wires or component leads (typically made of copper), a third metal, solder, must be added while in its molten state. Several different types of solder are available for each soldering technique, but the chosen solder must be compatible with the metals to be bonded; otherwise, a bond will not form. Lead and tin are two common and inexpensive metals that adhere very well to copper. However, neither metal by itself has the strength, hardness, and melting-point characteristics to make it practically useful. Therefore, lead and tin are combined into an alloy. A ratio of approximately 60% tin and 40% lead yields an alloy that offers reasonable hardness, good pliability, and a relatively low melting point that is ideal for electronics work. This is the solder that must be used.

While solder adheres very well to copper, it does not adhere well at all to the natural oxides that form on a conductor's surface. Even though conductors might look to be clean and clear, some amount of oxidation is always present. Oxides must be removed before a good bond can be achieved. A resin cleaning agent (flux) should be applied to the conductors before soldering. Resin is chemically inactive at room temperature, but becomes extremely active when heated to soldering temperatures. Activated flux bonds with oxides and strips them away from copper surfaces. As a completed solder joint cools, residual resin also cools and returns safely to an inactive state.

Never use an acid or solvent-based flux to prepare conductors. Acid fluxes remove oxides as well as resin does, but acids and solvents remain active after the joint cools. Over time, active acid flux dissolves copper wires and eventually causes a circuit failure. Resin flux can be purchased as a paste that is brushed onto conductors before soldering, but most electronic solders contain a core of resin flux. Prefabricated flux eliminates the mess of flux paste, and cleans the joint as the solder is applied.

Irons & tips

A soldering iron is little more than a resistive heating element built into the end of a long steel tube as shown in FIG. 4-6. When power Vac is applied to the heater, it warms the base of a metal tip. Any heat conducted down the cooldown tube (toward the handle) is dissipated harmlessly to the surrounding air, keeping the handle temperature low enough to hold comfortably.

Although some heat is wasted along the cooldown tube, most heat is channeled into a soldering tip similar to the one shown in FIG. 4-7. Tips generally have a solid copper core that is plated with iron. The plated

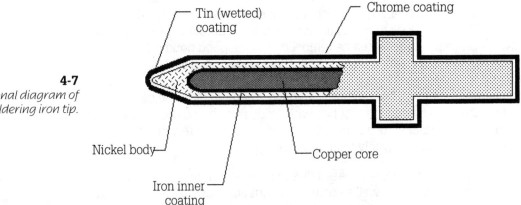

4-6
Cross-sectional diagram of a simple soldering iron.

Tip

ac heater coil

Cold-drawn metal tube

ac cord

Insulated handle

4-7
Cross-sectional diagram of a typical soldering iron tip.

Tin (wetted) coating

Chrome coating

Nickel body

Iron inner coating

Copper core

core is coated with a layer of nickel, to stop high-temperature metal corrosion. The entire assembly (except for the tip's very end) is finally plated with chromium, which gives a new tip its shiny chrome appearance. A chromium coating renders the tip "nonwettable"—solder will not stick to it. Since solder must stick at the tip's end, that end is plated with tin. A tin coating (a basic component of solder) makes the tip wettable so that molten solder will adhere. Tips are manufactured in a wide variety of shapes and sizes to handle different soldering tasks. Before you select the best tip for the job, you must understand ideal soldering conditions.

The very best soldering connections are made within a narrow window of time and temperature. A solder joint heated between 260°C to 288°C (500°F to 550°F) for 1 to 2 seconds makes the best connections. You should select a soldering iron with a wattage and tip shape to achieve these conditions. The purpose of soldering irons is not to melt solder.

Instead, a soldering iron is supposed to deliver heat to a joint, and the joint should melt the solder. A large solder joint (with larger or more numerous connections) requires a larger iron and tip than a small joint (with fewer or smaller connections).

If you use a small iron to heat a large joint, the joint might dissipate heat faster than the iron can deliver it, so the joint might not reach an acceptable soldering temperature. Conversely, using a large iron to heat a small joint will overheat the joint, which can melt wire insulation and damage printed circuit board traces. Match wattage to the application. Most general-purpose electronics work can be accomplished using a 25 to 30 W soldering iron.

Since the tip end actually contacts the joint to be soldered, the tip's shape and size can assist heat transfer greatly. When heat must be applied across a wide area (such as a wire splice), a wide-area tip should be used. A screwdriver (flat-blade) tip, such as shown in FIG. 4-8, is a good choice. If heat must be directed with pinpoint accuracy for small, tight joints or printed circuits, a narrow-blade or conical tip is best. Two tips for SMT desoldering are also shown in FIG. 4-8. More information on SMT soldering is presented later in this chapter.

Flat tip
(screwdriver tip)

Conical tip
(pointed tip)

4-8
Various soldering iron tips.

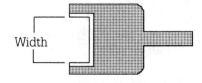

Surface-mount desoldering
tip for small-outline ICs
(SOICs)

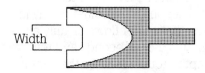

Surface-mount desoldering tip for
discrete components such as
resistors, capacitors, and transistors

Soldering Always keep your soldering iron in a secure holder while it is on! Never allow a hot iron to sit freely on a tabletop or anything that might be flammable. Make it a rule to always wear safety glasses when soldering. Active resin or molten solder can easily flick off the iron or joint and do permanent damage to your eyes.

Give your iron plenty of time to warm up. Five minutes is usually adequate, but small-wattage irons (or irons with larger tips) might need even more time. Once the iron is at its working temperature, coat the wettable portion of the tip with a layer of fresh solder—a process known as *tinning* the iron. Rub the tip into a sponge soaked in clean water to wipe away any accumulations of debris and carbon that might have formed. Then apply a thin coating of fresh solder to the tip's end. Solder penetrates the tip to a molecular level and forms a cushion of molten solder that aids in heat transfer. Re-tin the iron whenever its tip becomes blackened, perhaps every few minutes, or after several joints have been formed.

It might be helpful to tin each individual conductor before making the complete joint. To tin a wire, prepare it by stripping away ³⁄₁₆" to ¼" of insulation, being careful not to nick or damage the conductor. Heat the exposed copper for about 1 second, then apply solder into the wire—not into the iron! If the iron and tip are appropriate, solder will flow evenly and smoothly into the conductor. Apply enough solder to bond each of a stranded wire's exposed strands. When tinning a solid wire or component lead, apply just enough solder to lightly coat the conductor's surface. You will find that conductors heat faster and solder flows better when all parts of a joint are tinned in advance.

Completing a solder joint is just as easy. Bring together each of your conductors as necessary to form the joint. For example, if you are soldering a component into a printed circuit board, insert the component's leads into their appropriate PC board holes. Place the iron against all conductors to be heated, as shown in FIG. 4-9. For a printed circuit board, heat the printed trace and component lead together. After about 1 second, flow solder gently into the hot conductors, not the iron. Be sure that solder flows cleanly and evenly into the joint. Apply solder for another 1 or 2 seconds and remove the solder and the iron. Do not attempt to touch or move the joint for several seconds. Wait until the solder cools and sets. If the joint requires additional solder, re-heat the joint and flow in a bit more solder.

You can identify a good solder joint by its smooth, even, silvery-gray appearance. Any charred or carbonized flux on the joint indicates that your soldering temperature is too high (or heat is being applied for too

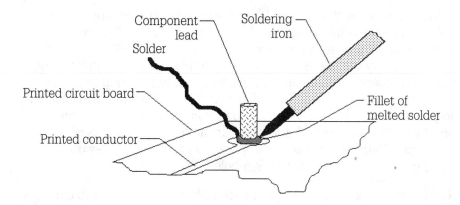

long). Remember that solder cannot flow unless the joint is hot. If the joint is not hot, solder will cool before it bonds. The result is a rough, built-up, dull gray or blackish mound that does not adhere to the joint very well. This is known as a cold solder joint. A cold joint can often be corrected by re-heating the joint properly and applying fresh solder.

Conventional printed circuits use through-hole components. Parts are inserted on one side of the PC board, and their leads are soldered to printed circuit traces on the other side. SMT components do not penetrate a printed circuit board. Instead, SMT components rest on one side of a PC board, as shown in FIG. 4-10. Metal tabs are used instead of long component leads. A full range of parts—from resistors and capacitors to transistors and ICs—are currently available in SMT packages. Even advanced ICs like microprocessors and ASICs are found in SMT packages. Many SMT PC assemblies are soldered using one of two soldering techniques: flow soldering or reflow soldering.

Surface-mount soldering

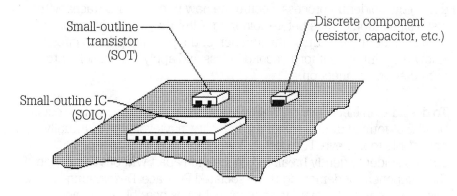

4-10
A view of surface-mount components on a printed circuit board.

In the *flow soldering* technique, SMT components are first glued into place on a PC board using automated assembly equipment. Gluing keeps each part in place and aligned with the proper PC board traces. The loaded PC board is then placed into a heating chamber and raised to soldering temperature. Molten solder is allowed to flow freely over the board, where it adheres to heated component leads and PC board traces. This effectively solders the components into place. The remainder of the board is physically and chemically masked prior to soldering to prevent solder from sticking elsewhere. A finished PC board is then cooled slowly to prevent excessive thermal shock to its components, its masks are stripped away, any through-hole parts are added, and then it is tested. This type of fabrication is similar in principle to the techniques used to mass produce conventional through-hole PC boards.

The technique of re-flow soldering uses a slightly different approach. Before any components are installed at all, a masked PC board is coated with a paste form of solder. The board is heated to soldering temperature which allows solder to adhere to each PC trace. This forms a little bead of solder under each component lead. Any masking is stripped away. Components are then glued into place using automatic assembly equipment (it would take a very long time for a person to do that by eye), and the board is quickly re-heated to soldering temperature. Solder melts again and "re-flows" to adhere at each component terminal. Re-flow establishes the component's connections. After slow, careful cooling, the board can be tested or through-hole components can be added.

While the specifics of each SMT soldering technique will have little (if any) impact on your troubleshooting, you should have some basic understanding of how SMT components are assembled in order to disassemble them properly during your repair.

Resoldering a new SMT component is just as easy as resoldering a conventional through-hole part, but SMT parts are often too small to hold during the soldering process. Secure the new part to its PC traces with just a small drop of glue before soldering. After the glue is dry, apply a regular soldering iron tip to the junction of the part and printed circuit. Allow the joint to heat for 1 second or less and apply a bit of solder to form the new connection.

Desoldering   To desolder an electronic connection, you must break the intermolecular bond that formed during soldering. In reality, however, this is virtually impossible to achieve. The best that you can hope for is to remove enough solder to gently break the connection apart without destroying the component or damaging the associated PC trace. Desoldering is basically a game of removing as much solder as possible—the more the better.

You will find that some connections are very easy to remove. For instance, a wire inserted into a printed circuit board can be removed easily by heating the joint and gently withdrawing the wire from its hole once the solder is molten. Use extreme caution when desoldering! Leads and wires under tension might spring free once the solder is molten, launching a bead of hot solder into the air. Always use safety glasses or goggles to protect your eyes from flying solder.

Desoldering other types of connections, such as with through-hole components, is usually more difficult. When desoldering a part with more than one wire, it is virtually impossible to heat all of its leads simultaneously while withdrawing the part. As a result, it becomes necessary to remove as much solder as possible from each lead, and gently break each lead free, as shown in FIG. 4-11. Grab hold of each lead with a pair of needlenose pliers. When the solder is molten, wiggle the lead back and forth gently until it breaks free. Solder can be removed using regular desoldering tools, such as a solder vacuum or solder wick, as shown in FIG. 4-12.

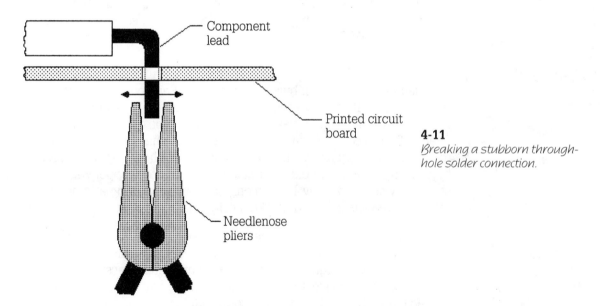

Component
lead

Printed circuit
board

4-11
Breaking a stubborn through-hole solder connection.

Needlenose
pliers

SMT components are typically small and are specialized enough for you to find a soldering tip to fit the desired part. Two simple SMT soldering iron tips are shown in FIG. 4-8. With a tip that precisely fits the part you wish to desolder, you can heat all the solder joints in the part simultaneously and move the part clear in one quick motion. Residual solder can be cleaned up later with conventional desoldering tools. There

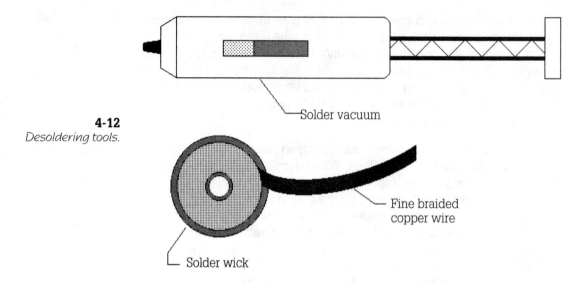

4-12
Desoldering tools.

Solder vacuum

Fine braided
copper wire

Solder wick

are also special tips for desoldering a selection of SMT IC packages. Instead of using fixed SMT tips, you could use SMT soldering tweezers, which is a special soldering iron that can be used to desolder and grasp a wide range of SMT parts.

Printed circuits

In the very early days of consumer electronics, circuit assemblies were manufactured by hand on bulky, metal frames. Each component was then wired by hand. If you have ever seen the chassis of a tube-driven television or radio, you probably have seen this type of construction. Eventually, the costs of hand-building electronic chassis became so high that a new technique was developed that used a photographic process to print wiring patterns onto copper-clad boards. Excess copper was chemically stripped away, leaving only the desired wiring patterns. Parts were inserted and soldered quickly, easily, and accurately.

Before long, manufacturers realized that these printed circuits appeared more uniform, were easier to inspect and test, required much less labor to assemble, and were lighter and less bulky than metal-chassis assembly. Today, practically all electronic equipment incorporates some type of printed circuit board. The size and complexity of the board depends on the function of the particular circuit. This section describes the major types of printed circuit boards that you might encounter, and presents a selection of PC board troubleshooting and repair techniques that you can use.

Types of printed circuits

Printed circuits are available as single-sided, double-sided, or multilayer boards. Your small computer most likely uses multilayer boards. Each type of board can hold SMT or through-hole components. Single-sided PC boards are the simplest and least expensive type of printed circuit. Copper traces are etched only on one side of the board. Holes are drilled through the board to accommodate the component leads. Components are inserted from the blank side of the board (the "component" side) so that their leads protrude on the copper trace side (the "solder" side). Component leads are then soldered to their copper traces to complete the printed circuit. Single-sided PC boards support SMT components.

When circuits are too complex to "print" all of the circuit traces on one side of the PC board, both sides of the board are used, resulting in a double-sided PC board. Plated (electrically conductive) holes are used to connect both sides of the board where needed. These plated holes are also used to hold through-hole component leads. Solder conducts up the plated hole through capillary action and ensures that a component lead is properly connected to both sides of the board, allowing the board to be soldered from one side only during manufacture. However, desoldering leads in plated holes is somewhat difficult, since solder adheres all the way through the hole.

All internal solder must be removed before a lead can be withdrawn. If you pull out a wire or component lead before solder is removed, you stand a good chance of ripping the plating right out of the hole. Double-sided PC boards are excellent for SMT components because components can be soldered on both sides of the board.

Even more complex circuit designs can be fabricated on *multilayer* PC boards. Not only will you find traces on both sides of the PC board, but there are more layers of etched traces sandwiched and interconnected between these two faces (each layer is separated by an insulating layer). As with double-sided boards, multilayer boards use plated through-holes to hold component leads and bond various layers together.

Typical printed circuits use etched copper traces on a base material of paper-based phenolic or epoxy. Other printed circuits incorporate a base of glass-fabric epoxy, or some similar plastic-based substance. These materials offer a light, strong, rigid base for printed circuits.

A fourth (but less commonly used) type of printed circuit is known as a *flexible* printed circuit. Copper traces are deposited onto a layer of plastic. Traces can be included on both sides of this base layer to form a single or double-sided circuit. Traces are then covered by an insulating layer of plastic. Using alternate layers of copper traces and flexible insulation, it is possible to form multilayer flexible printed circuits.

Flexible circuits can be folded to conform to tight or irregular spaces. As a result, flexible circuits are often used as wiring harnesses; that is, components are placed as needed, then a flexible circuit is inserted and attached by screws or solder to interconnect each component. Individual components are rarely soldered to a flexible PC as they are with a rigid PC board.

Printed circuit repairs

Printed circuits are generally very reliable structures; however, physical abuse can easily damage the rigid phenolic or glass base as well as any printed traces. If damage occurs to a PC board, you should know what signs of damage to look for, and what steps to take to correct any damage in your notebook, palmtop, or pen computer. There are four general PC board problems that you should know about: lead pull-through, printed trace break, board cracks, and heat damage.

Lead pull-through

Normally, a well-made solder joint will hold a wire or component lead tightly to its connection on a PC board. However, if that wire or lead is suddenly placed under a lot of stress, the solder joint can fail partially or completely, as shown in FIG. 4-13. Stress can be applied with sudden, sharp movements such as dropping or striking the computer.

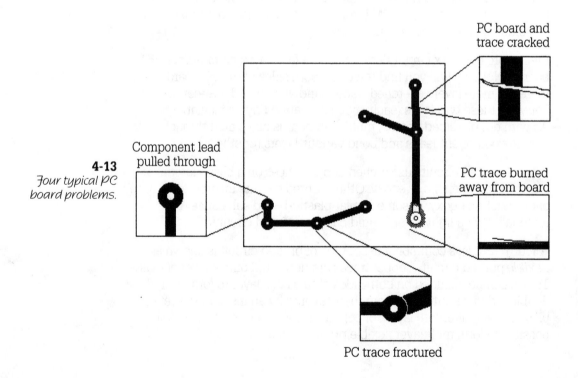

4-13
Four typical PC board problems.

Component lead pulled through

PC board and trace cracked

PC trace burned away from board

PC trace fractured

Lead pull-through is not always an obvious failure unless the lead or wire is entirely out of its through-hole. If the wire is still making contact with the PC board, its electrical connection might be broken or intermittent. Test an intermittent connection by exposing the PC board and gently rapping on the board or suspect conductor. By tapping different areas of the board, you might possibly focus on an intermittent connection in the area that is the most sensitive to the tapping. You can also test suspected intermittents by gently wiggling wires or component leads. The conductor most sensitive to the touch will probably be the one that is intermittent.

Another case of lead pull-through can occur on double-sided or multilayer PC boards during desoldering. Various layers are connected together by plated holes. Component leads are typically soldered into plated through-holes. If you pull out a conductor without removing all of the solder, you can rip out part or all of the hole's plating along with the conductor. When this happens, the electrical integrity at that point of the PC board is broken.

For double-sided PC boards, you will often fix intermittent connections by re-soldering the new component lead on both sides of the PC board. There is usually enough exposed copper on the component side to ensure a reasonable solder fillet. Unfortunately, there is no reliable way to solder a new lead to each layer of a multilayer board. As a result, a damaged through-hole on a multilayer board might be beyond repair, and the board will have to be replaced.

The best way to avoid damaging a plated through-hole is to heat a joint while removing the lead simultaneously. Grasp the lead with a pair of needlenose pliers while heating the joint. When solder is molten, pull out the component lead. You can then safely clean up any residual solder with conventional desoldering tools. Never grasp the component lead with your bare fingers. The entire lead will reach soldering temperatures almost immediately.

Another common problem that takes place in printed circuits is known as *trace break*. This can also be the result of a physical shock or sudden impact to the PC board. In this case, a portion of the printed trace (usually where a solder pad meets the remainder of the trace) can suffer a fine, hairline fracture that results in an open or intermittent circuit. What makes this particular problem especially difficult is that a trace break can be almost impossible to see upon visual inspection. You must often wiggle each solder pad until you find the fractured connection. Large, heavy components, such as transformers or relays, are often prime candidates for trace breaks, so start your search there.

Printed trace break

Do not attempt to create a bridge of solder across the break or jumper directly across the fracture. Solder does not adhere well to the chemical coatings often used with PC boards, so such quick fixes rarely last long. In order to repair a printed circuit trace break, you should desolder and remove the broken portion of the trace, then solder a jumper wire between two associated component leads—do not solder directly to the printed trace.

Board cracks Under extreme conditions, the phenolic or glass-epoxy circuit board itself might crack. This is not unusual for equipment that has been dropped or abused. When a crack occurs, the course of the crack might sever one or more printed traces. Luckily, board cracks are fairly easy to detect on sight. By following the crack, it is a simple matter to locate any severed traces.

As with trace breaks, the best, most reliable method of repairing broken traces is to solder a wire jumper between two associated solder pads or component leads. Never try to make solder bridge across a break. Solder does not adhere well to the chemicals used on many PC board tracks, so such fixes will not last long. If the physical crack is severe, you might want to work a bit of good-quality epoxy adhesive into the crack to help reinforce the board. Multilayer PC boards cannot be repaired practically.

Heat damage Printed copper traces are bonded firmly to the phenolic or glass epoxy board underneath. When extreme heat is applied to the copper traces, however, it is possible to separate the copper traces from the board. This type of damage usually occurs during soldering or desoldering when concentrated heat is applied with a soldering iron.

The only real remedy for this type of damage is to carefully cut off that portion of the separated trace to prevent the loose copper from accidentally shorting out other components, and solder a wire jumper from the component lead to an adjacent solder pad or component lead.

5 Batteries & power systems

Regardless of how simple or how sophisticated your notebook, palmtop, or pen computer might be, it requires a consistent source of power in order to function (FIG. 5-1). Batteries and power supplies are used to provide and control the power needed by your small computer. This chapter introduces you to various batteries used in today's systems and shows you the concepts and troubleshooting techniques needed to repair charging circuits, ac-powered supplies, inverter supplies, and dc-dc converters.

Batteries

The battery is perhaps the most common and dependable power source ever developed. In its simplest form, a battery (or *cell*) contains two dissimilar metals (called *electrodes*) encapsulated in a chemical catalyst paste (*electrolyte*), as illustrated in FIG. 5-2. The resulting chemical reaction causes a voltage differential to be developed across the electrodes. When a battery is attached to a circuit, the battery provides current. The more current required by the circuit, the faster the chemical reaction will occur. As the chemical reaction continues, the electrodes are consumed, eventually wearing out the battery.

In some battery types, the chemical reaction is irreversible. When the battery is dead, it must be discarded. These are known as nonrechargeable (or *primary*) cells. However, some types of batteries can

5-1
Color laptop computer.

Toshiba America Information Systems, Inc.

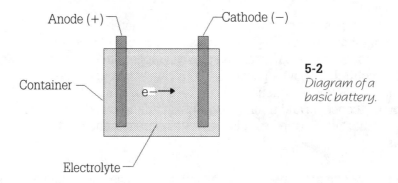

Anode (+)   Cathode (−)

Container

e→

5-2
Diagram of a basic battery.

Electrolyte

be recharged. By applying energy to the battery from an external source, the expended chemical reaction can be almost entirely reversed. Such rechargeable batteries are referred to as *secondary* cells, and are used to supply the main power in most small computers.

Batteries carry two important ratings: cell voltage and ampere-hour (A•h). *Cell voltage* refers to the cell's working voltage. Most everyday cells operate around +1.5 Vdc, but lithium cells supply +3.0 Vdc. *Ampere-hour* rating is a bit more involved, but reflects the energy storage capacity of a battery. A large A•h rating suggests a high-capacity battery, and vice versa.

As an example, suppose your battery is rated for 2 A•h. Ideally, you should be able to draw 2 amperes from the battery for 1 hour before it is exhausted. However, you should also be able to draw 1 ampere for 2 hours, 0.5 amperes for 4 hours, 0.1 amperes for 20 hours, etc. Keep in mind that the ampere-hour relationship is not always linear. Higher current loads might shorten the battery life to less than expected from the ampere-hour rating, while small loads might allow slightly more battery life than expected. Regardless of the ampere-hour rating, all batteries have an upper current limit—drawing excess current can destroy the battery. Physically large batteries can usually supply more current (and last longer) than smaller batteries.

Another way to express battery energy capacity is in Watt-hours per kilogram (W•h/kg), or Watt-hours per pound (W•h/lb). For example, a 1-kg battery rated at 60 W•h could provide 60 W for 1 hour, 30 W for 2 hours, 10 W for 6 hours, etc.

Alkaline batteries

Alkaline-manganese dioxide (alkaline) batteries have largely replaced carbon-zinc batteries in most consumer electronics applications. The alkaline cell is a primary battery using a zinc anode, a manganese dioxide cathode, and an extremely conductive electrolyte of potassium hydroxide. This formulation provides 1.5 Vdc with excellent energy density at about 130 W•h/kg (60 W•h/lb), as well as a shelf life approaching four years at room temperature. Alkaline cells have a high discharge rate, meaning that they can be discharged quickly by supplying significant amounts of current to a load. Ampere-hour ratings for alkaline cells can be quite high—from 560 mA•h (0.56 A•h) to 14,250 mA•h (14.25 A•h).

Figure 5-3 is a cutaway view of an alkaline cell. Notice the packed zinc anode material at the battery core, and packed manganese-dioxide cathode material around the anode. The voltage-producing chemical reaction takes place across a thin, porous separator membrane saturated with potassium hydroxide electrolyte. It is actually the separator that regulates the battery reaction. Separator quality affects the internal resistance of a battery. The entire electrode/separator assembly is enclosed in a PVC housing. A membrane vent is added to equalize the pressure developed within a battery during normal operation.

Lithium batteries

Lithium/manganese-dioxide (Li/MnO_2 or *lithium*) batteries are being used to assume two distinctly different roles in small-computer applications: system memory, or configuration backup; and main system power for palmtop computers. Lithium cells use a layer of lithium as the anode, a specially formulated manganese-dioxide alloy as the cathode, and a

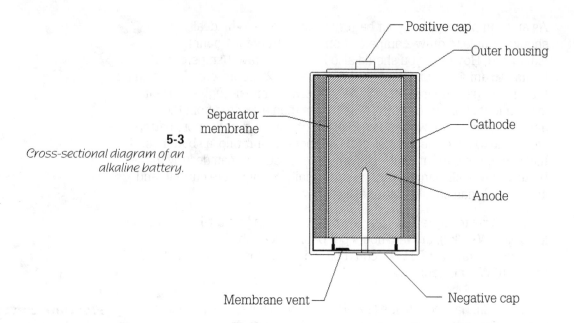

5-3
*Cross-sectional diagram of an
alkaline battery.*

Positive cap
Outer housing
Separator
membrane
Cathode
Anode
Membrane vent
Negative cap

conductive organic electrolyte. Depending on the overall size and shape
of the cell, a lithium battery can supply +3.0 Vdc at up to 230 W•h/kg (105
W•h/lb) of energy density. Lithium cells also offer a 5-year shelf life with
almost no loss of power. While their energy density is quite high, lithium
cells offer only low ampere-hour ratings between 70 mA•h (0.70 A•h) and
1300 mA•h (1.30 A•h). Limited ampere-hour ratings allow lithium cells to
maintain an almost constant output voltage over a long working life.

The classic type of lithium coin cell design is shown in FIG. 5-4. The
typical coin cell is designed in two halves with a lithium anode at the top

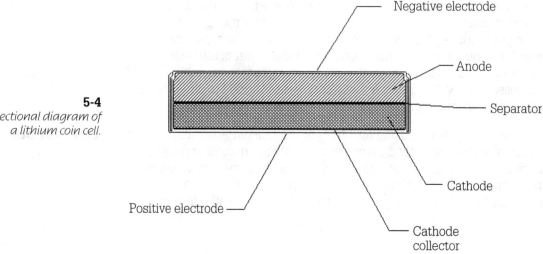

5-4
*Cross-sectional diagram of
a lithium coin cell.*

Negative electrode
Anode
Separator
Cathode
Cathode
collector
Positive electrode

and a manganese-dioxide cathode layer on the bottom. Both halves are separated by a thin membrane that contains a conductive electrolyte. The finished electrochemical assembly is packaged into a small metal can. The coin's lid forms the negative electrode, while the side walls and bottom of the coin form the positive electrode. The lid is physically isolated from the rest of the metal can by a thin insulating grommet—thus, the coin cell is not sealed. A grommet keeps moisture and contaminants out, yet will allow any pressure buildup to escape from the battery.

A cylindrical lithium cell is illustrated in FIG. 5-5. Long strips of anode, cathode, and separator material are sandwiched together and spiral-wrapped around a core. The positive cell top is insulated from the battery's main housing by a grommet. Any pressure accumulated in the cell during its chemical reaction is released through a vent diaphragm and a hole in the positive cap.

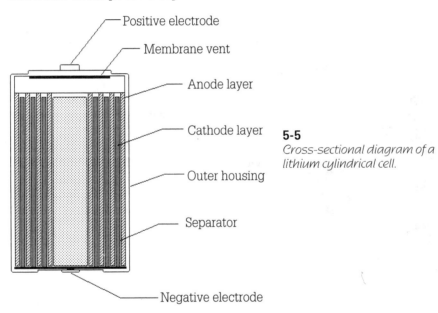

Positive electrode

Membrane vent

Anode layer

Cathode layer

Outer housing

Separator

Negative electrode

5-5
Cross-sectional diagram of a lithium cylindrical cell.

The Nickel-cadmium (NiCd) battery is one of the most cost-effective power sources in mass production today. Large NiCd battery packs are widely used as the main power source in small computers (primarily laptops and notebooks). Since NiCd cells can be manufactured in almost limitless shapes and sizes, they are ideal for systems requiring unusual battery configurations. Although NiCd batteries initially cost more than primary batteries, they can be recharged often—usually recovering their initial cost many times over.

Nickel-cadmium batteries

NiCd batteries are secondary (rechargeable) devices using an anode of nickel hydrochloride and a cathode consisting of a specially formulated cadmium compound. The electrolyte is made of potassium hydroxide. NiCd cells can supply up to +1.2 Vdc each, with ampere hour ratings from 500 mA•h (0.50 A•h) to 2300 mA•h (2.30 A•h). Energy densities in NiCd cells can approach 50 W•h/kg (23 W•h/lb). Respectable ampere-hour ratings allow NiCd cells to supply sizeable amounts of current, but their inherently low energy density means that NiCds must be recharged fairly often.

A standard NiCd cell is shown in FIG. 5-6. Both the positive and negative electrodes are long strips that are isolated by a thin, porous separator material. This long assembly is wrapped tightly around a core and inserted into a solid steel casing. Any pressure accumulated in the battery during normal operation is released through the cell's safety vent.

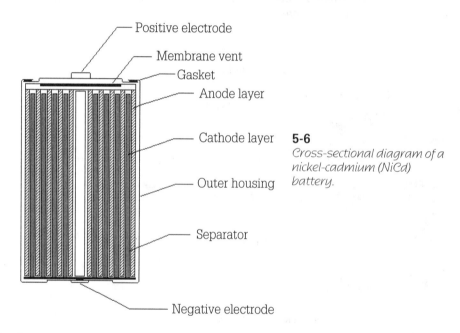

5-6
Cross-sectional diagram of a nickel-cadmium (NiCd) battery.

Nickel metal-hydride batteries

Nickel metal-hydride (NiMH) batteries are a fairly new type of rechargeable battery designed to offer substantially greater energy density than NiCd cells for small-computer applications. Since their introduction in 1990, NiMH cells have already undergone substantial improvements and cost reductions to make NiMH cells more competitive with NiCd batteries.

NiMH batteries are remarkably similar in construction and operating principles to NiCds. A positive electrode of nickel-hydroxide is the same as that used in NiCds, but the negative electrode replaces the cadmium with a metal-hydroxide alloy. When combined with a uniquely formulated electrolyte, NiMH cells are rated to provide at least 40% more capacity than similarly sized NiCd cells. NiMH batteries can provide +1.2 Vdc with discharge ratings from 800 mA•h (0.80 A•h) to more than 2400 mA•h (2.40 A•h) at continuous discharge currents of 9 A or more. Energy densities can exceed 80 W•h/kg (38.1 W•h/lb). Such specifications suggest widespread future use of NiMH batteries.

The general construction of a cylindrical NiMH cell is shown in FIG. 5-7. You might notice the similarities between NiMH and NiCd construction. The positive and negative electrodes are formed in long strips, with a porous separator membrane sandwiched between each electrode. The entire assembly is wrapped around a core and inserted into a nickel-plated steel case. A venting mechanism, virtually identical to NiCd devices, is used to bleed off any pressure buildup within the cell.

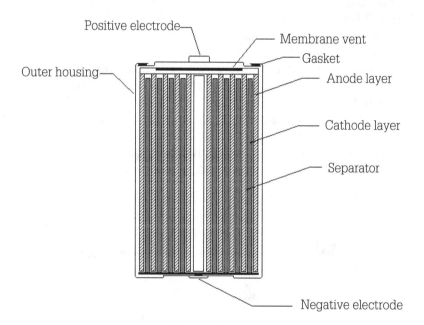

5-7
Cross-sectional diagram of a nickel metal-hydride (NiMH) cylindrical cell.

Battery protection & charging circuits

When a battery operates, it undergoes a chemical transformation that provides energy to a circuit. During the chemical reaction, the battery's electrodes are consumed, producing chemical by-products. For primary (nonrechargeable) cells, the chemical reaction is not reversible. By applying electrical energy across a secondary (rechargeable) cell, though, the chemical reaction can be reversed, restoring the integrity of the electrodes. The following sections show you common methods of battery protection and charging.

Protection circuits When primary batteries are used as a main power source or supplement to an ac-powered supply, great care must be taken to utilize the batteries properly. It is often not enough to simply strap one or more cells across a circuit and consider the circuit complete. Each battery must be protected from interference with other batteries, as well as power from ac line-powered supplies.

The main objective of all battery protection circuits is to prevent the current generated by one battery or power supply from feeding back into another battery. This sometimes happens when two or more batteries connected in parallel are not at precisely the same voltage level. When this unwanted current path occurs, the battery being backfed can be damaged, and in turn cause damage to the battery or power supply providing the current. The net result is extremely short battery life for your system.

Figure 5-8 illustrates a typical battery protection scheme for parallel sources. Four 3-volt lithium cells are used in sets of two cells each (each set producing 6 Vdc). The key elements in a battery protection circuit are rectifier-type diodes. Since diodes conduct current in one direction only, they act like one-way valves. Current from one set of batteries flows through diode D1 to the circuit, but that current will be blocked by D2 and D3. Current from the second set of batteries flows through D2 to the circuit, but will be blocked by D3 and D1. When an ac power supply is being used, its current flows through D3, but is blocked by D2 and D1. By allowing the power supply voltage to slightly exceed the battery voltage, the batteries will effectively be cut off as long as the ac power supply is

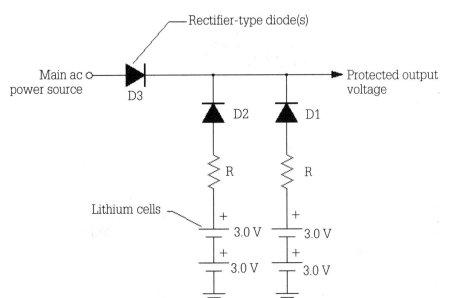

5-8
*A battery protection circuit
for parallel cells.*

used in the system. The resistors shown in the circuit are often optional as backup protection. If a diode in any leg should short circuit, the resistor limits the backfeed current into the battery, preventing catastrophic battery damage.

In its simplest sense, *charging* is the replacement of electrical energy in batteries whose stored energy has been depleted. By applying current to a discharged battery over a given period of time, it is possible to cause a chemical recombination at the battery's electrodes that restores the cell's potential. Essentially, you must backfeed the battery at a known, controlled rate. Keep in mind that recharging works only for secondary cells, such as nickel-cadmium or nickel metal-hydride batteries. Attempting to recharge a primary battery will quickly destroy it.

Charging circuits

Before you dive into an overview of charging circuits and troubleshooting, you must understand the concept of C. The term C designates the normal current capacity of a battery (in amperes). In most circumstances, C is the ampere-hour current level. For example, a battery rated for 1300 mA•h (1.30 A•h) would be considered to have a C value of 1.30 A, while a battery rated for 700 mA•h (0.70 A•h) would have a C of 0.70 A. Charging rates are based upon multiples of C.

To recharge a battery, you must apply a voltage across the cell that causes the proper amount of charging current to flow back into the battery, as shown in FIG. 5-9. Ideally, the battery should be charged at a rate of 0.1C. For batteries with a C of 500 mA (0.5 A), 0.1C is 50 mA (0.05 A). At 0.1C, the battery could be left in the charger indefinitely without damage occurring. Low-current charge rates, such as 0.1C are sometimes referred to as a "slow charge." Slow charging produces the least physical or thermal stress within a battery, and ensures the maximum possible number of charge-discharge cycles.

Many types of secondary batteries can be charged well above the 0.1C rate. The "quick charge" approach uses current levels of 0.3C (three times the slow charge rate) to recharge the cell in 4 to 6 hours. For a battery with a C of 600 mA (0.60 A), the slow charge rate is 60 mA (0.06 A), and the quick charge rate is 180 mA (0.18 A). However, the quick charge process runs the risk of overcharging a battery. Once a battery is fully recharged, additional current at or above the quick charge rate causes temperature and pressure buildups within the cell. In extreme cases, a severely overcharged cell might rupture and be destroyed. When quick charging, the 0.3C charging rate should be used only long enough to restore the bulk of a cell's energy. The rate should be reduced to 0.1C or less for continuous operation.

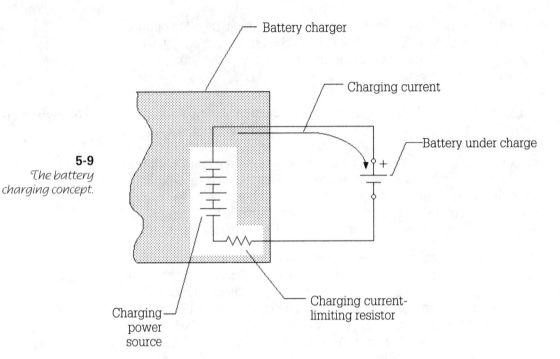

5-9
The battery charging concept.

Battery charger

Charging current

Battery under charge

Charging current-limiting resistor

Charging power source

New NiCd and NiMH batteries allow for an even faster charge of 1 hour. The 1-hour charge uses a rate of 1.5C, or 1.5 times the amount current that the cell is intended to provide. A battery with a C of 1400 mA (1.40 A) would use a 1-hour charge rate of 2100 mA (2.10 A). Remember that only specially-designed secondary cells can be safely charged in 1 hour or less. With 1-hour charging, current control and timing become critical issues. The battery charging current must be reduced as soon as the cell approaches its full charge, or catastrophic battery failure will almost certainly result. Rapid charging causes substantial temperature and pressure increases that eventually take their toll on a cell's working life. You should expect the working life of any cell to be curtailed when it is regularly operated in a 1-hour charge mode.

Constant current charging

The most efficient method of battery charging provides a constant source of charging current. As a battery charges, its terminal voltage increases. A constant-current charger keeps the charging current stable as the battery voltage increases. Figure 5-10 illustrates the design of a simple constant-current charging circuit. Since the circuit is designed only to provide one fixed current level, the charging current is typically set for the 0.1C level of the battery or batteries being charged (e.g., AA, C, or D).

In small computers, where small size, light weight, and low component counts are critical considerations, a simple battery charger circuit is often

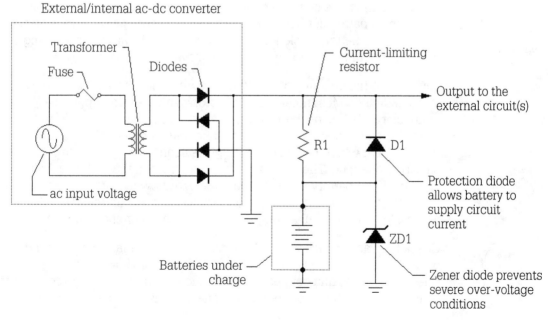

Output to the
external circuit(s)

External/internal ac-dc converter

Transformer

Fuse

Diodes

D1

R1

Q1

ZD1

Q2

R2   Batteries under
              charge

5-10
*A constant-current
charging circuit.*

preferred over a constant-current circuit. While constant current is an
ideal charging condition, it is not absolutely necessary. A variable-current
charging circuit is shown in FIG. 5-11. When a battery is deeply
discharged, there is a large voltage difference between the power supply
and the battery. This difference results in a sizeable voltage drop across
R1 and a corresponding large current flow into the battery. Charging

External/internal ac-dc converter

Transformer

Fuse

Diodes

Current-limiting
resistor

Output to the
external circuit(s)

R1   D1

ac input voltage

Batteries under
charge

Protection diode
allows battery to
supply circuit
current

ZD1

Zener diode prevents
severe over-voltage
conditions

5-11   *A variable-current charging circuit.*

might start out around the 0.3C rate; however, as the battery charges, the voltage difference across R1 falls, reducing the current flow to the battery. At a full charge, the current into the battery might be as low as 0.05C

Troubleshooting battery charging circuits

Fortunately, battery charging circuits are some of the easiest circuits to troubleshoot because there are generally so few parts. You will need a multimeter for charger testing. Keep in mind that many of the following procedures must be performed on powered circuitry. Although battery charging circuits primarily use low-voltage dc, take full precautions to protect yourself and your test equipment from accidental harm. If your small computer uses an external ac adaptor, an isolation transformer should not be needed (but might be used if you wish). When your power supply is incorporated into the small-computer assembly, using an isolation transformer is highly recommended for your own protection. If you have not read the electrical shock precautions in the service guidelines of chapter 4, familiarize yourself with that section now before continuing.

Start your repair by turning the computer off, removing the power plug from the receptacle, and removing or disconnecting the batteries. Disassemble the computer enough to expose your battery charging or power supply circuit. Be certain to insulate any loose assemblies or circuits to prevent accidental short circuits or physical damage.

Symptom 1: *The battery (or battery pack) does not charge.*
In this situation, the computer might run fine from the ac power supply, and from its battery (or batteries) when the ac power supply is removed. However, the battery pack does not charge when the ac supply is being used. Without recharging, the battery will eventually go dead.

Your clue to the charging situation comes from the computer's battery status indicator. Most notebook and laptop computers incorporate a multicolor LED to show battery information. For example, the LED might be red when the computer is operating from its internal battery. Yellow might appear when the ac power supply is connected to indicate the battery is charging. The LED might turn green when the battery is fully charged. If the battery status indicator fails to show a charging color when ac power is being used, it's often a good sign of trouble. The user's manual for your particular computer explains the charging indicators.

Check the battery pack with all computer power off. Make sure that the battery pack is inserted properly and completely into its compartment. Check any cables and connectors that attach the battery pack to the charging circuit. Loose or corroded connectors, as well as faulty cables,

can prevent energy current from reaching the battery. Reseat any loose
connectors and reattach any loose wires that you find.

After you are confident of your connections, provide power to your
computer. Trace the charging voltage from the ac power supply to the
battery terminals. If charging voltage does not reach the battery pack, it
can never charge. Set your multimeter to measure dc voltage (probably in
the 10 to 20 Vdc range) and measure the voltage across your battery pack
terminals. You should read some voltage below the pack's rated voltage
because the battery pack is somewhat discharged. Now, reconnect the
battery pack and once again measure the voltage across your battery
pack terminals. If charging voltage appears at the battery pack, the
voltage reading should climb above the battery pack's rated voltage. If the
battery pack still does not charge, try replacing the battery pack, which
might be worn out or damaged.

If charging voltage is not available to your battery pack, trace the
charging voltage from your ac power supply. The point at which the
charging voltage disappears is probably the source of the trouble. An
example of charging circuit is shown in FIG. 5-12. Refer to FIG. 5-12 for the
following troubleshooting procedures.

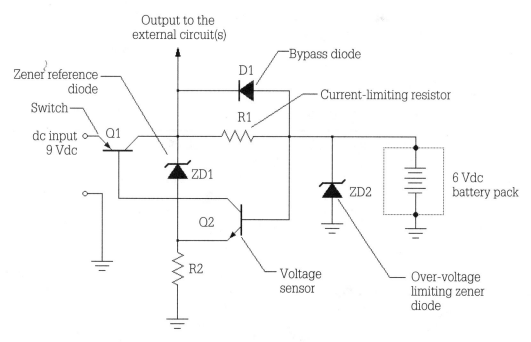

5-12 *A battery charging circuit (troubleshooting figure).*

Measure the dc voltage from the output of your ac power supply. You should read the voltage level specified on the supply output(s). To conserve space and reduce weight, most laptop and notebook computers use external power supplies. If you do not read the appropriate output voltage, disconnect the supply from the computer and read the output(s) again. An output that remains low when disconnected suggests a faulty power supply or poor ac input-voltage levels. Refer to the next section for power supply repair. If supply output voltage returns to a normal level, the charging circuit or some other part of the computer's power control circuitry is probably defective.

Measure voltage at the collector of Q1. When you can measure approximately the dc input voltage, you know Q1 is on and working. If you measure slightly less than battery voltage, Q1 is off. Q1 is activated by Q2, so check both transistors, replacing any defective ones. Check zener diode ZD1. A defective zener diode disrupts the charging circuit's reference level. Replace the zener if it is defective. Resistor R1 is a current-limiting resistor that protects the battery pack during charging. Check the connections at R1 and measure its value. If R1 is burned out or open circuited, the battery will not charge. As a last resort, you can replace the battery charger PC board.

Symptom 2: The system does not run on battery power, but runs properly from main power. This symptom suggests that your computer runs fine when the ac power supply is used, but does not run on a properly charged battery. The system might or might not initialize depending on the extent of the problem.

Before you disassemble the computer or attempt any sort of repair, make sure that you have a fully charged battery pack in the system. Remove the battery pack and measure the voltage across its terminals. You should read approximately the battery voltage marked on the pack. A measurably lower voltage might indicate that the battery is not fully charged. Recharge the battery pack or try a different battery pack. The charging process might take several hours on older systems, but newer small-computer battery systems can charge in an hour or so. If the discharged battery pack does not seem to charge, refer to symptom 1.

When you have a fully charged battery, check to be sure that it is inserted completely and connected properly. Inspect any wiring and connectors that attach the battery pack to the circuit.

At this point, it is perfectly safe to assume that battery power is not reaching the load circuit(s). Remove the battery pack, disconnect the ac power supply, and use your multimeter to check the bypass diode shown in FIG. 5-12. If the diode is open, battery current can backflow through R1. The resulting voltage drop across R1 might be too great to power the computer properly. Replace the bypass diode if necessary.

There might also be a zener diode across the battery pack to protect it from overcharging. A shorted zener diode will channel current away from the computer's circuit(s) and cause excessive battery heating. Remove the battery pack, disconnect the ac power supply, and use your multimeter to check any limiting diode(s), shown in FIG. 5-12 as ZD2. Replace any limiting diodes as necessary.

Symptom 3: The system suffers from a short battery life.
Today's small computers are designed to squeeze up to 6 hours of operation from every charge. Most systems get at least 4 hours from a charge. Short battery life can present a perplexing problem, especially if you do a great deal of computing on the road. All computer functions are assumed to be normal for this symptom.

Begin your investigation by inspecting the battery pack. Check for any damaged batteries. Make sure the battery pack is inserted properly into the computer, and see that its connections and wiring are intact. Replace the battery pack if necessary. Keep in mind that rechargeable batteries do not last forever—there are just so many charge-discharge cycles that a cell can physically withstand. Quick-charge battery packs are subject to the greatest abuse and can suffer the shortest life spans. It is possible that one or more cells in the battery pack might have failed.

The computer's configuration itself can largely determine the amount of running time available from each battery charge. An electroluminescent (EL) backlight, a spinning hard drive, and floppy drive access—each of these items consume a substantial amount of power. Most small computers are designed to shut down each major power consumer after some preset period of disuse. For example, an LCD screen might shut off if there is no keyboard activity for 2 minutes, or the hard drive might stop spinning after 3 minutes if there is no hard drive access, and so on. Even reducing CPU clock speed during periods of inactivity reduces power consumption. The computer's BIOS keeps track of elapsed time for each device, and initiates the appropriate shutdown sequence. The amount of time required before shutdown may be adjusted through setup routines in the computer.

Finally, use your multimeter to inspect any overvoltage zener diodes that might be across the battery pack, shown as ZD2 in FIG. 5-12. The zener is often used to protect the battery pack from overcharging. If the zener is partially or totally shorted, it will channel current away from the computer's circuit(s) and cause excessive battery heating. Remove the battery pack and disconnect the ac power supply before checking the zener. Replace any limiting diodes as necessary.

Linear power supplies

Batteries are certainly not the only source of energy for small computers. Just about every system can be powered from the ac line voltage available in your home, shop, or office. Unfortunately, conventional ac is not directly compatible with your computer, so the line power from an ac wall outlet must be converted into values of voltage and current suitable for your small computer. Such manipulation is the task of the power supply.

The term *power supply* is rather a misleading one. A power supply does not actually create power. Instead, a power supply converts commercially generated ac line power into one or more dc voltage levels needed to run your small computer.

This book covers three types of power supplies: conventional linear supplies, backlight inverters, and dc-dc converters. Some small-computer systems might use all three supplies. A fourth type of power supply known as a *switching* supply, is covered in the advanced book *Troubleshooting and Repairing Notebook, Palmtop, and Pen Computers: A Technician's Guide* (Windcrest #4427). Let's start with linear power supplies.

Linear supply construction & operation

Linear means "line" or "straight". As you see from the block diagram in FIG. 5-13, a linear supply essentially operates in a straight line from ac input to dc output(s). The exact component parts and supply specifications varies greatly from supply to supply, but all linear supplies contain the same basic subsections—a transformer, a rectifier, a filter, and a regulator.

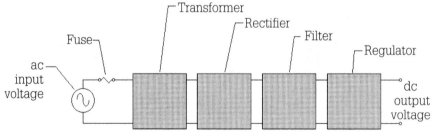

5-13
Block diagram of a linear power supply.

Linear supplies are sometimes designed into the small computer itself. When the supply is internal, you need only attach an ac cord between the nearest wall outlet and the computer. In many designs, the weight and bulk involved in a linear supply are removed from the computer and located in a standalone, remote power supply called an *ac adaptor* or *ac-dc converter*. When ac power is applied to this remote supply, its dc output(s) connect to the computer through a thin cable. Figure 5-14 shows an ac-adaptor.

5-14
A simple ac adaptor.
TandyCorp./RadioShack

Transformers

A transformer provides the vast majority of a power supply's weight and bulk. As discussed in chapter 2, a transformer uses the principles of magnetic coupling to alter the ac voltage and current levels of the input power. For example, it is usually desirable to transform the 120-Vac line voltage into one or more lower levels of ac voltage (e.g., 27 Vac or 18 Vac). Such transformations require a step-down transformer. By stepping the line voltage down, current is stepped up by the same factor. Suppose a 10:1 step-down transformer reduces 120 Vac to 12 Vac. An input current of 100 mA (0.10 A) would be increased to 1000 mA (1.00 A). Transformers are used only to handle ac signals—dc voltages will not work on a transformer.

Rectifiers

The secondary voltage from a transformer is still in ac form. The ac voltage and current must be converted into dc before powering electronic circuits. The process of converting ac into dc is known as *rectification*. To achieve rectification, only one polarity of the ac signal is allowed to reach the rectifier's output. Even though the rectifier's output can vary greatly, the output's polarity will remain either positive or negative. This fluctuating dc is called *pulsating dc*. Diodes are ideal for use as rectifiers since they allow current to flow in only one direction. You might encounter any of three classic rectifier circuits: half-wave, full-wave, and bridge.

A *half-wave* rectifier is shown in FIG. 5-15. It is the simplest and most straightforward rectifier, since only one diode is required. As secondary voltage from the transformer exceeds the diode's turn-on voltage (about 0.6 V), the diode begins to conduct current. This condition generates an output that mimics the positive half of the ac signal. If the diode is reversed, the output polarity is also reversed. The disadvantage with half-wave rectifiers is that it is very inefficient. Only half of the ac wave is handled; the other half is basically ignored. The resulting gap between pulses causes a lower average output voltage and a higher amount of ac noise contained in the final dc output. Half-wave rectifiers are rarely used in small computers.

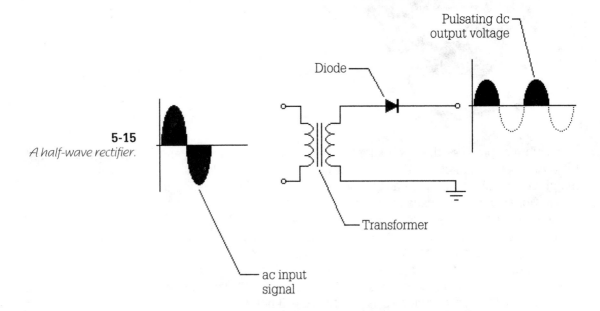

5-15
A half-wave rectifier.

Full-wave rectifiers, such as shown in FIG. 5-16, offer substantial advantages over the half-wave rectifiers. By using two diodes in the circuit, both polarities of the ac secondary voltage are changed into pulsating dc. Since a diode is at each terminal of the secondary, the polarities at each diode are opposite. When the ac signal is negative, the upper diode conducts and the lower diode is off. When the ac signal is

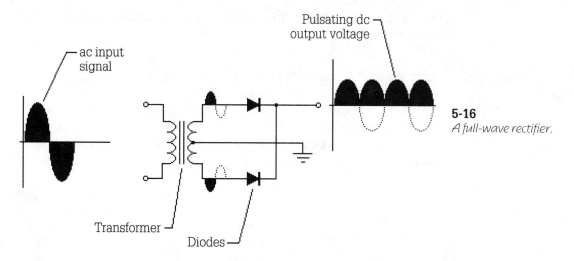

5-16
A full-wave rectifier.

negative, the upper diode is off and the lower diode conducts. This means that there is always one diode conducting, so there are no gaps in the pulsating dc signal. The only disadvantage to full-wave rectifiers is that a center-tapped transformer is needed. Tapped transformers are often heavier and bulkier than nontapped transformers.

Diode bridge rectifiers use four diodes in a bridge configuration to provide full-wave rectification without the hassle of a center-tapped transformer. Figure 5-17 illustrates a typical bridge rectifier. Two diodes provide forward current paths for rectification, while two other diodes supply isolation to ground. When ac voltage is positive, diode D1 conducts and D4 provides isolation. When ac voltage is negative, diode D2 conducts

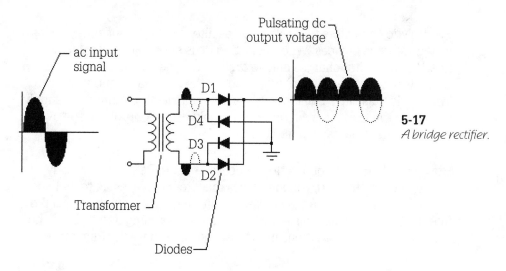

5-17
A bridge rectifier.

while D3 provides isolation. Bridge rectifiers are by far the most popular type of rectifier circuit.

Filters By strict technical definition, pulsating dc is dc because its polarity remains constant (even if its magnitude changes periodically). Unfortunately, pulsating dc is unsuitable for any type of electronic power source. Voltage magnitude must be constant over time in order to operate electronic devices properly. Pulsating dc is converted into smoothed dc through the use of a *filter*, as illustrated in FIG. 5-18.

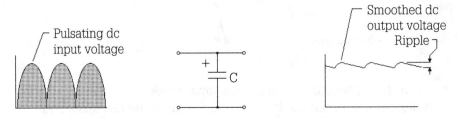

5-18
Capacitive filtering action.

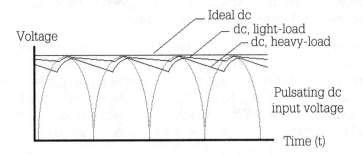

Electrolytic capacitors typically serve as filter elements since they act as voltage storage devices. When pulsating dc is applied to a capacitive filter, the capacitor charges and voltage across the capacitor increases. Ultimately, the capacitor's charge reaches the peak value of pulsating dc. When a dc pulse falls back toward zero, the capacitor continues to supply current to the load. This action tends to hold up the output voltage over time, and the dc voltage is filtered.

However, filtering is not a perfect process. As current is drained away from a filter by the load, voltage across the filter decreases. Filter voltage continues to drop until a new pulse of dc from the rectifier recharges the filter for another cycle. This action of repetitive charging and discharging results in regular fluctuations in the filter output. These fluctuations are called *ripple*, which is an undesirable noise component of a smoothed dc output.

Figure 5-18 also shows a sample plot of voltage versus time for a typical filter circuit. The ideal dc output would be a steady line indicating a constant dc output at all points in time. In reality, there will always be some amount of filter ripple. Just how much ripple is present depends on the load being supplied. For a light load (a circuit drawing low current), discharge is less between pulses, so the magnitude of ripple is lower. A large load (a circuit drawing substantial current), requires greater amounts of current, so discharge is deeper between pulses. This results in greater magnitudes of ripple. The relationship of dc pulses is shown for reference.

Beware of shock hazards from power supply filters. Large electrolytic capacitors tend to accumulate and hold substantial amounts of charge for a long time. If you touch the leads of a charged capacitor, it might discharge through you. While a capacitor shock is almost never dangerous, it can be very uncomfortable.

Before working on a power supply, make sure that the capacitor is discharged by placing a large-value resistor across the capacitor, as shown in FIG. 5-19. This bleeder resistor slowly drains off any charge

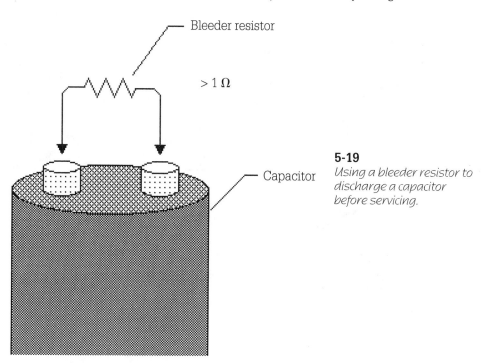

Bleeder resistor

$> 1 \, \Omega$

Capacitor

5-19
Using a bleeder resistor to discharge a capacitor before servicing.

remaining on the filter once the power supply is turned off. Never attempt to discharge a capacitor by shorting its leads with a screwdriver blade or wire. The sudden release of energy can actually weld a wire or screwdriver directly to the capacitor's leads, as well as damage the capacitor internally.

Regulators   A transformer, rectifier, and filter form the essentials of every power supply. These parts combined will successfully convert ac into dc capable of driving many electrical and electronic loads. However, such unregulated power supplies have two major disadvantages: ripple is always present on the supply's output, and the output level varies with the load. Even the most forgiving ICs might perform erratically if they are operated with unregulated dc. Ideal dc should be ripple-free and constant regardless of the load. A regulator is needed to fix dc from a filter's output.

Linear regulation is just as the name implies—current flows from the regulator's input to its output as shown in FIG. 5-20. When voltage is applied to the regulator's input, circuitry in the regulator manipulates input voltage to provide a steady, consistent output voltage. The output remains steady under a wide range of input conditions as long as the input voltage is above the desired output voltage (often by three volts or more). If input voltage falls to or below the desired output voltage, the regulator falls out of regulation. In such a case, the regulator's output signal tends to follow the input signal, including the ripple.

5-20
Typical regulator action.

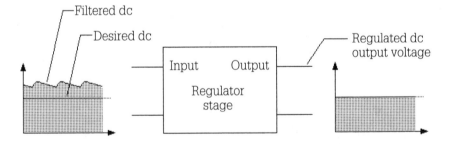

A linear regulator works by "throwing away" the extra energy provided by a filter; whatever is left over is the desired output. Energy is discarded in the form of heat. This explains why so many regulators are attached to large, metal heat sinks. Excessive heating also explains why so many power supplies are built as external, standalone ac adaptors instead of being built into the computer. While linear regulation is a simple and reliable operation method, it is also very inefficient. Typical linear power supplies are only up to 50% efficient, which means that for every 10 W provided to the supply, only 5 W is provided to the load. Most of this waste occurs in the regulation process itself.

Zener diodes make excellent voltage regulators because they limit the amount of voltage that occurs across them, illustrated in FIG. 5-21. Input voltage from the filter is applied across the zener diode through a current-limiting resistor. The zener clamps the voltage to its zener level. In turn, the zener potential turns on the proper transistor, allowing current to flow. Output voltage will equal the input voltage minus the diode drop across the transistor's base-emitter junction. You can change the regulator's output voltage by changing the zener diode.

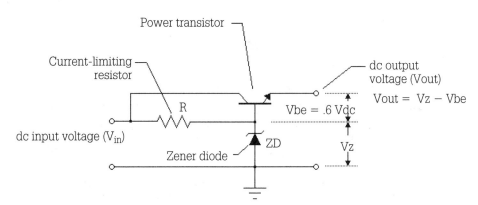

5-21
A simple transistor series regulator.

Vz: Zener voltage
Vbe: Base-emitter voltage
drop in a silicon transistor.

Regulator circuits can also be fabricated as integrated circuits, as shown in FIG. 5-22. Additional performance features such as automatic current limiting and overtemperature shutdown circuitry can be included to improve the regulator's reliability. Input voltages must exceed the desired output by several volts, but IC regulators are simple to use. One additional consideration for IC regulators is the use of small-value capacitors at the IC's input and output. Small capacitors (0.01 μF to 0.1 μF) filter high-frequency noise or signals that could interfere with the regulator's operation.

Under most circumstances, linear power supplies are reasonably simple and straightforward to troubleshoot. You can usually make use of your multimeter or oscilloscope to trace voltage through the supply. The point at which your expected voltage disappears is probably the point of failure. Keep in mind that many of the following procedures must be performed

Troubleshooting linear power supplies

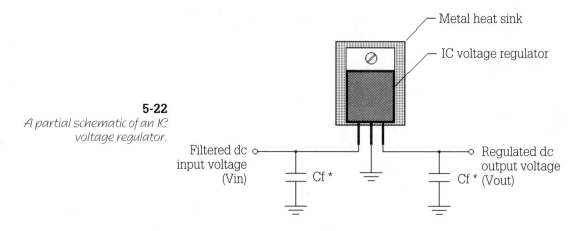

5-22
A partial schematic of an IC voltage regulator.

Metal heat sink

IC voltage regulator

Filtered dc input voltage (Vin)

Cf *

Regulated dc output voltage Cf * (Vout)

* High-frequency filter capacitors.

on powered circuitry. Therefore, take every precaution to protect yourself and your equipment before beginning your repair. The use of an isolation transformer to provide ac is highly recommended. If you have not read the precautions in the service guidelines of chapter 4, familiarize yourself with that section before continuing.

Start your repair by removing all power from the supply. Disassemble the power supply enough to expose the power supply circuit. For external power supplies, you will not have to touch your computer at this point. You might have to follow power into the computer circuits at a later point. Be certain to insulate any loose assemblies or circuits to prevent accidental short circuits or physical damage. For the following procedures, refer to the example linear power supply shown in FIG. 5-23.

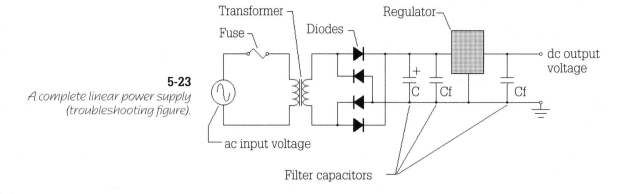

5-23
A complete linear power supply (troubleshooting figure).

Transformer

Fuse

Diodes

Regulator

dc output voltage

ac input voltage

Filter capacitors

Symptom 1: *The power supply is completely dead (no output).*   Begin by checking the ac line voltage into the power supply. Use your multimeter to measure ac voltage at the power supply's plug. If you are using an isolation transformer, check the transformer's ac output to your supply. You should normally read 105 to 130 Vac (210 to 240 Vac in Europe). More or less line voltage can cause the supply to malfunction. Use extreme caution whenever measuring ac line voltage levels.

For internal ac supplies, check the computer's power switch to be sure that it is in the ON position. This might sound silly, but it really is a common oversight. Unplug the power supply and inspect the main line fuse. For standalone ac adaptors, you will probably have to disassemble the supply's outer housing to reach the fuse(s). An integral (built-in) power supply might offer a panel-mount fuse that you can remove and test. In some cases, you must disassemble the built-in supply to check the fuse(s). Test a fuse by measuring its continuity. A working fuse should register as a complete short circuit (0 Ω). If you read infinite resistance, the fuse is defective and should be replaced. Replace defective fuses only with fuses of equal size and current rating.

With the supply disconnected, check all connectors and wiring to be sure that everything is intact. A loose connector or wire can sometimes disable the supply. If your supply has failed after being dropped or abused, consider the possibility of printed circuit board damage. Faulty soldering at the factory (or on your test bench) can also cause PC board problems. The PC board might be cracked, one or more component leads might have pulled away from its solder pads, or a trace (or traces) might have broken from impact stress. Use the PC board troubleshooting guidelines of chapter 4 to inspect your PC board assembly.

Apply power and use your multimeter to measure the dc output(s) from the supply. Each output is generally well marked, so you should have no trouble determining what the output should be. When an output is low or zero, disconnect the power supply from its load and measure its output(s) again. If you find the same measurements with the load disconnected, the trouble is probably in your supply. If the output returns to its rated value, the supply is probably being shorted by the load circuit(s). Check your computer's circuitry for damage or short circuits that might be ruining the supply.

If there are no obvious failures up to this point, you can try replacing the power supply outright, or attempt to troubleshoot the supply to the component level. For the purposes of this discussion, you should follow the procedure with FIG. 5-23. In linear-supply troubleshooting, it is often best to start your tracing at the supply output and work backward through the supply toward the ac input.

Measure dc voltage at the regulator's output and input. Regulator output should equal the final supply output measured earlier. If the regulator's input voltage is several volts higher than the expected output, and the actual output is low or nonexistent, your regulator is probably defective. Try replacing the regulator. If the regulator's input voltage is low or absent, examine the filter network. Assuming the PC board is intact, the filter voltage should roughly equal the regulator's input voltage. Remove all power from the supply, discharge all filter capacitors with a high-value resistor (100 KΩ or larger), and check each capacitor as outlined in chapter 3. Replace any faulty filter capacitors. If the filter circuit checks properly, check the junction of each rectifier diode. An open rectifier diode can disable the supply. Replace any faulty rectifier diodes.

Should your rectifier diodes check properly, reapply power to the supply, and measure ac voltage across the transformer's secondary (output) winding. The expected output is typically marked on the windings. Also check the ac voltage across the transformer's primary coil. You should find about 120 Vac across the primary (or 220 Vac in Europe). If there is no voltage across the primary, there will be no signal across the secondary. This suggests a faulty fuse or circuit breaker, or some other circuit interruption in the primary transformer circuit. When primary voltage is normal and secondary voltage is low or absent, suspect a failure in the transformer.

Finally, if ac is available to the supply, but you cannot find the point where ac or dc disappears, you can simply replace the power supply outright. Replacement is a simple matter for ac-adaptors—you need only to unplug the suspect supply and connect a new supply. Internal supplies are a bit more involved, but replacement should go fairly quickly.

Symptom 2: The power supply operates intermittently.
You might see the battery charging indicator LED blink on and off as the supply kicks in and out. Begin by checking the ac input voltage into the power supply. Exercise extreme caution whenever measuring ac line voltage. Use your multimeter to measure ac voltage at your power supply's plug. If you are using an isolation transformer as recommended, check the transformer's ac output to your supply. You should normally read 105 to 130 Vac (210 to 240 Vac in Europe). More or less line voltage can cause the supply to malfunction.

Consider the possibility of a PC board failure—especially if your supply has only recently been dropped or severely abused. Faulty soldering at the factory (or on your test bench) can also cause PC board problems. The PC board might be cracked, one or more component leads might have pulled away from its solder pads, or a trace (or traces) might have broken from the stress of the impact. Use the PC board troubleshooting guidelines of chapter 4 to inspect your PC board assembly.

In addition to physical intermittents, you should also check the supply for thermal intermittent problems. Thermal problems typically occur in semiconductor devices such as transistors or ICs, so your supply's regulator(s) are likely candidates. A thermal failure usually occurs when the supply works once turned on, then cuts out after some period of operation. The supply might then remain disabled until it is turned off, or might cut in and out while running. Often, a thermally-defective regulator might operate when cool (room temperature), but as it runs and dissipates power, its internal temperature climbs. When temperature climbs high enough, the device might stop working. If you remove power from the supply and let it cool again, the supply might resume operation.

If you detect any hot components in your intermittent supply, you might suspect a thermal intermittent problem. Spray the suspect part with electronics-grade refrigerant. Leave power applied to the part and spray in short, controlled bursts. Many short bursts are better than one long burst. If the supply stabilizes or stops cutting out, you have probably identified the faulty part. Replace any thermally intermittent components, or replace the entire power supply.

Symptom 3: *The computer's operation is erratic.* The system may run fine on batteries, but not from the ac-powered supply. Batteries might not charge properly. Begin by checking the ac voltage at your power supply's plug. Use extreme caution whenever measuring ac line voltage. If you are using an isolation transformer as recommended, you should check the transformer's ac output to your supply. You should normally read 105 to 130 Vac (210 to 240 Vac in Europe). More or less line voltage can cause the supply to malfunction.

Disconnect power from the supply and inspect all cables and wires to be certain that everything is intact. A loose connector or wire can sometimes disable your supply. If you cannot find an obvious failure at this point, you can replace the suspect power supply outright, or attempt to troubleshoot the supply to the component level. For the purpose of this discussion, you should follow the procedure with FIG. 5-23.

Measure dc voltage at the regulator's output and input. Regulator output should equal the final supply output measured earlier. If the regulator's input voltage is several volts higher than the expected output and the actual output is low or nonexistent, your regulator is probably defective. Try replacing the regulator. If the regulator's input voltage is low or absent, examine the filter network. Assuming the PC board is intact, the filter voltage should roughly equal the regulator's input voltage. Remove all power from the supply, discharge all filter capacitors with a high-value resistor (100 KΩ or larger), and check each capacitor as outlined in chapter 3. Replace any faulty filter capacitors. If the filter circuit checks properly, check the junction of each rectifier diode. An open rectifier diode can disable the supply. Replace any faulty rectifier diodes.

Should your rectifier diodes check properly, reapply power to the supply and measure the ac voltage across the transformer's secondary (output) winding. The expected output is typically marked on the windings. Also check the ac voltage across the transformer's primary coil. You should find about 120 Vac across the primary (or 220 Vac in Europe). If there is no voltage across the primary, there will be no signal across the secondary. This suggests a faulty fuse or circuit breaker, or some other circuit interruption in the primary transformer circuit. When primary voltage is normal and secondary voltage is low or absent, suspect a failure in the transformer.

Finally, if ac is available to the supply, but you cannot find the point where ac or dc disappears, you can simply replace the power supply outright. Replacement is a simple matter for ac-adaptors—you need only unplug the suspect supply and connect a new supply. Internal supplies are a bit more involved, but replacement should proceed quickly.

Backlighting power supplies

Liquid crystal displays are visible because light is reflected to your eyes. Whatever light emanates from the display is interpreted as being transparent. Light that is absorbed by energized liquid crystal material appears opaque. Light will not always fall evenly or regularly across your small-computer's display, so artificial light is used to produce a consistent light source for the display. The artificial lighting used to illuminate LCDs is known as *backlighting*. This part of the chapter covers the power supplies used to drive typical backlighting.

Supply requirements & principles

Just about all major backlighting schemes require a high-voltage, low-current signal to power the light source. In many cases, an ac voltage in excess of 200 V is needed. To supply a constant ac level, your small computer uses an inverter circuit similar to the one shown in FIG. 5-24. The dc from your power supply or dc-dc converter is fed to an oscillator that "chops" the dc into low-voltage pulsating dc. Pulsating dc is applied across a small, high-ratio, step-up transformer that multiplies the

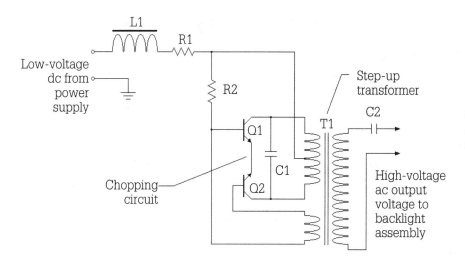

pulsating dc into a rough ac signal. This high-voltage ac signal can then be used to run a cold cathode fluorescent tube (CCFT) or electroluminescent (EL) panel. Keep in mind that the conversion of dc into ac is virtually opposite to the process used in linear power supplies (thus the term inverter) where ac is transformed into dc.

Backlight problems usually manifest themselves in the LCD itself. Without lighting, the contrast and brightness of a display will be extremely poor. The display might appear clearly in strong daylight, but might disappear in low light or darkness. When backlight problems occur, investigate your inverter supply as well as the particular mechanism producing your light.

Troubleshooting inverter supplies

Symptom 1: The backlight appears inoperative. The LCD might seem washed out or invisible in low light. Disassemble your system to expose the inverter board (typically located behind or next to the LCD). Apply power to the system and use your multimeter to measure the inverter's dc input voltage. Input voltage usually runs from 12 to 24 Vdc, depending on your particular system and backlight type. Input voltage might be developed directly in the system's power supply or from a dc-dc converter (covered in the next section). In any case, you would expect to measure a strong dc voltage. If input voltage is low or absent, your power supply or dc-dc converter might be faulty.

Next, use your multimeter to measure the inverter's ac output voltage. Fluorescent tubes and EL panels typically require from 200 to 400 Vac for proper illumination. If output voltage is low or absent, the inverter circuit is probably defective. You might simply replace the inverter circuit outright, or attempt to troubleshoot the inverter to the component level. If output voltage measures an acceptable level, your inverter board is probably working correctly and the trouble might exist in the light source itself. For example, a CCFT might have failed, or an EL panel might be damaged. Try replacing the suspect light source.

If you elect to try troubleshooting the inverter board itself, you might see from FIG. 5-24 that there is little to fail. Remove all power from the computer and check the oscillator transistors. A faulty transistor can stop your inverter from oscillating, so no ac voltage will be produced. Replace any defective transistors. Beyond faulty transistors, inspect any electrolytic capacitors on the inverter board. A shorted or open tantalum or aluminum electrolytic capacitor might prevent the oscillator from functioning. The transformer might also fail, but transformers are often special components that are difficult to find replacements for. If you are unable to locate any obvious component failures, go ahead and replace the inverter board.

dc-dc converters

With most battery-powered small computers (and many ac power systems), it is necessary to generate one or more dc voltage levels in order to operate the computer's circuitry. However, there might only be one available dc power source, so dc-dc converters are used to manipulate a single dc source voltage into other dc voltage levels needed by your computer. Suppose your new palmtop computer uses two alkaline cells as its main power source. Two alkaline batteries yield only +3.0 Vdc. A dc-dc converter can be used to convert the 3 volt source into a 5 volt source that the computer's circuitry needs. By adding dc-dc converters, other voltages can also be generated. Figure 5-25 illustrates the concept of a dc-dc converter.

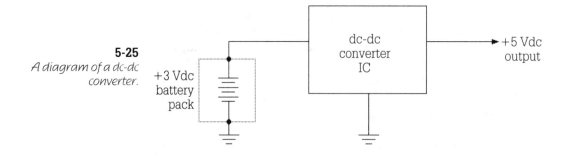

5-25
A diagram of a dc-dc converter.

+3 Vdc battery pack

dc-dc converter IC

+5 Vdc output

Converter concepts

A dc-dc converter is an extraordinary device. It combines the functions of an inverter supply and a linear supply in one convenient IC package. A source of dc—either from a battery pack or an ac power supply—is inverted (chopped) into ac, stepped up or down to some desired level, and reconverted into a new dc level. The actual techniques used to implement dc-dc conversion are beyond the scope of this book, but it is important that you understand the principles of conversion. Since IC packages are used, converters cannot handle significant amounts of power. With today's low-power computer systems, however, dc-dc converters are an excellent fit.

Typically, dc-dc converters are implemented on the computer's motherboard, remote from the actual power supply. You will need a schematic diagram of your computer or manufacturer's data sheet to locate and identify each pin on the converter. A dc-dc converter circuit is illustrated in FIG. 5-26. To complete the package, the converter is shown in conjunction with a regulator IC. As discussed in the section on linear power supplies, a regulator maintains a stable output voltage even though its input might vary somewhat.

Troubleshooting dc-dc converters

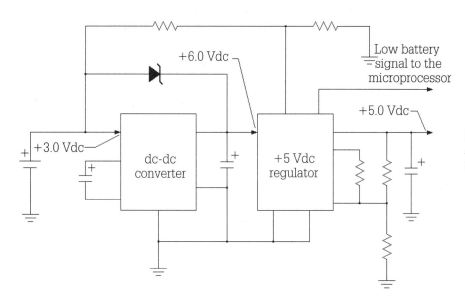

5-26
A practical dc-dc converter (troubleshooting figure).

Symptom 1: The computer is dead or acting erratically.
Both the ac power supply and the battery pack check properly. This symptom picks up where battery and linear supply troubleshooting leave off. Once you are confident that your power sources are working properly, you should suspect your dc-dc converter(s) next. For this procedure, refer to the schematic of FIG. 5-26.

Before testing each IC, remove all power from the system and use your multimeter to check the condition of zener diode ZD1. The zener helps to clamp the converter's output at a known maximum level so the regulator will not be overloaded. Replace any defective zener diode(s). When the zener diode(s) checks properly, you reapply power and test the converter IC.

Start by using your multimeter to measure dc input voltage from your battery pack. When the dc input voltage is low or absent, power from your ac power supply or battery pack might not be reaching the dc-dc converter. Inspect your PC board, connectors, and wiring very carefully for any interruptions that might cut off the input voltage. When dc input voltage is present, check the converter's output. You should measure an output of about 1 or 2 volts above the regulator's rated output. In the case of FIG. 5-26, you should expect to measure roughly 6 Vdc. If the converter's output is low or absent, replace the faulty dc-dc converter. If the converter's output is at the expected level, the regulator might be defective.

When the converter's output is normal, check the regulator's output. Should the output appear low or nonexistent, remove all power from the system and check the regulator's filter capacitor, which should be replaced if faulty. If the capacitor measures correctly, replace the defective regulator. If the regulator's output remains defective, there is probably a short circuit or severely defective IC elsewhere on the motherboard.

6 Display systems

For a small computer to be of any use, the results of its processing and computations must be made available to you at some point. Although there are numerous computer output devices, the visual display has proven to be the most versatile and effective (see FIG. 6-1). With desktop systems, the visual display is called a monitor. Unfortunately, monitors are entirely inappropriate for small computer applications because of their relatively large size, significant weight, and hideous power requirements.

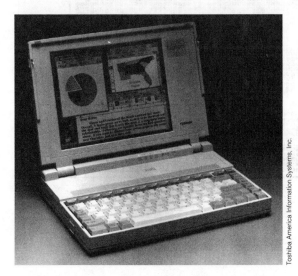

Toshiba America Information Systems, Inc.

6-1
A Toshiba T2200SX notebook computer.

Flat-panel displays offer the small size, light weight, reasonably low power consumption, and general ruggedness that are ideal for notebook, palmtop, and pen systems. Two families of flat-panel displays that have evolved for use in small computers are liquid crystal displays (LCDs) and gas plasma displays (GPDs). This chapter shows you the technology behind LCD and GPDs, and presents a series of troubleshooting procedures.

Display characteristics

Before jumping into detailed discussions of flat-panel display technologies, it is helpful for you to have a clear understanding of a display's major characteristics. This chapter also presents a set of cautions for handling displays. Even if you are already familiar with flat-panel specifications, take a moment to review their handling precautions.

Pixel organization

The images formed on a flat-panel display are not solid images. They are formed as an array of individual picture elements called *pixels* or *dots*). Pixels are arranged in a matrix of rows (top-to-bottom) and columns (left-to-right) as illustrated in FIG. 6-2. Each pixel corresponds to a location in video RAM (not the core memory, which holds programs and data). As data is written into video RAM, pixels in the array turn on and off. The on/off patterns that appear in the array form letters and graphics. You see more about video RAM and the display controller IC later in this chapter.

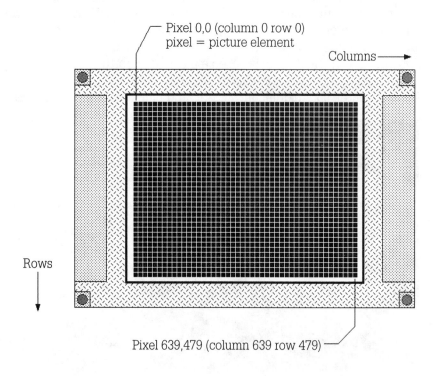

6-2
Flat-panel display organization.

Each alphanumeric character (letters, numbers, symbols, and punctuation) is formed using a unique pattern of dots. Figure 6-3 shows the character generation of a capital "A." In total, 16 pixels are activated to display an "A" in this letter style. The exact number of pixels required for a character depends on the character being displayed and the letter style being used. By combining dot patterns over a large area, intricate symbols and graphic images are presented.

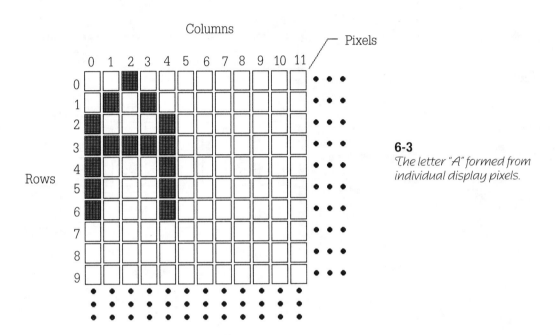

6-3
The letter "A" formed from individual display pixels.

The *resolution* of a flat-panel display is little more than the number of pixels that can be displayed. More pixels allow the display to present finer, higher-quality images. As an example, most notebook computer displays are capable of showing 307,200 dots arranged in an array of 640 columns by 480 rows, while older laptop and notebook displays are capable of only 128,000 pixels arranged as 640 columns by 200 rows (or less).

Aspect ratio is basically the "squareness" of each pixel and, indirectly, the squareness of the display. For example, a display with perfectly square pixels has an aspect ratio of 1:1. A rectangle 100 pixels wide and 100 pixels high appears as a square. However, pixel aspect ratios are not always 1:1. Normal pixels are somewhat higher than they are wide. For a display with 320×200 resolution, a pixel width of 0.34 mm and height of 0.48 mm (1:1.41) is not uncommon. Higher resolution displays use smaller

Aspect ratio

dots to fit more pixels into roughly the same viewing area. As a result, smaller pixels tend to have 1:1 aspect ratios with typical dimensions of 0.27 mm high and 0.27 mm wide. Aspect ratio might not be shown as an individual display specification. Figure 6-4 illustrates the concept of aspect ratio.

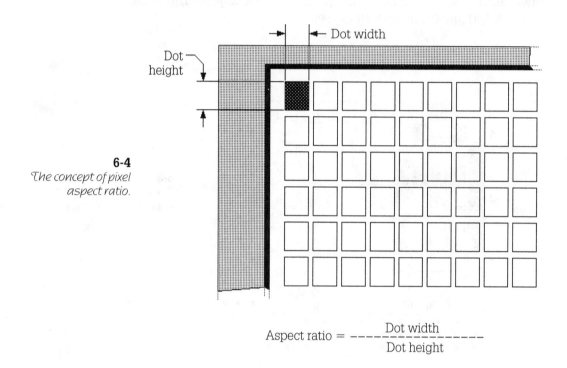

6-4
The concept of pixel aspect ratio.

$$\text{Aspect ratio} = \frac{\text{Dot width}}{\text{Dot height}}$$

Viewing angle   Every display has a particular *viewing angle*. It is the angle through which a display can be viewed clearly, as shown in FIG. 6-5. Viewing angle is rarely a concern for bright, crisp displays such as CRTs and gas plasma flat-panels. These displays generate light, so they can be from a very wide angle (usually up to 70 degrees from center). For LCDs, viewing angle is a critical specification. LCDs do not generate their own light, so the display contrast tends to degrade quickly as you leave a direct line of sight.

Position yourself or your small computer so that you look directly at the display (a perpendicular orientation). Tilt the screen up and away from you. Do you see how the contrast and brightness of the display decreases as you tilt the screen? The angle the display is at when the picture just becomes indiscernible is the negative vertical limit ($-\theta$). Return the screen to a direct line of sight, then slowly tilt the screen down toward you. Once again, you will see the display degrade. The angle the display is at when

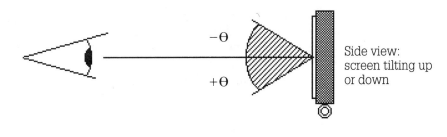

Side view:
screen tilting up
or down

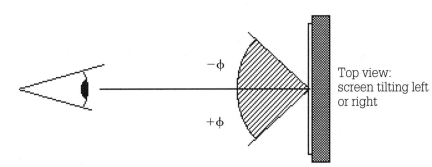

Top view:
screen tilting left
or right

the display becomes indiscernible is the positive vertical limit ($+\theta$). Ideally, both vertical limits should be the same. Return the display to a direct line of sight and repeat this test in the horizontal orientation. Swing the display left or right until the image becomes indiscernible. These are the negative and positive horizontal limits respectively, $-\phi$ and $+\phi$. Ideally, both horizontal limits should be the same. As a general rule, the larger a viewing angle is, the easier the display is to look at.

Contrast

The *contrast* of an image is loosely defined as the difference in luminous intensity between pixels that are fully on (black) and pixels that are fully off (white). The greater this difference is, the higher the contrast is, and the sharper the image appears. Many graphic, flat-panel LCDs offer contrast ranging from a low of 4 up to 9 and higher. In this book, contrast is a number without units. Since luminous intensity is strongly dependent on a display's viewing angle, a reference angle is typically added to the contrast specification.

Remember that contrast is a comparison of black and white. It is desirable (especially with monochrome displays) to simulate 16, 32, 64, or more gray levels that are somewhere between black and white. Any gray level other than black and white provides a lower contrast versus white—do not confuse gray scale levels with poor contrast.

Response time   The *response time* of a display is the time required for a display pixel to reach its on or off condition after the pixel has been addressed by the corresponding driver circuitry. Such on/off transitions do not occur instantaneously. Depending on the vintage and quality of the display, pixel response times can vary anywhere from 40 ms to 200 ms. Gas plasma and active-matrix LCDs typically offer the shortest response times, while older passive-matrix LCDs provide the slowest performance (longest response times). You see much more about the various display types and techniques a bit later in this chapter.

Handling   Next to magnetic hard drives, flat-panel displays are some of the most
precautions   sophisticated and delicate assemblies in the computer industry. While most GPDs and LCDs can easily withstand the rigors of everyday use, there are serious physical, environmental, and handling precautions that you should be aware of before attempting any repair work.

You must be extremely careful with all LCD assemblies. Liquid crystal material is sandwiched between two layers of fragile glass, which can be fractured easily by abuse or by careless handling. If a fracture should occur and liquid crystal material happens to leak out, use rubber gloves and wipe up the spill with soap and water. Immediately wash off any LCD material that comes in contact with your skin. Do not, under any circumstances, ingest or inhale LCD material. Avoid applying pressure to the surface of an LCD. You risk scratching the delicate polarizer layer covering the display's face. If the polarizer is scratched or damaged in any way, it will have to be replaced. Excessive pressure or bending forces can fracture the delicate connections within the display.

You can use very gentle pressure to clean the face of a display. Lightly wet a clean, soft, lint-free cloth with fresh isopropyl alcohol or ethyl alcohol and gently wipe away the stain(s). You might prefer to use photographic lens wipers instead of a cloth. Never use water or harsh solvents to clean a display. Water drops can accumulate as condensation, and high-humidity environments can corrode a display's electrodes. When a display assembly is removed from your system, keep the assembly in an antistatic bag at room temperature. Never store your small computer in a cold vehicle, room, or other similar environment. LCD material thickens at low temperatures (below 0°C or 32°F). Exposure to such low temperatures can cause black or white bubbles to form in the material.

Flat-panel display circuitry is very susceptible to damage from electrostatic discharge (ESD). Make certain to use all of the static electricity control techniques outlined in chapter 4. Use an antistatic wrist strap to remove any charges from your body, and use a grounded soldering iron and tools. Work on an antistatic workbench mat (if possible). Try to avoid working in cool, dry environments where static charges can easily accumulate. If you use a vacuum cleaner around your display, make sure that the vacuum is static-safe.

Liquid crystal is an unusual organic material that has been known to scientists for many years. While it is liquid in form and appearance, liquid crystal exhibits a crystalline molecular structure that resembles a solid. If you were to look at a sample of liquid crystal material under a microscope, you would see a vast array of rod-shaped molecules, as shown in FIG. 6-6. In its normal state, LC is virtually clear—light passes right through a container of liquid crystal. When liquid crystal material is assembled into a flat panel, the molecules have a tendency to twist.

Top view

Side view

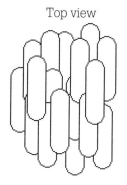
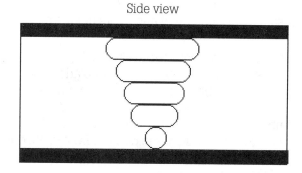

6-6
View of a liquid crystal structure.

Quite by accident, it was discovered that a voltage applied across a volume of liquid crystal forces the molecules between the electrodes to straighten. When the voltage is removed, the straightened LC molecules return to their normal twisted orientation. It would have been a simple matter to have dismissed the liquid crystal effect as little more than a scientific curiosity, but further experiments revealed an interesting phenomenon when light polarizing materials (or polarizers) are placed on both sides of the liquid crystal layer: areas of the LC material excited by an external voltage became dark and visible. When the voltage was removed, the area became clear and invisible again. A polarizer is a thin film that allows light to pass in only one orientation.

By using electrodes with different patterns, various images can be formed. The earliest developments in commercial liquid crystal displays were simply referred to as *twisted nematic* (TN) displays. A typical LCD assembly is illustrated in FIG. 6-7. Notice that an array of transparent electrodes are printed and sealed on the inside of each glass layer.

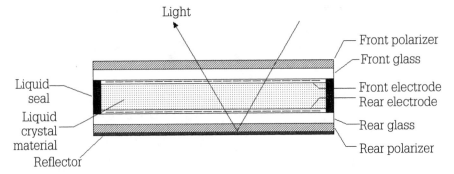

6-7
A conventional twisted nematic LCD assembly.

Light

Front polarizer
Front glass
Front electrode
Rear electrode
Rear glass
Rear polarizer

Liquid seal
Liquid crystal material
Reflector

There are four major varieties of liquid crystal assemblies that you should know about: twisted nematic (TN), super twisted nematic (STN), neutralized super twisted nematic (NTN or NSTN), and film-compensated super twisted nematic (FTN or FSTN). Each of these variations handles light somewhat differently and offers unique display characteristics.

TN LCDs   The TN display is illustrated in FIG. 6-8. Light can originate from many different sources and strike the front polarizer, but the vertically oriented polarizer allows only light waves in the vertical orientation to pass through into the LC cell. As vertically oriented light waves enter the LC assembly, its orientation twists 90 degrees, following the molecular twist in the LC material. As light leaves the LC cell, its orientation is horizontal. Since the rear polarizer is aligned horizontally, light passes through and the LCD appears transparent.

When a pixel is activated, the LC material being energized straightens its alignment, twist becomes 0 degrees, and light does not change its polarization in the LC cell. Vertically polarized light is blocked by the horizontally oriented rear polarizer, which action makes the activated pixel appear dark.

TN technology is appealing for its low cost, simple construction, and good response time, but it is limited by poor viewing angle and low contrast in high-resolution displays. Today, TN displays have been mostly replaced by any one of the three following technologies.

STN LCDs   An STN approach is shown in FIG. 6-9. Initially, the STN approach appears identical to the TN technique, but there are two major differences. First, the super twisted LC material used provides more than 200 degrees of twist instead of only 90 degrees as with the TN formulation. The rear polarizer is changed to match the twist of the LC material. For example, if

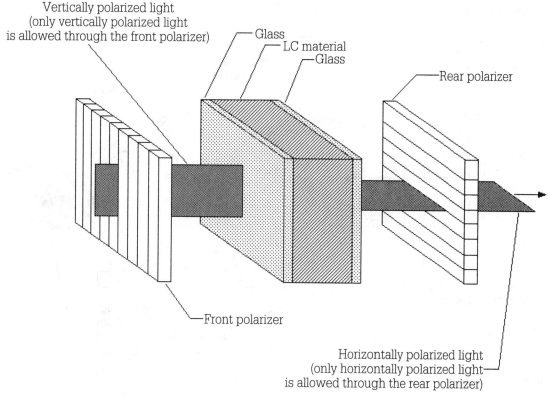

Vertically polarized light
(only vertically polarized light
is allowed through the front polarizer)

Glass
LC material
Glass

Rear polarizer

Front polarizer

Horizontally polarized light
(only horizontally polarized light
is allowed through the rear polarizer)

6-8 *Light path in a twisted nematic (TN) LCD assembly.*

the LC material has a twist of 220 degrees, the rear polarizer must be aligned to that same orientation.

In STN operation, the vertically oriented light passing through the front polarizer enters the LC cell. As light passes through the LC cell, its orientation changes following the formulation's particular twist. The twist might be as little as 200 degrees or as much as 270 degrees. Light leaving the LC cell then passes through the customized rear polarizer, making the display appear transparent. If a pixel is activated, the LC material at that point straightens completely. Light no longer twists to match the rear polarizer, so the pixel appears dark.

STN displays offer much better contrast and viewing angle than TN versions because of the additional twist. STN technology also performs very well at high resolutions (up to 1024×800 pixels). However, STN displays cost more than regular TN displays, and the response time to activate each pixel is somewhat slow.

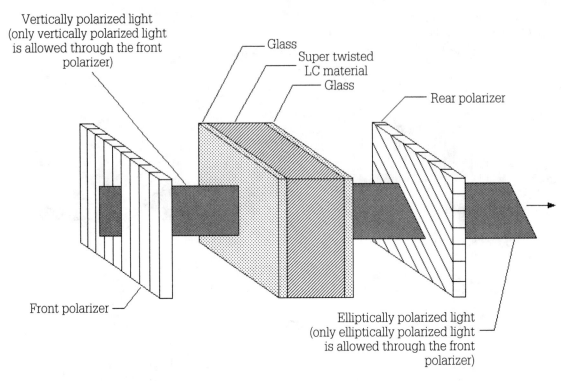

Vertically polarized light
(only vertically polarized light
is allowed through the front
polarizer)

Glass

Super twisted
LC material

Glass

Rear polarizer

Front polarizer

Elliptically polarized light
(only elliptically polarized light
is allowed through the front
polarizer)

6-9   *Light path in a super twisted nematic (STN) LCD assembly.*

NTN LCDs   The neutralized super twisted nematic (NTN or NSTN) display is shown in FIG. 6-10. Light is vertically oriented by the front polarizer before being admitted to the first LC cell. Light entering the first LC cell is twisted more than 270 degrees. A second LC cell (known as a compensator cell) adds extra twist to light polarization, resulting in a horizontally oriented light output. Light that passes through the second LC cell also passes through the rear polarizer and results in a clear (transparent) display. Keep in mind that only the first LC cell offers active pixels. The compensator cell only adds twist.

When a pixel is activated in the first LC cell, the LC molecules align so light at that point is not twisted. The untwisted light is not twisted enough by the compensator cell, so that point is blocked by the rear polarizer and appears dark. Light passing through an idle pixel is twisted, then twisted again by the compensator cell. With this additional twist, light passes through the rear polarizer and the inactivated points appear transparent.

NTN displays produce some of the finest, high-contrast, high viewing angle images available, but NTN displays are also much heavier, thicker,

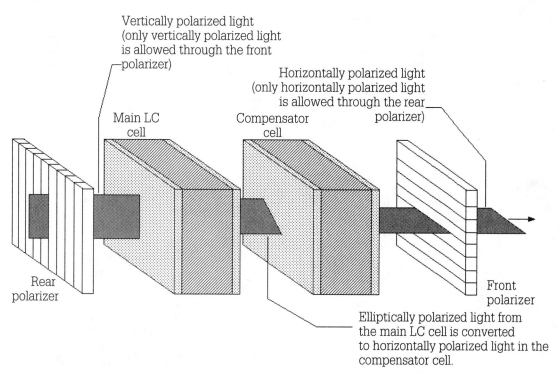

Vertically polarized light (only vertically polarized light is allowed through the front polarizer)

Horizontally polarized light (only horizontally polarized light is allowed through the rear polarizer)

Main LC cell

Compensator cell

Rear polarizer

Front polarizer

Elliptically polarized light from the main LC cell is converted to horizontally polarized light in the compensator cell.

6-10   *Light path in a neutralized super twisted nematic (NSTN or NTN) LCD assembly.*

and costlier than other displays. It is also difficult to backlight this LC cells configuration. For most small-computer applications, FTN displays are preferred over NTN models.

Figure 6-11 illustrates the basic structure of a film-compensated super twist nematic (FTN or FSTN) display. As you might see, the FTN display is very similar to the NTN display shown in FIG. 6-10. However, an FTN display uses a layer of optically compensated film instead of a second LC cell to achieve horizontal light polarization. Vertically oriented light passes through the front polarizer and is twisted more than 200 degrees by the LC cell. When the light emerges from the LC cell, it passes through a compensator film. Assuming that light is oriented properly from the LC cell, the compensator layer changes light polarization to a horizontal orientation. Light then passes through the horizontal polarizer, causing a clear (transparent) display.

When a pixel is activated, the LC material at that point straightens and light polarization does not twist. As unaltered light passes through the compensation film, it does not twist enough to pass through the rear polarizer, so the pixel appears dark.

FTN LCDs

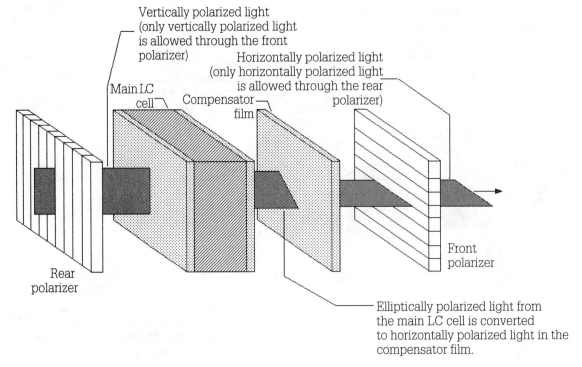

Vertically polarized light
(only vertically polarized light
is allowed through the front
polarizer)

Horizontally polarized light
(only horizontally polarized light
is allowed through the rear
polarizer)

Main LC cell

Compensator film

Rear polarizer

Front polarizer

Elliptically polarized light from
the main LC cell is converted
to horizontally polarized light in the
compensator film.

6-11 *Light path in a film-compensated super twisted nematic (FSTN or FTN) LCD.*

FTN LCDs are much lighter, thinner, and less expensive than their NTN counterparts. The FTN display does not have nearly as much optical loss as NTN versions, so FTN displays are easy to backlight. The only major disadvantage to an FTN display is that its contrast and viewing angle are slightly reduced because of the compensating film.

Viewing modes It is important to realize that light plays a critical role in the formation of liquid crystal images. The path that light takes through the LC assembly and your eye has a serious effect on the display's image quality as well as the display's utility in various environments. There are three classic viewing "modes" to understand: reflective LCD, transflective LCD, and transmissive LCD. Figure 6-12 illustrates the action of each mode.

In the *reflective* viewing mode, only available light is used to illuminate the display. A metallized reflector is mounted behind the display's rear polarizer. Light from the outside environment that penetrates the LC assembly is reflected back to your eye, resulting in a clear (transparent) image. Light that is blocked due to an activated pixel appears dark.

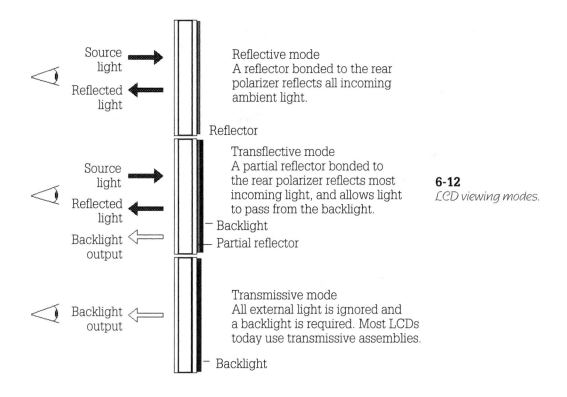

Source light →
Reflected light ◀—

Reflective mode
A reflector bonded to the rear polarizer reflects all incoming ambient light.

Reflector

Source light →
Reflected light ◀—
Backlight output ⇐

Transflective mode
A partial reflector bonded to the rear polarizer reflects most incoming light, and allows light to pass from the backlight.

— Backlight
— Partial reflector

Backlight output ⇐

Transmissive mode
All external light is ignored and a backlight is required. Most LCDs today use transmissive assemblies.

— Backlight

6-12
LCD viewing modes.

Reflective displays work best when used in an outdoor or well-lit environment. If light is blocked from the display, the image virtually disappears. However, since no backlighting is used, the display consumes very little power.

The *transflective* viewing mode uses a partial reflector behind the LC cell's rear polarizer. This partial reflector will reflect light provided by the outside environment, and pass any illumination provided from behind the assembly (the backlight). Transflective operation allows the display to be operated in direct light with the backlight turned off. The backlight can then be activated in low-light conditions.

A *transmissive* LCD uses a transparent rear polarizer with no reflector. Light entering the LCD assembly from the outside environment is not reflected back to your eye. Instead, a backlight makes the image visible. When pixels are off, backlight illumination passes directly through the display to your eye, resulting in clear (transparent) pixels. Activated pixels block the backlight and result in dark points. The backlight can be overpowered by bright light or sunlight, so the transmissive display might appear pale or washed out when used outdoors.

Backlighting *Backlighting* is the process of adding a known light source to an LCD in order to improve the display's visibility in low-light situations. There are three primary approaches to backlighting: electroluminescent (EL) panels, cold-cathode fluorescent tubes (CCFTs), and light emitting diodes (LED).

Electroluminescent (EL) panels are very thin and light-weight, and produce a very even light output across their surface area. EL panels are available in several colors, but white is preferred for notebook or pentop displays. The EL panel is usually mounted directly behind the display's rear polarizer (or transflector if used) as shown in FIG. 6-13. EL panels are reasonably rugged and reliable but require a substantial ac excitation voltage in order to operate. An ac inverter supply is used to convert low-voltage dc into a high-voltage ac level of 100 Vac or more. Chapter 5 presents some concepts and troubleshooting techniques for inverter circuits. A disadvantage to EL panels is their relatively short working life of 2000 to 3000 hours before a serious loss of backlight intensity occurs.

6-13
Construction of a typical EL (or LED) backlight assembly.

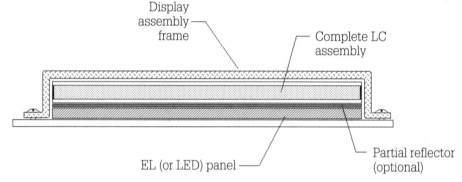

Display assembly frame

Complete LC assembly

EL (or LED) panel

Partial reflector (optional)

An array of light emitting diodes (LEDs) might be used for backlighting small displays. As with EL panels, LED arrays are thin and light-weight. They offer better brightness than most comparable EL panels, and have a working life of more than 50,000 hours. Unfortunately, LED backlight assemblies draw much more power and shed more heat than EL panels, even though the LEDs will run from +5.0 Vdc. Also, LEDs are not yet available in the white-light configurations favored for laptops and notebooks. Instead, most LED backlight panels produce a yellow-green color. As of this writing, LED backlights are primarily used in small, character-oriented displays for such devices as fax machines or photocopiers.

Cold-cathode fluorescent tubes (CCFTs) offer a very bright white light and consume reasonably little power. CCFTs also enjoy a long life of 10,000 to 15,000 hours. These characteristics make CCFTs very popular in a great many notebook and pen-computer displays. As FIG. 6-14 illustrates, there are two common methods of mounting CCFTs: edgelighting and backlighting.

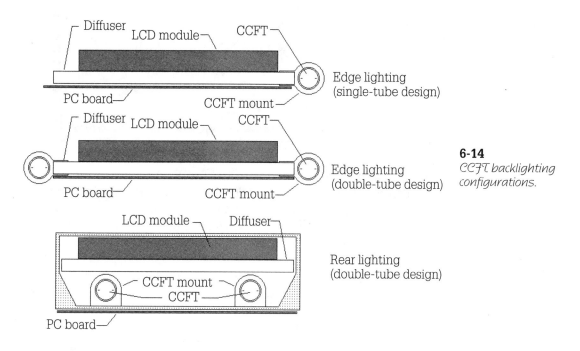

6-14
CCFT backlighting configurations.

Edgelighting is favored in thin or low-profile displays. A layer of translucent material referred to as the *diffuser* distributes the lamp's light evenly behind the LC cell. To create an even brighter display, a second CCFT is added to the opposite edge of the diffuser. If a smaller, thicker display assembly is preferred, one or two CCFTs may be mounted in a cavity directly behind the LC cell. A diffuser is still used to spread light evenly behind the LC cell. CCFTs need a high-voltage ac source in order to operate, so an inverter supply can be used to provide the 270 to 360 Vac that most CCFTs need. Inverter supplies are covered in chapter 5.

So far, this chapter has given you much of the background information and technology associated with monochrome (black & white) LCDs (FIG. 6-15). Now that you understand what liquid crystal displays are and how they are constructed, you must understand how each pixel in a display is controlled (or addressed). There are two methods of addressing LCDs: passive addressing and active addressing. You will probably encounter both types of addressing at one time or another.

Passive & active matrix operation

6-15
*A Seiko Instruments
low-power monochrome
LCD module.*

A *passive matrix* LCD is illustrated in FIG. 6-16. Each layer of glass in an LC cell contains transparent electrodes deposited on the inside of the glass sheet. The upper (or front) glass contains column electrodes, and the lower (or rear) glass contains the row electrodes. The two sheets of glass are fitted together, forming a matrix. Every point where a row electrode and a column electrode intersects is a potential pixel. To light a pixel, the appropriate row and column electrodes must be energized. Wherever an energized row and column intersect, a visible pixel appears.

6-16
*Structure and operation of
a passive-matrix LCD.*

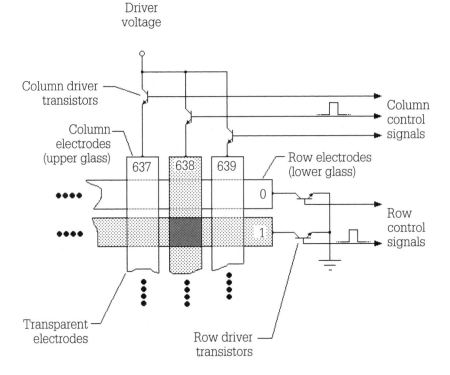

In order to excite a pixel, a voltage is applied across the LC material. For the example of FIG. 6-16, if a voltage is applied to column 638 and row 1 is connected to ground, pixel (638,1) appears.

A small transistor is used to switch power to each electrode. These driver transistors are operated by digital control signals generated in a matrix control IC that is usually located on the LCD panel. When a row electrode is selected, multiple column electrodes can be addressed along that row. In this way, a complete display can be developed a row at a time instead of a pixel at a time. The passive matrix display is updated constantly by scanning rows in sequence and activating each column necessary to display all of the pixels in the selected row. Most displays can update row data about 30 times per second.

While passive matrix displays are simple and straightforward to design and build, the inherent need to scan the display slows down its operation. It is difficult to display computer animation or fast graphics on many passive monochrome displays. Even a mouse cursor might disappear while moving around a passive matrix LCD.

To overcome the limitations of passive LCDs, the *active matrix* display was developed. As shown in FIG. 6-17, each pixel is handled directly by a dedicated electrode instead of common row and column electrodes.

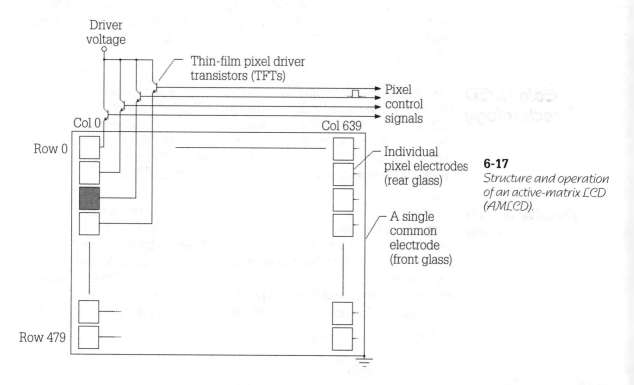

6-17
Structure and operation of an active-matrix LCD (AMLCD).

Individual electrodes are driven by their own transistors, so there is one transistor driver for every pixel in a monochrome display. Driver transistors are deposited onto the rear glass substrate in much the same way that integrated circuits are fabricated. For a display with 640×480 resolution, 307,200 thin film transistors (TFTs) are fabricated onto the rear glass. A single, huge, common electrode is deposited on the front glass. To excite the desired pixel, it is only necessary to activate the corresponding driver transistor. The ICs that manage operation of the driver transistor array are generally included in the display panel.

When a driver transistor is fired, a positive potential is applied to the corresponding electrode. This potential establishes an electric field between the electrode and the common electrode on the front panel. Referring to FIG. 6-17, the pixel in row 3 and column 0 is activated simply by applying a control signal to its driver transistor. Since each pixel in an active matrix LCD can be addressed individually, there is no need to constantly update the display, as is needed with passive displays.

Active matrix addressing is much faster than passive matrix addressing. As a result, active matrix displays offer impressive response time with extremely good contrast. Unfortunately, active matrix LCDs are also some of the most expensive parts of your small computer. As of this writing, active matrix displays suffer from poor manufacturing yields—many of the display panels manufactured do not work at the factory. Such low yields tend to keep active matrix display prices high. Once manufacturers work out their manufacturing limitations, you will see a significant price drop.

Color LCD technology

The desire for high-quality flat-panel color displays continues to be somewhat of a quest for display designers. While two very effective color LCD techniques are well-established, both types of color displays offer their own particular drawbacks. Passive matrix FSTN and active matrix TFT color displays are the two dominant color LCD technologies currently available. This section describes these color technologies.

Passive matrix color

Passive matrix color LCD technology is based on the operation of film-compensated super twisted nematic (FSTN or FTN) LCDs, presented earlier in this chapter. The most striking difference between color and monochrome LCDs is that the color LCD uses three times as many electrodes as the monochrome display. This is necessary because three colors (red, green, and blue) are needed to form the color of each "dot" that you see. As shown in FIG. 6-18, each colored dot is made up of three tiny pixels.

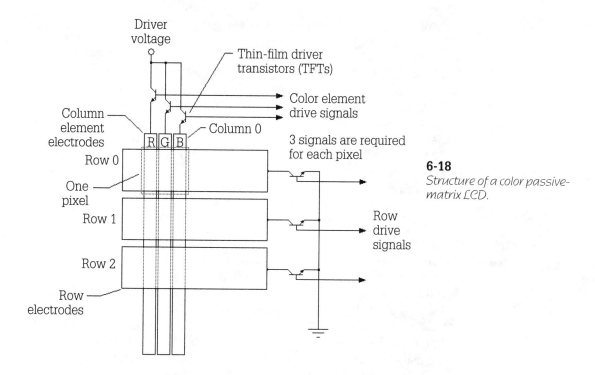

Driver voltage

Thin-film driver transistors (TFTs)

Color element drive signals

Column element electrodes

Column 0

R G B

3 signals are required for each pixel

Row 0

One pixel

Row 1

Row drive signals

Row 2

Row electrodes

6-18
Structure of a color passive-matrix LCD.

Pixels do not actually generate the colors that you see. Rather, it is the white light passing through each pixel that is filtered to form the intended color. The front glass is coated with color filter material in front of each red, green, and blue pixel. For example, if the dot at row 0 column 0 is supposed to be red, the green and blue pixels turn on at that point to block white light through all but the "red" filter. White light travels through the red filter on the front glass, where it emerges as red. When the red, green, and blue pixels are all on, all light is blocked and the dot appears black. If all three pixels of a dot are off, all light passes through and the dot appears white. By controlling the three pixel elements at each dot, up to eight colors can be produced (including black and white). Intermediate color shades are produced using color hatching schemes between adjacent dots.

The red, green, and blue (RGB) column electrodes for each pixel are deposited onto the front glass, while a single row electrode for each dot is fabricated onto the rear glass. As you might imagine, tripling the number of column electrodes complicates the manufacture of passive color displays. Not only is electrode deposition more difficult because electrodes are closer together, but three times the number of column driver transistors and IC driver signals are needed. Like monochrome LCDs, the color display is updated by scanning each row sequentially and manipulating the RGB elements for each column. Typical color LCD data can be updated 30 times per second.

FSTN color displays suffer from many of the same disadvantages as monochrome passive matrix displays. First, response time is slow (about 250 ms). This means that no matter how fast data is delivered to the display, the image changes only change four times per second. Such slow update times make passive displays poor choices for fast graphic operations or animation. Their contrast ratio is a poor 7:1 that generally results in washed out or hazy displays. Viewing angles for color passive matrix LCDs are also poor at around 45 degrees. Your clearest view of the display comes when you look straight at it.

Active matrix color

Active matrix color LCD technology takes the contents of monochrome active panels one step further by using three electrodes for every dot. Each electrode is completely independent, and is driven by its own TFT. The three elements provide the red, green, and blue light sources for each dot that you see. Figure 6-19 illustrates the structure of a TFT active matrix color LCD. Every electrode driver transistor and all interconnecting wiring is fabricated onto the rear glass plate. With three transistors per dot, a 640-column by 480-row color display requires 640×480×3, or 921,600 individual transistors. Essentially, the rear plate of a TFT color

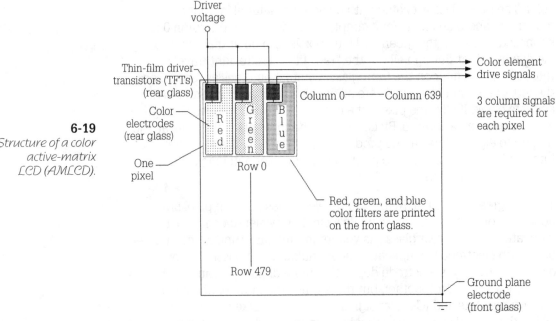

6-19
Structure of a color active-matrix LCD (AMLCD).

display is one large 25.4 cm (10") diagonal integrated circuit. The front glass plate is fabricated with a single, large common electrode that every screen element references to.

As with passive matrix displays, the LC material used in active matrix displays do not actually generate color. The individual elements simply turn white light on or off. White light that is permitted through an element is filtered by colored material applied to corresponding locations on the front glass. When the red, green, and blue elements are all off, white light shines through the three elements and the dot appears white. If the red, green, and blue elements are all on, all light is blocked, and the dot appears black. The ability to closely control contrast in individual dots allows active matrix color LCDs to produce 512 individual colors, with 256 colors being standard.

Active matrix color displays do away with many of the limitations of passive matrix displays. Response time is very fast, on the order of 30 ms or better. Such fast response times allow the screen image to change more than 30 times per second, providing excellent performance for graphics or animation applications. The control afforded by active matrix screens provides a brilliant contrast ratio of 60:1 with a comfortable viewing angle of approximately 80 degrees. Color active matrix displays will most likely reflect the state-of-the-art in small computer technology for quite some time.

Gas plasma (or simply, plasma) displays use points of ionized gas to form images. Although plasma displays are a somewhat older display technology, you will still find many larger notebook computers offering them. Plasma displays offer some advantages over LCDs. First, plasma displays operate in a fully transmissive viewing mode. Since ionized gas actually generates light, no backlighting is needed, and the display is easily visible in bright light or direct sunlight. Contrast is very good (usually a minimum of 50:1), and the viewing angle is at least 120 degrees. However, plasma displays are not without their disadvantages. Since only one gas is used, the display has only one color. While several gray-scale schemes do exist, plasma displays are limited to monochrome operation. Power supply requirements are also much more involved for plasma displays. Two high-voltage dc supplies (80 to 100 Vdc and 130 to 150 Vdc) are needed to drive the display. This part of the chapter introduces operating principles of gas plasma displays (GPDs).

Plasma display technology

Construction & operation

The typical construction of a gas plasma display is shown in FIG. 6-20. Column electrodes are etched onto the front glass layer and coated with a dielectric material and a layer of magnesium oxide (MgO). Magnesium oxide prolongs display life by preventing ion shock damage to the electrodes during gas discharge. Anode row electrodes are fabricated onto the rear glass in a similar manner. The two glass assemblies are sealed together and separated by small spacers placed at regular intervals between the layers. The discharge gap formed between the two glass layers is filled with the primary discharge gas, usually neon with a small amount of xenon. Neon produces the characteristic orange-red color that GPDs are noted for. Xenon stabilizes the neon's discharge characteristics and improves the display's light emissions.

6-20
Cross-section of a conventional neon gas plasma display (GPD) assembly.

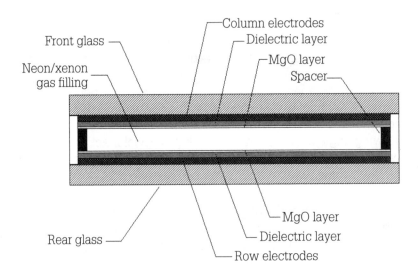

Front glass —
Neon/xenon gas filling —
Column electrodes
Dielectric layer
MgO layer
Spacer —
MgO layer
Dielectric layer
Rear glass —
Row electrodes

The structure of a passive matrix GPD is illustrated in FIG. 6-21. With passive matrix designs, each row electrode is scanned in sequence. When a row is made active, each column where a pixel must be written is fired with a writing voltage (Vw, typically 130 to 140 Vdc). Writing-voltage levels will ionize the gas at desired points. Points that are already lit need only be refreshed with a sustain voltage (Vs, usually 80 to 100 Vdc). Sustain voltage maintains the gas ionization level at a reasonable brightness level. Dots that must be extinguished are left unpowered. An absence of sustaining voltage stops the ionization of gas at that point.

Troubleshooting flat-panel displays

Up to now, you have learned about the LCD and plasma display panels. Each display type requires a substantial amount of circuitry to perform properly in a computer system. This part of the chapter shows you the ICs

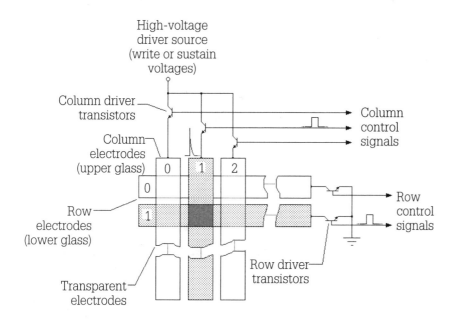

High-voltage
driver source
(write or sustain
voltages)

Column driver
transistors

Column
electrodes
(upper glass)

Row
electrodes
(lower glass)

Transparent
electrodes

Column
control
signals

Row
control
signals

Row driver
transistors

6-21
Structure and operation of a passive-matrix gas plasma display (GPD).

and circuitry that interface a flat-panel display to the computer. Once you understand how flat-panel displays are driven, you will be ready to start troubleshooting.

There are seven major parts of an LCD system, shown in FIG. 6-22: a CPU, a system controller (if used), some video RAM, a backlight voltage source, a highly integrated display controller IC, a contrast control, and the display assembly. If the system is a gas plasma display, the contrast control is replaced with a brightness control, and a single ac backlight voltage is replaced with two, high-voltage dc sources.

The CPU is responsible for executing the instructions contained in BIOS or core memory (RAM). As the CPU executes its program(s), it directs the operations of a system controller IC, which is a sophisticated ASIC used to handle the majority of small computer's overhead operations. While it is not mandatory that a computer utilize a system controller, a single controller IC can effectively replace dozens of discrete logic ICs.

The display controller IC is addressed by the system controller over the common system address bus. Once the display controller is addressed, the system controller writes display information and commands over a secondary (or peripheral) data bus. A clock and miscellaneous control signals manage the flow of data into the display controller. Display data is interpreted and stored in video RAM (VRAM). Each pixel in the display can be traced back to a specific address in VRAM. As new data is written

A display system

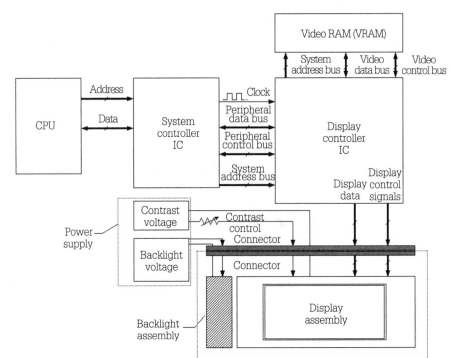

6-22
Block diagram of a typical display system.

to the display controller, VRAM addresses are updated to reflect any new information. During an update, the display controller reads the contents of VRAM and sends the data to the flat-panel display.

There are two other signals required by an LCD assembly, those being contrast voltage and backlight input voltage. If the display is gas plasma, it requires a brightness control voltage, a high-voltage dc write voltage (Vw), and a high-voltage dc sustain voltage (Vs).

A complete flat-panel display assembly is shown in FIG. 6-23. The plastic outer housings (marked K1 and K22) form the cosmetic shell of the display panel. An LC cell with its driver ICs and transistors (E6) is mounted to the front housing. A number of insulators might be added to protect the LC cell from accidental short circuits. Note that the front polarizer layer is built into the LC cell. A rear polarizer (K15) is placed directly behind the LC cell, followed by the translucent backlight diffuser panel (K16). The backlight mechanism is a long, thin CCFT (K13) located along the bottom of the diffuser. Several spacers/brackets are used to secure the diffuser panel and tie the entire assembly together. Finally, a rear housing is snapped into place to cover the display. A cable (K19) connects the display assembly to the motherboard.

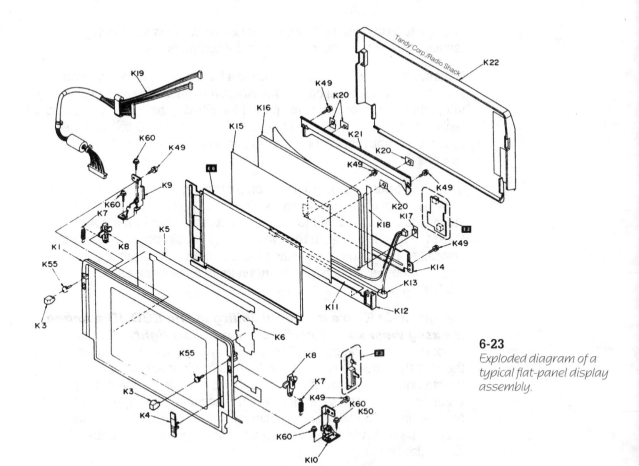

6-23
Exploded diagram of a typical flat-panel display assembly.

Now let's look at some symptoms. Refer to FIGS. 6-22 and 6-23 for the following procedures.

Symptom 1: One or more pixels is defective. The defective pixel might be black (opaque), white (clear), or fixed at some color.

Before beginning any repair procedure, turn off your computer and turn it on again. A cold start ensures that your pixels are not being locked up due to any possible software glitch. If the questionable pixels disappear, there might be a bug in your application software, not in your hardware.

This is a symptom that commonly occurs with active matrix display panels. Since each screen dot is driven by either one or three individual driver transistors, the loss of one or more drivers will ruin a pixel. For monochrome displays, the single driver transistor might be open (pixel will not turn on) or shorted (pixel will not turn off). For color displays, damage to a driver transistor might cause a certain color to appear and remain fixed on the screen as long as the computer is on.

Unfortunately, there is no way to repair a failed screen driver transistor. Active matrix flat-panel circuitry is fabricated much the same way as any integrated circuit, so when any part of the IC fails, the entire IC must be replaced. Your best course is to replace the suspect LCD cell. In some systems, it might simply be easier to just replace the entire flat-panel assembly.

If a new flat-panel display fails to correct the trouble, replace the VRAM IC(s). One or more address locations might be defective, resulting in faulty video data being provided to the display. It is unusual for a problem in VRAM to manifest itself in this way, but you should be prepared for this possibility. If you do not have the proper tools or inclination to perform surface-mount soldering, you might prefer to replace the entire motherboard.

Symptom 2: There is poor visibility in the LCD. The image is easily washed out in direct or ambient light.   The vast majority of small computer LCDs operate in the transmissive mode, where the light that you see is generated from a backlight system. As a result, the strength and quality of the backlight directly effects the display's visibility. If the computer is older and has accumulated a great deal of running time, the EL backlight panel or CCFT(s) might be worn out or failing. The high-voltage power supply that is operating the backlight might also be faulty.

Check your LCD's contrast control. Contrast adjusts the amount of driver voltage that is used to straighten the LCD material. Less driver voltage straightens the liquid crystal less, resulting in lower contrast. If contrast is already high or maximum, disassemble the display to expose your contrast adjustment. Measure contrast voltage across the adjustment. Your multimeter should read the entire contrast display voltage. If contrast voltage is low or absent, troubleshoot your dc-dc converters as described in chapter 5. Measure contrast voltage from the center (adjustable) leg of the control with respect to ground and vary the adjustment. If voltage is zero or remains fixed while the adjustment is varied, replace the defective contrast control.

Disassemble your small computer to expose the backlight unit (either an EL panel or a CCFT assembly) as well as the inverter power supply. Gently brush away any dust or debris that might have accumulated on the EL panel, CCFT(s), or diffuser. If the light source has been badly fouled by dust, retry the system with the cleaned light source. Use your multimeter to measure the ac output voltage from your inverter power supply. A working inverter should output 150 to 200 Vac for an EL panel, or 250 to 350 Vac for CCFTs. If your inverter output is low or nonexistent, troubleshoot your faulty inverter supply with the procedures in chapter 5. If the inverter's output voltage appears normal, replace the defective backlight mechanism.

Symptom 3: There is poor visibility in the gas plasma display. The image is not bright. Gas plasma displays generate their own light as a natural by-product of ionized gas. The brightness shown by the display is heavily dependent on the voltage levels used to ionize (write) and light (sustain) the gas. By adjusting the sustain voltage level, the display's brightness should vary. Check the plasma display's brightness control. If brightness is already set high or at maximum, disassemble the display to expose the brightness adjustment. Use your multimeter to measure the brightness control voltage across the adjustment. If the brightness control voltage is low or absent, check the plasma write and sustain power supplies. Measure the brightness control voltage at the center of the adjustment versus ground and vary the adjustment. If voltage is zero or remains fixed while the adjustment is being varied, replace the faulty brightness control.

Measure your plasma drive voltages. You should measure the sustain voltage (Vs) and the write voltage (Vw). Sustain voltage should measure 80 to 100 Vdc, and write voltage should measure between 130 and 150 Vdc. Some plasma displays use ac drive voltages, so consult your owners manual or service manual for the particular display specifications. If you are unable to correct a low supply voltage with the output adjustments on the supply, or if the supply outputs measure very low, repair or replace your plasma power supply.

Symptom 4: The display is completely dark. There is no apparent display activity. This symptom assumes that your computer has plenty of power and attempts to boot up with all normal disk activity, but the display does not come on. If there are no active LEDs to indicate power or disk activity, there might be a more serious problem with your system. Refer to chapter 5 for power system troubleshooting.

Begin by removing all power from your system. Remove the outer housings of the computer and inspect all connectors and wiring between the motherboard and the display. Tighten any loose connectors and reattach any loose or broken wiring. Defective connections can easily disable your display.

Reapply power to your small computer and check the display voltage(s) powering your display system. Typical LCDs use +5 Vdc (or +3.0 or +3.3 Vdc for low-voltage systems), and +12 Vdc. Plasma displays use high dc voltages, around 80 to 100 Vdc and 130 to 150 Vdc. If your display is not receiving the appropriate voltages, check your power supply and/or dc-dc converter(s). Replace any defective power components.

When your display is connected securely and is receiving the appropriate voltage levels, you should suspect a fault in the display controller IC, or somewhere within the display assembly itself. Use your logic probe to check the data lines and control signals from the display controller to the display assembly. If you have service charts available for the controller, you should have no difficulty locating the appropriate signals. Expect to see high-frequency pulse signals on each of the data and control lines, since the display must be updated continuously. If you see one or more data lines frozen in a logic 1 or logic 0 state, it might indicate a defective display controller. A faulty logic state on any of the display controller's outputs also suggests a faulty display controller IC. In either case, the controller should be replaced. If you do not have the tools or inclination to perform surface-mount soldering, you should probably replace the entire motherboard.

If you find the signals from the display controller to be intact, the circuitry within the display assembly itself is probably faulty. Your best course would be to replace the entire display assembly.

Symptom 5: The display appears erratic. It displays disassociated characters and garbage.   This is another symptom that assumes your small computer has plenty of power and attempts to boot up with normal disk activity. Your display is simply acting erratically. If no power indicators or disk activity LEDs are lit, there might be a much more serious problem in your system. Refer to chapter 5 for power supply troubleshooting. Remove all power from your system and remove the outer housings to expose the motherboard and display assembly. Inspect all cables and connectors between the motherboard and display assembly. Tighten any loose connectors and secure any loose or broken wiring. Defective connectors or wiring can easily interfere with normal display operation. You might also wish to check the voltage levels powering your display.

When all connections are intact, you should suspect a fault in the display controller or VRAM. Unfortunately, the great volume of data flowing from the system controller to the display controller, from VRAM to the display controller, and from the display controller to the display makes a comprehensive test virtually impossible without sophisticated test equipment. On a symptomatic basis, you should replace the display controller since it is at the crux of the display system. If a new display controller IC does not correct the problem, try replacing the VRAM IC(s). Defective memory can cause erratic display performance. If you are unable to perform surface-mount soldering, replace the motherboard. A motherboard change will change both the display controller and VRAM. If all else fails, try replacing the display assembly itself.

7 *Hard, floppy, & card drives*

Mass-storage devices are a vital part of every small-computer system (see FIG. 7-1). With mass-storage devices, you can maintain a huge library of application programs and data files in your computer. You can also transfer programs and data from your small computer to other systems as needed. Floppy disk drives, hard disk drives, and memory cards are the three types of mass-storage systems in widespread use today. In fact, most small computers utilize a hard drive along with a floppy drive or a memory card. This chapter explains the technology behind each type of drive and presents a series of troubleshooting procedures.

7-1
A Tandy 3800HD notebook computer.

Tandy Corp./Radio Shack

Floppy drives (floppies) are perhaps the most reliable form of mass-storage ever developed for computers. Although floppies are relatively large mechanical devices, they offer the convenience of a removable storage media—the floppy disk (diskette). Programs or data can be recorded onto a diskette and transferred to the floppy drive of another computer. Floppy drive systems have evolved through a number of sizes and recording densities, but this book focuses on 8.89 cm (3.5"), high-density (1.4Mb) drives.

An 8.89 cm (3.5") floppy drive is shown in FIG. 7-2. As you might see, the drive is not terribly complex. Most of the drive is filled by a mechanical chassis, along with simple linkages and coverings. There are two motors: a head motor and a spindle motor. The head motor is a stepping motor used to position the drive's read/write heads. A spindle motor is a synchronized dc motor that spins the diskette at a fixed rate of 300 or 360 rpm. The diskette spins only during access (reading or writing operations). The heart of a floppy drive is a set of precision magnetic

Drive construction

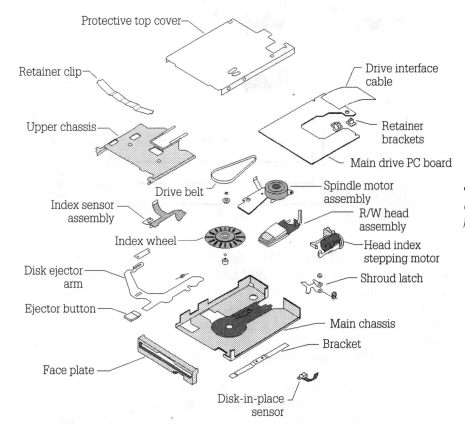

7-2
Exploded diagram of a 3.5" floppy drive.

read/write (R/W) heads. A diskette is inserted between the heads, which are moved radially (along the diskette's radius) by the head motor.

The Main Drive PC Board handles all of the drive's physical operations and interprets inputs from the drive's various sensors. Figure 7-3 is a block diagram for floppy drive control circuitry. Signals to and from the motherboard take place over a single, 34-pin ribbon cable. Remember that special drive systems might use unusual cable assemblies, but the 34-pin configuration is considered IBM PC/AT-compatible. A separate four-conductor cable supplies power to the drive.

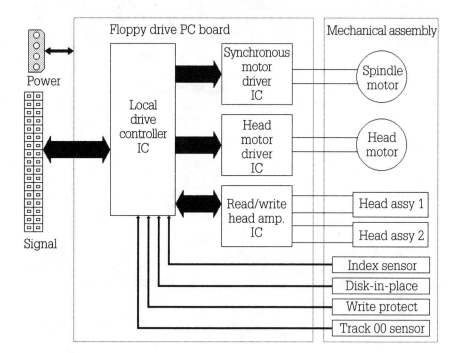

7-3
Block diagram of floppy drive control circuitry.

There are three mechanisms that a floppy drive controls: the R/W heads, a stepping motor, and a disk spindle motor. The floppy drive directs each of these mechanisms with a main disk controller IC, which not only handles communications with the motherboard, but also communicates with the drive's sensors. Many floppy drives use one IC for each mechanism, but newer drives use highly integrated devices that combine several (or all) functions into a single IC.

Typical floppy drives incorporate four sensors: an index sensor, a disk-in-place sensor, a write protect sensor, and a track 00 sensor. An *index sensor* is basically an optoisolator that monitors the diskette's rotation rate when it is spinning. A small, notched index wheel spins with the diskette and causes a known pulse signal to appear at the controller IC. If this pulse rate is too fast or too slow, the controller adjusts the spindle motor's speed to maintain rotation at 300 or 360 rpm. The *disk-in-place sensor* is little more than a switch that closes when a diskette is inserted. The drive will not operate without a diskette. A *write protect sensor* is either a switch or optoisolator. When the write-protect notch on a 8.89 cm (3.5") diskette is uncovered, the drive inhibits all write operations—the diskette can only be read. The *track 00 sensor* is an optoisolator that generates a signal whenever the R/W heads are in the track 00 position. This allows the head motor to initialize to a known location whenever needed before seeking the desired track for reading or writing.

The drive mechanism is not capable of holding data. It is the recording media inside the drive assembly that holds the information. The floppy drive is merely a tool for accessing the media. In this case, the *media* is a small disk of plastic (usually mylar) coated on both sides with a thin layer of magnetic oxide. The coated disk is mounted in a hard plastic jacket that protects the disk (see FIG. 7-4). A metal shroud shields the media when diskette is not in the floppy drive. When the diskette is inserted in a floppy drive, a mechanical linkage slides the shroud aside to allow the

Magnetic diskettes

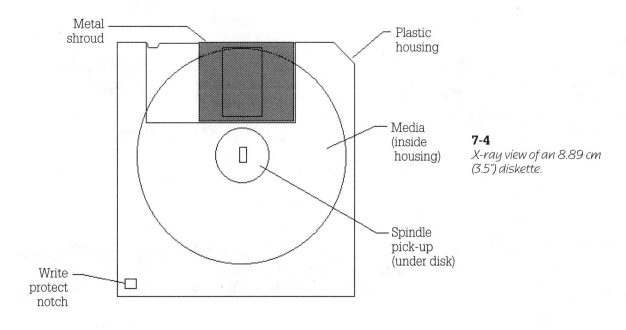

7-4
X-ray view of an 8.89 cm (3.5") diskette.

R/W heads access to the disk. The magnetic disk is rotated using the metal spindle pick-up in the diskette's center.

Magnetic recording principles

A floppy disk is a circular piece of mylar, only a few thousandths of an inch thick, coated on both sides with a thin layer of permeable material—often some kind of high-quality magnetic oxide. These layers of magnetic oxide hold the information. You might know that a magnet has two poles (north and south). The fascinating aspect of a permeable material is that every molecule acts as an independent magnet. When an external magnetic field crosses the oxide, the area subjected to the field takes on a definite north/south orientation, which depends on the magnetic field's orientation. It is very important that you understand this concept because it is basic to floppy and hard drive operation.

For floppy disks, an external magnetic field is generated in the R/W head, as shown in FIG. 7-5. A head is little more than a coil of fine wire wrapped around a soft iron core material. When the head is energized by current from an R/W head driver IC, a path of magnetic flux is established in the head. The direction of the flux depends on the coil's polarity. If the current direction is reversed, the flux orientation is reversed.

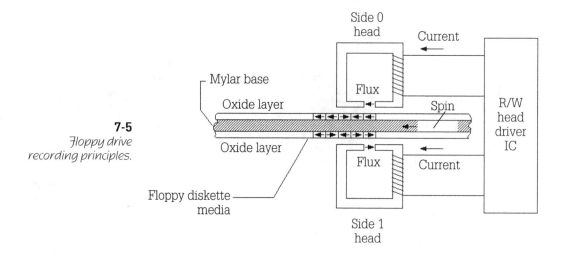

7-5
Floppy drive recording principles.

As magnetic flux is generated in the head, the tightly focused field aligns particles in the disk's oxide at that point. Binary 1s and 0s are defined by the flux patterns laid down on the media. In practice, both R/W heads are actually in contact with the oxide layers. The drive signal duration is extremely small—so small that each magnetized point on a disk is microscopic. Once an R/W head orients the diskette's particles, the disk "remembers" that information.

To read a floppy disk, the heads pass over the diskette while it spins. Magnetic fields stored on the disk move past the heads and induce a current in each head winding. The direction of induced current depends on the orientation of each flux element. Induced current is proportional to the flux density (how closely each bit is placed) and the velocity of the media as it passes the heads. In other words, the signal strength depends on the rate of change of flux with respect to time.

You will encounter two major recording techniques used with floppy drives: frequency modulation (FM) and modified frequency modulation (MFM). Both of these techniques define how data is encoded and synchronized on the diskette. FM and MFM encoding are beyond the scope of this book, but keep in mind that MFM encoding approach is used with all 8.89 cm (3.5") floppy disks.

Data organization

Of course, you cannot place data just anywhere on a diskette. Information must be organized into known, standard locations, which allows a diskette recorded on one computer to be read by another computer, even if their floppy drives are made by different manufacturers.

Data is recorded in *sectors*, each of which holds up to 512 bytes and is the smallest division of recording area on a floppy disk. A *track* is composed of multiple sectors arranged in concentric circles around the disk. For the 8.89 cm (3.5") high-density floppy disk shown in FIG. 7-6, there are 80 tracks on each side of the diskette, for a total of 160 tracks. Each track has 18 sectors. The entire diskette then contains 18×160, or 2880 sectors. At 512 bytes per sector, a 3.5" high-density diskette should hold 2880×512, or 1,474,560 bytes. The computer inserts "housekeeping" information, which acts rather like labels and notes on a file folder, into each sector and track. The computer can then quickly and efficiently locate and keep track of the files for which it is looking. The disk also holds the file allocation table (FAT), which is the disk's table of contents. The specifications for the major drive types are compared in TABLE 7-1. Although 5.25" floppy drives are not incorporated into small computers, they are often available as peripheral devices.

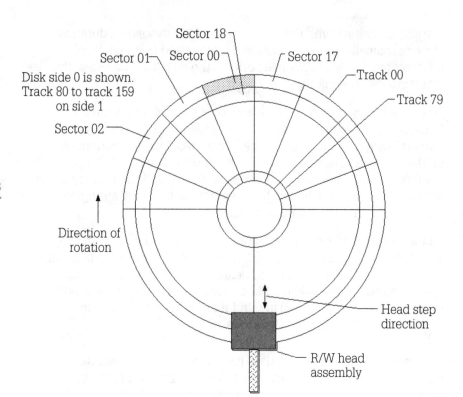

Sector 18

Sector 01   Sector 00   Sector 17

Disk side 0 is shown.
Track 80 to track 159
on side 1   Track 00

                                            Track 79

Sector 02

7-6
*Data organization on a 3.5"
high-density floppy disk.*

Direction of
rotation

                                            Head step
                                            direction

                                            R/W head
                                            assembly

Table 7-1
Comparison of floppy drive specifications.

Parameter	3.5" drives		5.25" drives	
	HD	DD	HD	DD
Drive spindle speed (rpm)	300	300	360	300
Megabytes/drive	1.4	.720	1.2	.360
Encoding format	MFM	MFM	MFM/FM	MFM/FM
Tracks/inch (tpi)	135	135	96	96
Bits/inch (bpi)	17,434	8717	9870	5922
Tracks/side	80	80	80	40
Sectors/tracks	18	9	15	9
Bytes/sector	512	512	512	512
Data transfer rate (Kbits/sec)	500	500	500 (MFM) 250 (FM)	250 (MFM) 125(FM)

Newest<————————————————>Oldest

It takes much more than just a floppy drive assembly to make mass-storage possible. The transfer of information into or out of a floppy drive is an intricate and involved process requiring the interaction of a CPU (and system controller) as well as core memory. Overall operation of the drive is handled by a sophisticated floppy drive controller IC, which is typically located on the motherboard, external to the drive assembly. A complete floppy disk system is illustrated in FIG. 7-7.

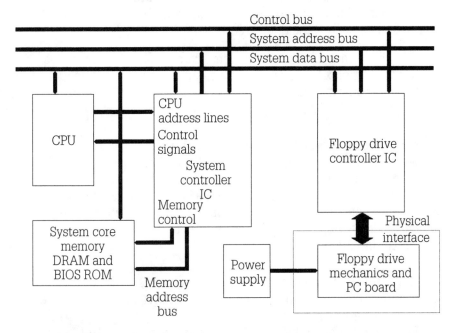

As with most computers, the CPU is the key component of the entire system; however, the CPU does not interact directly with the floppy drive. Instead, the CPU directs the system controller to begin the appropriate data transfer into or out of the floppy drive. Any instructions or routines needed to operate the floppy drive are taken by the CPU from the BIOS ROM in core memory. The system controller, in turn, addresses the floppy disk controller, which performs all of the data preparation and interpretation for the floppy drive.

Data being loaded into a floppy drive is taken one byte at a time from core memory (RAM) by the floppy disk controller, translated into serial form, and sent one bit at a time over the drive's physical interface. Other control signals are sent simultaneously along the interface to handle the drive's motors, sensors, etc. After TTL data bits arrive at the floppy drive, they are converted into driver signals that are written to the disk as points of magnetic flux.

When data is read from a floppy drive, the process is reversed. The CPU orders the system controller to load a program or data file. The system controller instructs the floppy disk controller to initiate drive activity and seek the desired track and sector containing the necessary record. Once the beginning location is found, the disk's R/W head produces signals based on the disk's flux variations. Circuitry on the floppy drive PC board converts these current signals into 1s and 0s. Data is sent in serial form across the physical interface to the floppy disk controller, which converts data into parallel form and extracts the data from the housekeeping information and sends the data to core memory.

Actually, the formal process of signalling, data transfer, and control is much more complex than just described, but at least you get an idea of the many important points involved. These concepts of floppy drive system operation will be invaluable to you during troubleshooting.

The physical interface   The connections between the floppy disk controller IC on the motherboard and the floppy drive assembly is referred to as the *physical interface*. This interface is a standard set of connections used by most floppy drives and controller ICs. By using a standard interface, any floppy drive will operate properly in any computer using the standard interface. Standards allow floppy drives and controllers to be designed and built by many manufacturers.

For floppy drives, the physical interface is composed of two cables— power and signal. Both cable pinouts are shown in FIG. 7-8. The power connector is a 4-pin, mate-n-lock connector. A floppy drive requires +5.0 Vdc for logic (+3.3 or +3.0 Vdc for low-voltage systems) and +12 Vdc for the motors. The return (ground) for each supply is also provided at the connector. The signal connector is typically a 34-pin, insulation displacement connector (IDC) cable. Notice that the odd-numbered pins are ground lines, while even-numbered pins carry the signals. Such a cable arrangement helps to reduce interference between interface signals.

The physical interface handles TTL-level input and output signals. There are up to four drive-selection inputs ($\overline{\text{DRIVE SELECT}}$ 0 to $\overline{\text{DRIVE SELECT}}$ 3) that determine which drive in the system is active. For a small computer, only one select line is needed, so any other drive select lines may simply be ignored. A $\overline{\text{MOTOR ON}}$ input instructs the floppy drive to start the spindle motor turning. The diskette must be spinning properly before any read or write operations can take place.

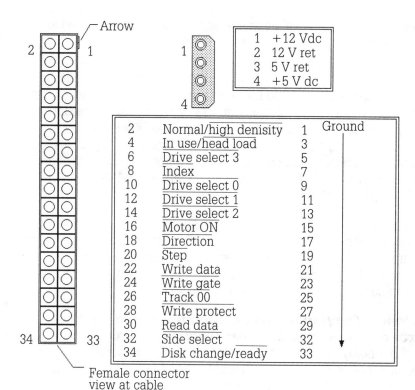

1	+12 Vdc		
2	12 V ret		
3	5 V ret		
4	+5 V dc		

2	Normal/high denisity	1	Ground
4	In use/head load	3	
6	Drive select 3	5	
8	Index	7	
10	Drive select 0	9	
12	Drive select 1	11	
14	Drive select 2	13	
16	Motor ON	15	
18	Direction	17	
20	Step	19	
22	Write data	21	
24	Write gate	23	
26	Track 00	25	
28	Write protect	27	
30	Read data	29	
32	Side select	32	
34	Disk change/ready	33	

Female connector
view at cable

7-8
Pinout diagram for a typical (IBM PC/AT) floppy drive interface.

The head assembly must also be manipulated. A DIRECTION SELECT signal tells the head stepping motor whether it should be moving in (toward the spindle) or out (away from the spindle) while a STEP pulse signal tells the head stepping motor how many steps to take. STEP and DIRECTION controls position the R/W heads precisely over the diskette. A WRITE DATA line carries information to the diskette, and a WRITE GATE signal tells the drive to accept data on the WRITE DATA line. Finally, the SIDE SELECT signal determines which side of the diskette is to be written or read.

There are also a number of output signals that you should understand. A NORMAL/HIGH-DENSITY SELECT signal tells the floppy controller IC what type of media is in use. The IN USE/HEAD LOAD line indicates the R/W head status. An INDEX signal provides a chain of index pulses back to the floppy controller to regulate the spindle speed. A TRACK 00 signal is the reference to indicate when the head assembly is positioned at track 00. A WRITE PROTECT signal prevents the floppy controller from writing to the diskette if the diskette is write protected. Any data read from the disk are provided to the floppy disk controller over the READ DATA line. A DISK

CHANGE/READY signal shows when the disk is ready to be accessed for reading or writing.

Troubleshooting floppy drive systems

Typically, there are four problems that plague floppy drives: the drive is entirely dead, the R/W heads do not seek, the drive does not read, or the drive does not write. This book concentrates on the floppy drive controller or the floppy drive as a complete assembly, and does not present disk alignment or drive repair procedures. If you wish repair floppy drives themselves, obtain the advanced version of this book, *Troubleshooting and Repairing Notebook, Palmtop, and Pen Computers: A Technician's Guide* (Windcrest #4427).

To perform some of the following tests, you should have a good, properly formatted diskette, which may contain files. Be certain that those files are backed up properly on a hard drive or another floppy disk—if you can't afford to loose the files don't use the disk. For the following procedures, refer to the floppy drive block diagram in FIG. 7-7.

Symptom 1: The floppy drive is completely dead—the diskette does not even initialize when inserted. Begin troubleshooting by inspecting the diskette. When a 3.5" diskette is inserted into a drive, a mechanism should pull the disk's metal shroud away and briefly rotate the spindle motor. Make sure that the diskette is properly inserted into the floppy drive assembly. If the diskette does not enter and seat just right within the drive, disk access will be impossible. Try several diskettes to ensure that test diskette is not defective. It may be necessary to partially disassemble the computer to access the drive and allow you to see the overall assembly. Free or adjust any jammed assemblies or linkages to correct diskette insertion. If you cannot get diskettes to insert properly, change the floppy drive.

If the diskette inserts properly but fails to initialize, carefully inspect the drive's physical interface cabling. Loose connectors or faulty cable wiring can easily disable a floppy drive. Use your multimeter to measure dc voltages at the power connector. Place your meter's ground lead on pin 2 and measure +12 Vdc at pin 1. Ground your meter on pin 3 and measure +5 Vdc at pin 4 (+3.0 or +3.3 Vdc on low-voltage systems). If either or both of these voltages is low or missing, troubleshoot your power supply or dc-dc converter as discussed in chapter 5.

With appropriate power and proper mechanical operation, the trouble is probably in the floppy drive PC board, or the floppy drive controller IC located on the motherboard. Try replacing the floppy drive assembly entirely. This is not the least expensive avenue in terms of materials, but it is the fastest and simplest. If a new floppy drive corrects the problem, reassemble the computer and return it to service. You should retain the old floppy drive for parts. Read/write heads, motors, and mechanical drive parts can be rather difficult to obtain as individual parts.

If a new floppy drive assembly fails to correct the problem, replace the floppy controller IC on the motherboard. You have to disassemble your computer to expose the motherboard. A schematic or block diagram of your system will probably be required for you to locate the floppy drive controller IC. If you do not have the tools or inclination to perform surface-mount work, replace the motherboard.

Symptom 2: The floppy drive rotates the diskette but does not seek to the desired track.   This type of symptom usually suggests that the head-positioning stepping motor is inhibited or defective, but that all other floppy drive functions are working properly. Begin by disassembling your small computer and removing the floppy drive. Carefully inspect the head-positioning assembly to be certain that there are no broken parts or obstructions that could jam the R/W heads. You might want to examine the mechanical system with a diskette inserted to be certain that the trouble is not a disk alignment problem that might be interfering with head movement. Gently remove any obstructions that you find. Be careful not to accidentally misalign any linkages or mechanical components while clearing an obstruction.

Remove any diskette from the drive and reconnect the drive's signal and power cables. Apply power to the computer and measure drive voltages with your multimeter. Ground your multimeter on pin 2 of the power connector and measure +12 Vdc at pin 1. Move the meter ground to pin 3 and measure +5 Vdc on pin 4. You might measure +3.0 or +3.3 Vdc in low-voltage systems. If either voltage is low or absent, troubleshoot your power supply or dc-dc converter as discussed in chapter 5.

Once confident that the drive's mechanics are intact and appropriate power is available, determine whether the trouble is in the floppy drive PC board or the floppy drive controller IC on the motherboard. Use your logic probe to measure the $\overline{\text{STEP}}$ signal in the physical interface (standard interfaces use signal pin 20). When drive access is requested, you should detect a pulse signal as the floppy drive controller attempts to position the R/W heads. If $\overline{\text{STEP}}$ pulses are missing, the floppy drive controller IC is probably defective and should be replaced. You will probably need a schematic or block diagram of your system to identify the floppy drive controller. If you lack the tools or inclination to perform surface-mount work, you can replace the entire motherboard. If $\overline{\text{STEP}}$ pulses are present at the interface but the heads are not moving, replace the faulty floppy drive assembly. Feel free to save the old drive for parts.

Symptom 3: The floppy drive heads seek properly, but the spindle does not turn.   This symptom suggests that the spindle motor is inhibited or defective, but that all other functions are working properly. Remove all power from the computer. Disassemble the system enough to remove the floppy disk drive. Carefully inspect the spindle motor, drive belt (if used), and spindle assembly. Make certain that there are no broken parts or obstructions that could jam the spindle. If there is a belt between the motor and the spindle, make sure the belt is reasonably tight—it should not slip. Examine the floppy drive with a diskette inserted to be certain that the diskette's insertion or alignment is not causing the problem. You can try this with several diskettes. Gently remove any obstructions that you find. Be careful not to cause any accidental damage while clearing an obstruction. Do not add any lubricating agents to the assembly, but gently vacuum away any accumulations of dust or dirt.

Remove any diskette from the drive and reconnect the floppy drive's signal and power cables. Restore power to the computer and measure drive voltages with your multimeter. Ground your multimeter on pin 2 and measure +12 Vdc on pin 1. Move the meter ground to pin 3 and measure +5 Vdc on pin 4 (+3.0 or +3.3 Vdc in low-voltage systems). If either voltage is low or absent, troubleshoot your power supply or dc-dc converter as shown in chapter 5.

Once you are confident that the floppy drive is mechanically sound and appropriate power is available, determine whether the trouble is in the floppy drive PC board or the floppy drive controller IC on the motherboard. Use your logic probe to measure the MOTOR ON signal in the physical interface (standard interfaces use signal pin 16). When drive access is requested, the MOTOR ON signal should appear (in most cases an active low). If the MOTOR ON signal is missing, the floppy drive controller IC is probably defective and should be replaced. If you lack the tools to perform surface-mount work, you should replace the motherboard. If the MOTOR ON signal is present but the spindle does not turn, replace the faulty floppy drive. Feel free to save the old drive for spare parts.

Symptom 4: The floppy drive will not read from or write to the diskette and all other operations appear normal.   This type of problem can manifest itself in several ways, but your computer's operating system usually informs you when a disk read or write error has occurred. Begin by using a good, properly formatted diskette in the drive. A faulty diskette can generate some very perplexing read/write problems.

If a good diskette does not resolve the problem, try cleaning the R/W heads with a commercial, nonabrasive head cleaning kit. Do not run the drive with a head cleaning disk inserted for more than 30 seconds at a time, or you risk damaging the heads with excessive friction.

When a fresh diskette and clean R/W heads do not correct the problem, you must determine whether the trouble exists in the floppy drive assembly or the floppy controller IC. When you cannot read data from the floppy drive, use your logic probe to measure the READ DATA signal (standard interfaces use signal pin 30). When the disk is idle, the READ DATA line should read as a constant 1 or 0. During a read cycle, you should measure a pulse signal as data moves from the drive to the floppy controller IC. If no pulse signal appears on the READ DATA line during a read cycle, replace the defective floppy drive assembly. Feel free to retain the old drive for spare parts. If a pulse signal does exist during a read cycle, the floppy disk controller IC on the motherboard is probably defective and should be replaced. If you do not have the tools to handle surface-mount work, you can replace the entire motherboard.

When you cannot write data to the floppy drive, use your logic probe to measure the WRITE GATE and WRITE DATA lines (standard interfaces use signal pins 24 and 22 respectively). During a write cycle, the WRITE GATE should be 0 and you should read a pulse signal as data flows from the floppy controller IC to the drive. If the WRITE GATE remains at 1 or there is no pulse on the WRITE DATA line, replace the defective floppy controller IC on the motherboard. If you do not have the tools to perform surface-mount work, replace the motherboard. When the two WRITE signals appear as expected, replace the defective floppy drive assembly.

Hard drives

Floppy drives are slow. It takes a relatively long time to spin up the diskette, seek the desired track and sector, and transfer the necessary information to or from the disk. Floppy drives are also limited by low storage capacity. Although a high-density diskette can save a respectable 1.4Mb of data, the vast majority of today's software demands much more disk space. Hard disk drives (or hard drives) evolved in the early 1980s to answer the limitations posed by floppy drive systems (FIG. 7-9).

Hard drives have a great range of sizes and shapes (known as *form factor*), as well as storage capacity. TABLE 7-2 provides a comparison of popular form factors. Large drives can provide 1 gigabyte (Gb) or more of storage, mid-sized drives typically can provide from 80 to 280Mb, and small drives usually offer 80Mb or less. This part of the chapter teaches about hard drives and their common interface standards.

7-9
*Three general-purpose
hard drives.*

Table 7-2
Comparison of form factor
nomenclature to actual drive dimensions.

Form factor nomenclature	Approximate dimensions		
	Height (mm) (in)	Width (mm) (in)	Depth (mm) (in)
5.25" full height*	82.60	145.54	202.69
	3.25	5.73	7.98
5.25" half height*	41.28	145.54	202.68
	1.63	5.73	7.98
3.5" half height**	41.28	101.60	146.05
	1.63	4.00	5.75
3.5" low profile**	25.40	101.60	146.05
	1.00	4.00	5.75

Table 7-2 Continued.

Form factor nomenclature	Approximate dimensions		
	Height (mm) (in)	Width (mm) (in)	Depth (mm) (in)
2.5" low profile	19.05	70.10	101.85
	0.75	2.76	4.01
1.8" low profile	15.00	51.00	77.00
	0.59	2.00	3.03
1.3" low profile	10.50	36.50	50.80
	0.41	1.44	2.00

*used in desktop systems only
**used in desktops and some older laptops

A typical hard drive is illustrated in FIG. 7-10. Most of the drive is composed of mechanical components and assemblies, such as the frame, case, spindle, platters, heads, etc. Hard drives use one synchronized dc motor to drive the spindle. Older hard drives used stepping motors to position their R/W heads, but stepping motors have long since been replaced by moving coil motors. Rotary coil actuation allows a head assembly to be positioned just as precisely as a stepping motor, but in much less time. Rotary coil actuators also eliminate the weight and bulk encountered in stepping motors.

Drive construction

Each disk in the hard drive is called a *platter*. There can be from one to five platters in a hard drive assembly. Instead of flexible mylar, platters are made of aluminum, glass, or ceramic, in order to withstand the centrifugal forces of high rotation velocity. Each platter is coated on both sides with a high-quality magnetic oxide media. One R/W head is provided for each platter side. For example, a drive with three platters can have up to six R/W heads. A spindle assembly spins the entire platter arrangement at about 3600 rpm.

In order to support the incredible recording density found on most hard drives (some densities can exceed 48,000 bits per inch), the R/W head travels on a cushion of air within fractions of a millimeter above the disk surface. An air cushion is created by the rotation of the platters, as shown in FIG. 7-11. Since it is critically important that the heads do not contact the platters during operation, all hard drives are designed with a specific landing zone—a track on each platter where the heads are positioned during spindown and spinup. No data are stored or accessed on the landing zone, so head contact does not cause damage. Once the disk is at running speed, the heads can then track normally along the drive.

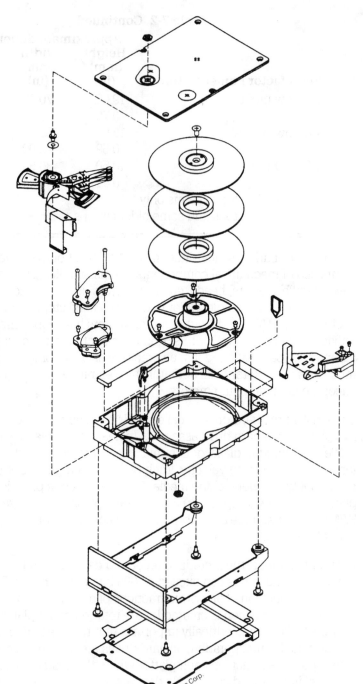

7-10
*Exploded view of a typical
hard drive.*

Quantum Corp.

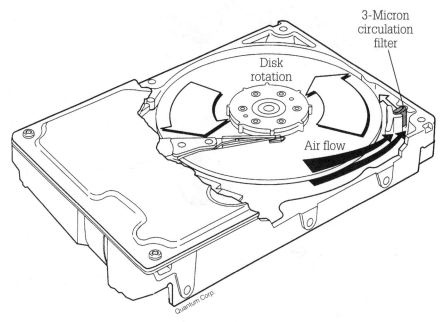

Disk rotation

3-Micron circulation filter

Air flow

Quantum Corp.

7-11
View of air flow in a hard drive.

Many hard drive head assemblies today are dynamically loaded; that is, the R/W heads are mechanically loaded to an appropriate distance from each platter only when the spindle is at running speed. When the drive spins down, the heads are unloaded so that they cannot contact the platters. However, vibration from rough handling can still shock the heads into contact with the platters, so the use of a landing zone is still mandated. The process of parking the drive to its landing zone before spindown is now accomplished automatically in small computers.

A rotary moving coil provides much faster track-to-track seek times than stepping motors. Figure 7-12 illustrates a greatly simplified rotary moving coil actuator. With no drive current from the head actuator IC, the R/W arm moves to some known position as determined by the arm's mounting. As drive current is applied, each coil magnet takes on a magnetic field that drives the arm. The more drive current applied to the actuator, the farther the arm travels. If drive current is reversed, the arm turns in the opposite direction. Drive controller circuitry is responsible for keeping the arm properly positioned at all times. This principle is almost identical to the operation of an analog meter movement.

The hard drive requires a substantial amount of circuitry to ensure proper operation. An R/W controller, a disk controller/interface ASIC, a spindle motor controller IC, and a head actuator/driver IC are minimum

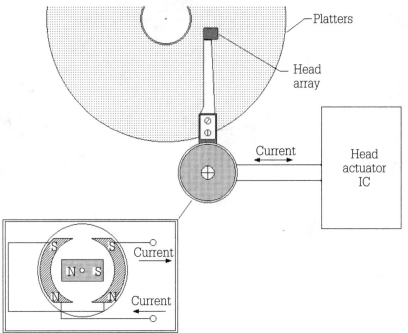

Platters

Head array

Current

Head actuator IC

Current

Current

requirements. Many new drives also employ a microcontroller to oversee the drive's operation as shown in FIG. 7-13. Notice that a small Programmable Read Only Memory (PROM) is added to provide instructions for microcontroller operation. Also notice another small portion or memory called a *disk cache*. The only other electronics within a hard drive is the read preamplifier/write driver IC, which is usually located next to the head actuator inside the sealed platter case. Let's look at each part of the circuitry.

Data enters and leaves the hard drive through the disk controller/interface IC. This controller is a complex ASIC, specially designed according to the drive's physical interface. The drive shown in FIG. 7-13 is designed to operate over the SCSI physical interface. The IDE interface is another standard used in many low-to-medium cost hard drives. The disk controller/interface IC also controls the head actuator driver circuit and spindle motor driver.

Another key element in a hard drive is the R/W controller IC. The R/W controller works directly with the head preamplifier and driver circuits to convert the analog electrical patterns from read heads into useful binary logic levels. The R/W controller also separates any clock and synchronization information from raw data. When data must be written to

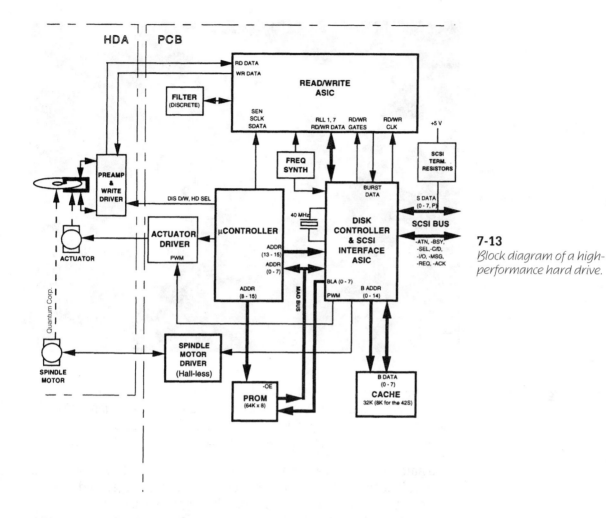

7-13
Block diagram of a high-performance hard drive.

the platters, the R/W controller generates properly shaped write signals that are amplified by write driver circuits. Binary data enters and leaves the R/W controller through the disk controller/interface IC.

An on-board microcontroller serves to coordinate the drive's electronics by synchronizing the disk controller/interface and the R/W controller. The microcontroller is also used to implement drive spinup and spindown, as well as any other power management features with which the drive might be equipped. In practice, the microcontroller is typically a custom version of a microprocessor. Some hard drives, however, use an off-the-shelf microprocessor. For small drives, such as the 1.3" form factor unit of FIG. 7-14, much of the circuitry is integrated onto one or two extremely sophisticated surface-mount ASICs.

Hewitt-Parkard Company

Data organization

You cannot simply place data anywhere on a hard drive. Information must be organized into known, standard groups and locations. Organization helps to ensure that data recorded on one hard drive will be readable by another computer using the same physical interface.

Since hard drives evolved to increase the storage offered by floppy drive systems, it seems only natural that hard drive data be organized in a similar way, shown in FIG. 7-15. A sector is still the smallest block of storage space offering 512 bytes. Sectors are formed in concentric rings (tracks) around a platter. There are sectors and tracks on each side of a platter. Where floppy drives utilize only one floppy disk, a hard drive can use from one to five platters. Large hard drives might use six or more platters. Every platter is mounted on the same spindle. Hard drives also introduce the concept of *cylinders*, which are groups of concentric rings (tracks) visualized to pass through every platter. In practice, the number of cylinders equals the number of tracks on one surface of one side of one platter. Typical hard drives hold hundreds of cylinders.

As an example, a 3.5" form factor drive might provide 83,045 sectors in a 42.5Mb (formatted) assembly. Such a drive can offer 977 tracks per

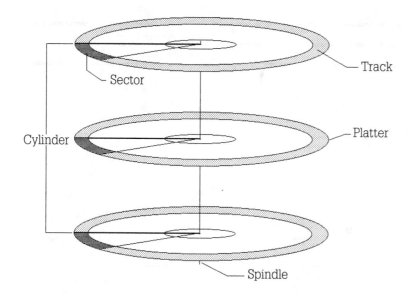

surface (cylinders) with 17 sectors per track. With a storage capacity of 512 bytes per sector, one platter surface can hold 17×977 or 16,609 sectors. At 512 bytes per sector, this is equivalent to 8.5Mb (formatted). If there are three platters, there can be up to six surfaces (not every surface has to be used). If five surfaces are used in a six-platter assembly, the drive will hold 8.5×5, or 42.5Mb (formatted).

The term *formatted* means that the drive can actually hold more data than the amount specified, but that additional space (often several megabytes for a hard drive) is used during the operating system's format process to encode sector and track information and establish a FAT to serve as the disk's table of contents. When the drive needs to access a file for reading or writing, the FAT provides the starting track and sector of the file as well as file length.

The transfer of information into and out of a hard drive is an extremely intricate process. Since a hard drive is designed to provide much greater speed and storage capacity than a floppy drive, the circuitry required to form a complete hard drive system is much more sophisticated and stringent. The CPU, system controller, and core memory are used in conjunction with a powerful hard drive controller IC. The hard drive controller located on the system motherboard is primarily responsible for connecting a standard hard drive to the computer's busses. Figure 7-16 illustrates a block diagram for a hard drive system.

A hard drive system

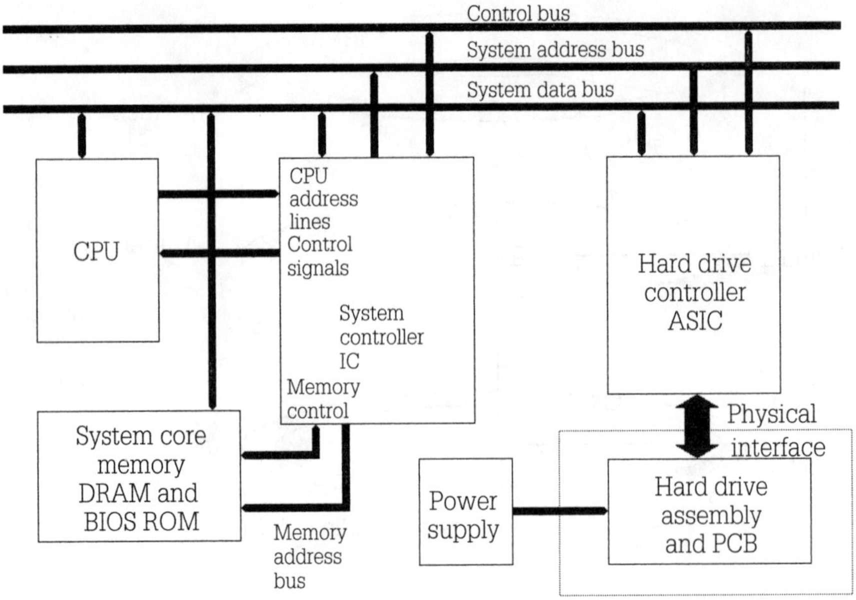

7-16
Block diagram of a complete hard drive system.

Control bus
System address bus
System data bus

CPU

CPU address lines
Control signals

System controller IC

Memory control

Hard drive controller ASIC

System core memory DRAM and BIOS ROM

Memory address bus

Power supply

Physical interface

Hard drive assembly and PCB

Hard drive control begins at the CPU, which executes the instructions needed to handle data transfer (note that the CPU does not interact with the hard drive directly). Instead, the CPU instructs the system controller to begin data transfer into or out of the drive. It is the system controller that actually manages the hard drive controller IC. Any machine code needed to operate the hard drive is taken by the CPU from BIOS ROM in core memory.

A hard drive controller connects the computer's main busses (control, system address, and system data) to a physical interface with which the drive is compatible. Data and commands read from the drive are translated into appropriate computer bus signals by the hard drive controller IC. Circuitry on the hard drive is used to operate the drive's mechanics and to convert digital information from the physical interface into microscopic points of magnetic flux that can be recorded on a platter (and vice versa).

In practice, the process of drive signalling, data transfer, and control is much more complex than just described, but you can see the important concepts that are involved. The next part of this chapter describes two popular physical interface standards. TABLE 7-3 presents a comparison of typical interface characteristics.

Table 7-3
Comparison of hard drive interface characteristics.

Parameter	ESDI	IDE	SCSI-1	SCSI-2	SCSI-3
Data bus width (bits)	1	8/16	8	8/24	8/32
Interface cable conductors	34/20	40	50	50/68	50/68
Maximum cable length (meters)	3.0	0.5	6.0	6.0	?
Data transfer rate (Mbps)	10.0	?	32.0	80/320	?
Data transfer rate (MHz)	10.0	?	4.0	10.0	?

?—a highly variable or not well-established parameter.

The Intelligent Drive Electronics or Integrated Drive Electronics (IDE) interface is one of the most popular and widely used interfaces in small computers today. All the circuitry required to operate an IDE drive is located on the hard drive PC board. An IDE interface connects a hard drive to the motherboard with a 40-pin connector. Software routines needed to communicate with an IDE drive are already embedded in the BIOS ROM of any IBM PC/AT (or compatible) system.

The IDE interface

A complete IDE interface is composed of two cables: a 4-pin power cable and a 40-pin signal cable. Both cable pinouts are illustrated in FIG. 7-17. The standard power connector is a 4-pin mate-n-lock connector. To maintain conventions with floppy drive systems, IDE hard drives use +5 Vdc and +12 Vdc. In a low-voltage system, you might see +3.0 or +3.3 Vdc instead of +5.0 Vdc. The return (ground) for each supply is also provided on the power connector.

The signal cable is typically a 40-pin insulation displacement connector (IDC) cable. Both the even- and odd-numbered wires are signal-carrying lines. Also note that some of the signal labels have dark bars over their names. The bar indicates that the particular signal is active low; that is, the signal is TRUE in the logic 0 state instead of being TRUE in the logic 1 state. All signal lines on the IDE interface are fully TTL-compatible, where a logic 0 is 0.0 to +0.8 Vdc, and a logic 1 is +2.0 to V_{cc}.

The hard drive is addressed using the Drive Address bus lines (DA0 to DA2) in conjunction with the Chip Select inputs ($\overline{\text{CS1FX}}$ and $\overline{\text{CS3FX}}$). When a TRUE signal is sent along the Drive I/O Read ($\overline{\text{DIOR}}$) line, the drive executes a read cycle, while a TRUE on the drive I/O write (DIOW) line

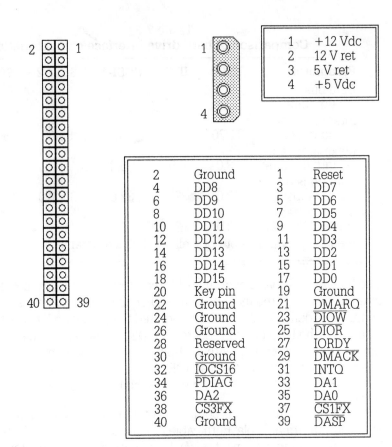

7-17
Pinout diagram for an IDE hard drive interface.

1	+12 Vdc		
2	12 V ret		
3	5 V ret		
4	+5 Vdc		

2	Ground	1	Reset
4	DD8	3	DD7
6	DD9	5	DD6
8	DD10	7	DD5
10	DD11	9	DD4
12	DD12	11	DD3
14	DD13	13	DD2
16	DD14	15	DD1
18	DD15	17	DD0
20	Key pin	19	Ground
22	Ground	21	DMARQ
24	Ground	23	$\overline{\text{DIOW}}$
26	Ground	25	$\overline{\text{DIOR}}$
28	Reserved	27	IORDY
30	Ground	29	$\overline{\text{DMACK}}$
32	$\overline{\text{IOCS16}}$	31	INTQ
34	PDIAG	33	DA1
36	DA2	35	DA0
38	$\overline{\text{CS3FX}}$	37	$\overline{\text{CS1FX}}$
40	Ground	39	$\overline{\text{DASP}}$

initiates a write cycle. The IDE interface provides TTL-level input and output signals. Sixteen bidirectional data lines (DD0 to DD15) are used to carry data bits into or out of the drive. Once a data transfer is completed, a DMA ACKNOWLEDGE ($\overline{\text{DMACK}}$) signal is provided to the drive from the hard disk controller IC. Finally, a TRUE signal on the drive's reset line will restore the drive to its original condition at power on. A $\overline{\text{RESET}}$ is sent when the computer is first powered on or rebooted.

The IDE physical interface also provides a number of outputs back to the motherboard. A Direct Memory Access Request (DMARQ) is used to initiate the transfer of data to or from the drive. The direction of data transfer is dependent on the condition of the $\overline{\text{DIOR}}$ and $\overline{\text{DIOW}}$ inputs. A $\overline{\text{DMACK}}$ signal is generated in response when the DMARQ line is asserted (made TRUE). IORDY is an I/O Ready signal that keeps a system's attention if the drive is not quite ready to respond to a data transfer request. A Drive Interrupt Request (INTQ or INTRQ) is asserted by a drive when there is a drive interrupt pending (i.e., the drive is about to transfer information to or from the motherboard). The Drive Active line (DASP) becomes logic 0 when any hard drive activity is occurring. A Passed Diagnostic (PDIAG) pin provides the results of any diagnostic command or reset action. When PDIAG is logic 0, the system knows that the drive is ready to use. Finally, the 16-bit I/O control line (IOCS16) tells the motherboard that the drive is ready to send or receive data.

The Small Computer Systems Interface (SCSI, pronounced "scuzzy") is more than just a hard drive interface. SCSI is a standalone bus architecture capable of transmitting 8-bit data words at speeds up to 4 million bits per second. In operation, SCSI is very much like a regular computer bus where a formal protocol (sequence of events) is needed to communicate between devices. As a result, the computer is not concerned with the particular aspects or conditions of the drive—the hard drive contains its own comprehensive on-board intelligence to complete each task. A host system sends high-level commands to the SCSI bus and waits for the results. The original specification for SCSI was published in 1986. Two other enhanced versions, SCSI-2 and SCSI-3 are now available. Like the IDE interface, a SCSI drive needs only to be connected to a motherboard using a standard cable.

The SCSI interface

Figure 7-18 illustrates a typical SCSI connector pinout for the signal and power cables. The typical power connector is often the 4-pin mate-n-lock connector. To maintain conventions with standard power supplies and floppy systems, SCSI hard drives use +5.0 Vdc and +12 Vdc. A low-voltage system might use +3.0 or +3.3 Vdc instead of +5.0 Vdc. The return (ground) for each supply is also provided on the connector.

The signal cable is usually a 50-pin insulation displacement connector (IDC) cable. Notice that all of the odd-numbered lines are ground lines. This cable scheme helps to reduce electrical noise in the cable and ensures data integrity throughout the range of data transfer speeds. SCSI signals are carried over the even-numbered lines. Notice that some of the label names have dark bars over them. Such bars indicate that the particular signal is active low. An active low signal is true in the logic 0 state instead of being true in the logic 1 state. Every signal in the SCSI interface is fully TTL-compatible.

The communications protocol that takes place between an SCSI hard drive and motherboard is much different than that for an IDE system. When an SCSI system needs to access its hard drive, it brings its SELECT (SEL) signal to a logic 0 state. The drive can also control the SEL line to

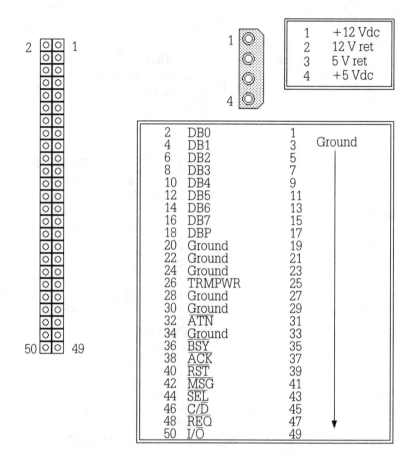

7-18
Pinout diagram for an SCSI hard drive interface.

1	+12 Vdc
2	12 V ret
3	5 V ret
4	+5 Vdc

2	DB0	1	
4	DB1	3	Ground
6	DB2	5	
8	DB3	7	
10	DB4	9	
12	DB5	11	
14	DB6	13	
16	DB7	15	
18	DBP	17	
20	Ground	19	
22	Ground	21	
24	Ground	23	
26	TRMPWR	25	
28	Ground	27	
30	Ground	29	
32	ATN	31	
34	Ground	33	
36	BSY	35	
38	ACK	37	
40	RST	39	
42	MSG	41	
44	SEL	43	
46	C/D	45	
48	REQ	47	
50	I/O	49	

initiate data transfer—but that is almost never done. The Attention (ATN) pin then becomes logic 0, and the drive responds by pulling the Request (REQ) line to a logic 0. When the drive must send back a particular control response to the system, an 8-bit message can be placed on the bidirectional data bus (DB0 to DB7), and the MESSAGE (MSG) signal is pulled to logic 0. A DATA BIT PARITY (DBP) signal is used in conjunction with the data bits to provide data error checking.

The Control/Data line (C/D) is controlled by the hard drive. A logic 1 on the line indicates that the drive has placed a control byte on its data lines, while a logic 0 says that data is being placed on the bus. The direction of data transfer is determined by the Input/Output (I/O) pin. A logic 1 will input data from the hard drive, while a logic 0 outputs data to the hard drive. After a data transfer has taken place, the motherboard forces the Acknowledge (ACK) line to a logic 0 state to indicate that data has been transmitted or received. Whenever the SCSI bus is in use, the BUSY (BSY) signal becomes logic 0. When power is first applied to the SCSI drive or the computer system is rebooted, a RESET ($\overline{RST}$) pulse forces the drive's circuitry to initialize.

In order for an SCSI bus to operate properly, bus lines must be terminated with pullup resistors, which help ensure that each logic line behaves as expected. The power needed for each pullup resistor is provided by the Terminator Power (TRMPWR) line.

As a final note, always remember that some small computers might not utilize the standard interface connector scheme for their particular interface, even though the same major signals are required. If your computer uses a nonstandard interface connector arrangement, you will need a schematic diagram to identify the appropriate pins.

There are many serious problems that can plague a hard drive (FIG. 7-19). Bad media (platters), head crashes due to excessive shock or abuse, spindle or head actuator failure, or electronic failures can permanently disable your hard drive. The hard drive controller IC on the motherboard might also be faulty. For the purposes of this book, however, you will concentrate on the hard drive as an assembly, the interface cable, and the

Troubleshooting hard drive systems

MiniStor Peripherals, PORTables Series™ of 1.8″ hard disk drives

7-19
An assortment of permanent and removeable hard drives.

hard drive controller IC. If you wish to study hard drives in more detail, refer to the advanced version of this book, *Troubleshooting and Repairing Notebook, Palmtop, and Pen Computers: A Technician's Guide* (Windcrest #4427).

Symptom 1: The hard drive does not function properly (if at all). All other functions appear to be normal. Most DOS hard drive error messages are not terribly specific in describing exactly what is occurring during hard drive failures. The following procedures can be used to help you isolate just about any hard drive problem. As you read through the procedures, refer to the block diagram of FIG. 7-16.

If your small computer will not boot from its hard drive, boot the computer using a DOS system floppy diskette (or memory card) and check your system's setup. Almost all small computers save their configuration parameters in a small section of battery backed-up CMOS RAM. Part of the setup information includes descriptions of each installed drive type. If the small lithium backup battery supporting your configuration memory fails, the setup information might be lost. As a result, your system might "forget" how it should be setup and not recognize the installed hard drive. If you find that your system's configuration has been lost, replace the CMOS RAM backup battery, reenter and resave the necessary setup information, and reboot the computer from its hard disk. You will probably have to disassemble at least some small part of your computer to install a new battery.

Here is a trick to help you with setup information: check your system's setup parameters before a problem arises and copy the setup information into your system's DOS or User's Manual. That way, you need only refer to your written notes when it is time to reload or modify a missing or corrupt setup parameter.

When setup parameters check properly, remove all power from the computer and disassemble the system to expose the hard drive assembly. Check the signal and power cable installations. This check is especially important if you have just finished a repair that required you to disconnect your drive cables. Make certain that each cable is installed properly and oriented correctly. Check for any loose or broken wiring. Correct any wiring problems that you encounter.

Remove the power cable from the hard drive, reapply power to the computer, and measure dc voltages at the power connector. Place your meter's ground lead on pin 2 and measure +12 Vdc on pin 1. Ground your meter at pin 3 and measure +5 Vdc on pin 4. Low-voltage systems might use +3.0 or +3.3 Vdc instead of +5 Vdc. If either voltage is low or absent, troubleshoot your power supply or dc-dc converters as discussed in chapter 5.

At this point, your hard drive assembly is probably defective. However, you can test the drive by substitution. Since hard drives use standard physical interfaces, you can install the questionable drive into another computer (even a desktop) using the same physical interface and power levels. For example, never install a low-voltage hard drive in a conventional (+5 Vdc) system, or vice versa. Either the drive circuitry or the motherboard circuitry might be destroyed. If you are able to find a compatible system (you can call it the test system), you might have to change the test system's setup parameters before it will recognize the suspect drive. Once the testing is complete, remember to restore and recheck the test system's original drive and setup parameters. If you must change a test system's setup parameters, make it a point to keep careful notes of the original configuration for later reference.

If your suspect drive is functioning properly (and holds the files needed to boot the computer), it should be able to boot the test system, and you should have normal access to the drive. Remember that the suspect drive must be the only boot device in the test system. When you prove that the suspect drive does work, try replacing the hard drive signal cable, then try replacing the hard drive controller IC located on the small-computer's motherboard. If you do not have the tools or inclination to tackle surface-mount work, you may wish to replace the entire motherboard.

If you encounter the same hard drive failure in the test system, you should replace the hard drive entirely. You will then need to reformat the new drive in your system and reload all of the applications software and data files contained on the original drive. (Of course, you should always back up your hard drive on a regular basis.) As long as the replacement drive is identical to the faulty drive, you will not need to alter any setup parameters.

Without a test system to verify operation of the hard drive, your best course is simply to replace the hard drive. This is not the least expensive answer, but it is much faster and easier to obtain a replacement drive than struggling to find and replace the hard drive controller IC.

Solid-state memory cards

Platters and diskettes do not last forever—over time and use, magnetic oxides break down and wear away, and magnetic particles eventually loose their orientation. Stray magnetic fields can also upset the alignment of magnetic particles. All it takes is one bad bit to render a program or data file unusable. Wide, frequent fluctuations in environmental conditions can also contribute to oxide breakdown. Magnetic media requires relatively large, intricate, and delicate mechanisms to transport the media and heads. Such drawbacks make floppy and hard drives susceptible to failures from natural wear and tear, as well as impact shock and physical abuse. Finally, magnetic drives require motors and electronic driver circuitry to read or write, and motors require substantial amounts of power to operate. Even with the many power reduction features found in many of today's small computers, mechanical drives consume a large part of every battery charge.

Solid-state memory cards take advantage of advanced memory ICs and packaging to provide mass-storage in the form of solid-state cards (FIG. 7-20). Integrated circuits are reaching a level of sophistication where they can now handle the large volume of information once handled only by magnetic media. Small, credit card-sized memory cards are generally considered to be an efficient and reliable alternative to magnetic media. After all, memory cards have no moving parts, and they require no drive mechanism, so there is nothing to wear out except, perhaps, the card's connectors. Memory cards use very little power as compared to magnetic drives. Cards are not influenced by external magnetic fields, and they are more rugged than floppy disks. This part of the chapter introduces you to conventional memory card technology, as well as mass-storage flash cards (up to 20Mb per card). Both classes of memory card are quickly gaining acceptance in palmtop and pen-computer designs.

7-20
A selection of Maxell SRAM cards.

Maxell Corp. of America, Fairlawn, NJ

Memory card types   Memory cards are divided into two general classes: temporary (volatile) and permanent (nonvolatile). Volatile memory cards utilize static or dynamic RAM, or some variation of erasable ROM ICs, while nonvolatile memory cards employ nonerasable ROM components. Both types of cards have their own particular niche in small-computer applications. A volatile memory card can be erased and rewritten many times, yet information is retained on the card when the small computer is powered down or when the card is removed from the system. Reusable operation makes volatile cards extremely popular. A nonvolatile memory card is much more limited in its operation. Once nonvolatile cards are programmed, they cannot be rewritten. The following descriptions explain each type of memory card in more detail.

Static random access memory (SRAM) cards use static RAM ICs to store information. All RAM is volatile, so static RAM can be read or written as needed. Small lithium coin cells are used within the memory card to maintain RAM contents after power is removed. SRAM cards are typically available in capacities ranging from 32K to 2Mb or more.

Dynamic random access memory (DRAM) cards use dynamic RAM ICs to store information. DRAM is at least twice as fast as SRAM, and can pack much more memory in the same card area. Although DRAM cards have their advantages, a substantial amount of circuitry is needed to periodically refresh DRAM contents. Since it is not economical to package such circuitry in the card itself, DRAM cards do not retain their information once power is removed. Even with such a limitation, DRAM cards can pack 12Mb or more onto a single card. DRAM cards usually serve as compact, convenient expansion memory for a small computer.

Electrically erasable programmable read-only memory (EEPROM) cards are somewhere between volatile and nonvolatile memory cards. With limited memory capacity up to 192K, an EEPROM card can be written to by a small computer, then erased and rewritten as needed. Yet, the EEPROM card retains its information when removed from the system without the use of a battery backup. Unfortunately, conventional EEPROMs are somewhat slow to erase and rewrite.

The masked read-only memory (ROM) card is the simplest form of nonvolatile memory card. A masked ROM card is fabricated at the IC factory already programmed—the program is provided by the company purchasing the cards for sale. Once manufactured, the card's contents can never be altered. This may sound extremely limited, but masked ROM cards can be quite economical for distributing large, well-established software packages, such as Lotus 1-2-3. Masked ROM capacities can be found up to 16Mb or more.

One-time programmable read-only memory (OTPROM) is a user-programmable version of the masked ROM. Instead of preprogramming the memory ICs at the factory before being incorporated into memory cards, memory ICs are manufactured blank. A company can purchase an OTPROM programmer and create its own cards (no small computer is yet able to program (or burn) an OTPROM). Once an OTPROM is programmed, it can never be altered. OTPROM cards are available in medium sizes up 4Mb.

Perhaps the most exciting development in memory cards has been the flash EEPROM card (flash card). A flash card uses a recent variation of EEPROM technology that can be erased and rewritten very quickly and easily. Flash EEPROMs also offer lower power dissipation and much higher storage capacity than conventional EEPROMs. Since EEPROMs retain their data once power is removed, batteries are not needed (although some flash card designs use batteries to support small quantities of on-board SRAM). Two such applications of flash technology are in high-capacity, mass-storage cards such as the 20Mb IDE-series solid-state mass-storage system that is compatible with a hard drive's IDE interface. Another popular flash card is the 14.6Mb SDP series solid-state mass-storage system intended to be directly compatible with the PCMCIA card interface. Both mass-storage cards are manufactured by SunDisk Corporation of California. Figure 7-21 shows a close-up view of a SunDisk SDP mass-storage card.

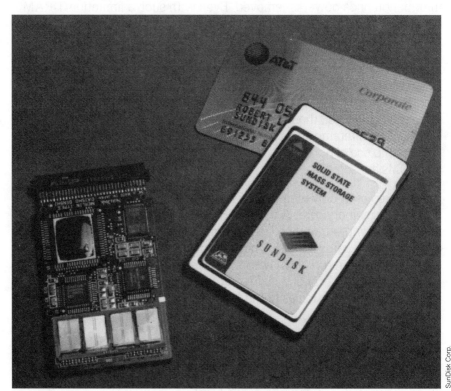

7-21
A solid-state mass-storage unit from SunDisk Corp.

SunDisk Corp.

Card construction   One of the key advantages of a memory card is its small size, as shown in FIG. 7-22. With a form factor only 86-mm (3.44") long, 54-mm (2.16") wide, and 3.8-mm (0.152") deep, the typical memory card is actually smaller

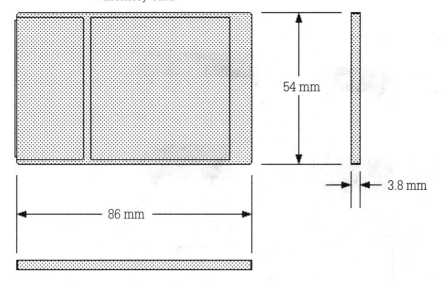

PCMCIA-compatible
memory card

54 mm

86 mm

3.8 mm

7-22
*Form factor of a typical
memory card.*

than an 8.89 cm (3.5") diskette. Memory cards make extensive use of the most sophisticated ICs and SMT techniques in order to pack all the necessary components into such an incredibly small package. Keep in mind that other card products may often be somewhat longer or higher than standard cards depending on the particular product.

A memory card is a stunningly complex assembly, but just about every memory card can be broken down into four major areas: memory ICs, support logic ICs, a power source/backup, and a connector. Figure 7-23 illustrates each of these four areas. To understand memory cards, you should understand the importance of each section.

Memory

Memory ICs are the most important elements of every solid-state memory card. The capacity and data bus width (8 or 16 bits) is determined by the choice of memory ICs. For example: eight, 256K×8 bit SRAM ICs can be configured to provide 2Mb×8 bits or 1Mb×16 bits. Various sizes of memory ICs can provide many possible card configurations. The type of memory ICs that are used determines the type of memory card that is constructed (such as SRAM, OTPROM, or flash).

The memory card illustrated in FIG. 7-23 is configured for a data bus 8-bits wide (D0 to D7). A 16-bit data bus would be D0 to D15. Memory array size determines how many address lines are needed. Twenty address lines (A0 to A19) can address 2^{20} or 1,048,576 unique memory addresses. Memory

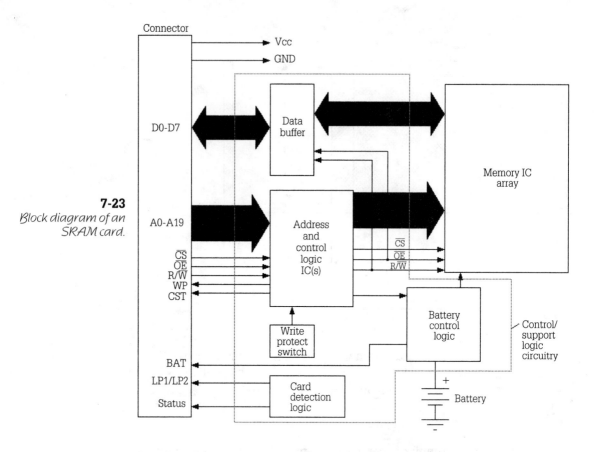

Connector

Vcc
GND

D0-D7

Data
buffer

Memory IC
array

7-23
*Block diagram of an
SRAM card.*

A0-A19

Address
and
control
logic
IC(s)

$\overline{CS}$
$\overline{OE}$
$\overline{R/W}$

$\overline{CS}$
$\overline{OE}$
R/W
WP
CST

Write
protect
switch

Battery
control
logic

Control/
support
logic
circuitry

BAT

LP1/LP2

Status

Card
detection
logic

+
Battery
−

cards use a standard interface for the same purpose as floppy or hard drives do, so there might be more address lines available to the card than it can use. For example, a 256K×8-bit memory card requires only 18 address lines (A0 to A17) to address the card's 2^{18} or 262,144 bytes. As long as the interface provides enough address lines to operate the inserted card, any additional lines from the interface are simply unused.

Support logic Memory alone is not enough to make a memory card. Multiple memory ICs must be addressed and activated as needed by the card interface. Support logic is needed to ensure that the memory card ICs are properly interfaced to your small computer's data, address, and control busses. Data travelling to and from the memory card is handled within the card by a bidirectional data buffer that does not alter data, but merely amplifies the existing data to guarantee signal integrity.

A write cycle causes data on the card controller's data bus to be read into the memory card and stored at the memory location specified on the card's address pins. A read cycle allows data at the location specified in the memory card's address pins to be sent to the card controller's data bus.

Address decoding and control logic are incredibly important aspects of a memory card's supporting logic. When there are multiple memory ICs on a card, each memory IC shares data and address lines. Decoding logic determines exactly which of the common ICs need to be activated. Control logic in the card interprets the variety of control signals coming from the motherboard's card controller IC. The desired memory IC is activated with a CHIP SELECT ($\overline{CS}$) signal. A logic 0 selects an IC while a logic 1 allows the IC to remain idle. The READ/WRITE (R/$\overline{W}$) signal defines whether data is entering (write) or leaving (read) the card. A logic 0 indicates a write operation and a logic 1 will cause a read. During a read operation, an OUTPUT ENABLE ($\overline{OE}$) signal allows the addressed data in the selected memory IC to be available at the bidirectional data buffer that directs data out of the card.

Memory cards also generate some control signal outputs that are interpreted by the memory card controller IC. A WRITE PROTECT (WP) signal is available on most volatile memory cards. WRITE PROTECT signals are generated by a small switch on the card and serves much the same purpose as the write protect notch on floppy diskettes. A logic 1 on the write protect line prevents new data from being written to the card. The card's overall condition is fed back to the memory card controller using a Card Status (CST) line.

A small circuit is added to the card for identification. When a card is inserted into a small computer, card select and status signals tell the memory card controller IC exactly which card is inserted in the system. Logic is needed to control card power. A voltage sensing/comparison circuit within the card detects when external power is available. When external power is applied (the card is plugged into a system), the card stops drawing backup power from its internal battery. If your small computer is turned off or the card is removed from its slot, the voltage detector monitors external power loss and reconnects the card's battery.

Power source

Solid-state memory cards have one main source of power, the host computer system. Ideally, a memory card should not require any power when it is removed from a system, but SRAM cards (and some flash card designs) use one or more lithium coin cells to maintain memory contents when system power is not available (see FIG. 7-24). Under normal circumstances, SRAM batteries should support a card's contents for one or two years.

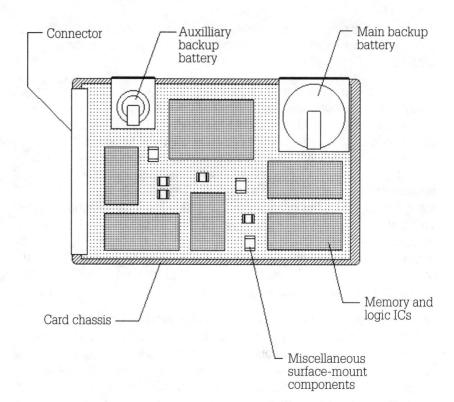

Connector

Auxilliary backup battery

Main backup battery

7-24
Internal view of a typical SRAM card.

Card chassis

Miscellaneous surface-mount components

Memory and logic ICs

Connector You might think that connectors are rather trivial. However, connectors are a critical concern in memory cards. A typical 60- or 68-pin memory card must be able to withstand many regular insertion and removal cycles over a period of many years. If even one pin in the computer or receptacle in the card should become loose or intermittent, the entire card could be made useless. Most commercial-grade memory cards are rated for 10,000 insertion/removal cycles. Some industrial-grade cards designed for harsh environments can withstand only 5,000 insertion/removal cycles. Be suspicious of connectors and sockets whenever you are troubleshooting memory card systems. Figure 7-25 shows an AMP memory card connector interface.

Variations The major memory card elements presented above might not be needed for every type of memory card. For instance, nonvolatile card, such as OTPROM cards, do not require an internal backup battery. DRAM cards cannot support a battery at all. Support logic also varies widely from card to card depending on the data bus width and memory IC arrangement. A DRAM card does not need a write protect switch. Finally, the connector used on a memory card reflects the interface for which the card is designed. You might encounter 34-pin, 60-pin, 68-pin, or 88-pin connectors.

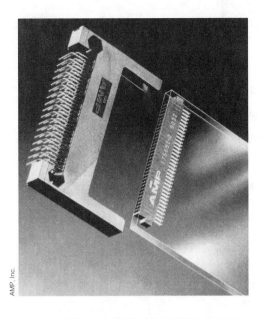

7-25
The connector interface for a typical memory card.

AMP, Inc.

While DRAM cards have direct access to your small computer's busses, most other memory cards interact with your system through a sophisticated controller IC, as illustrated in the block diagram of FIG. 7-26. The data transfer to or from a memory card begins at the microprocessor,

A card drive system

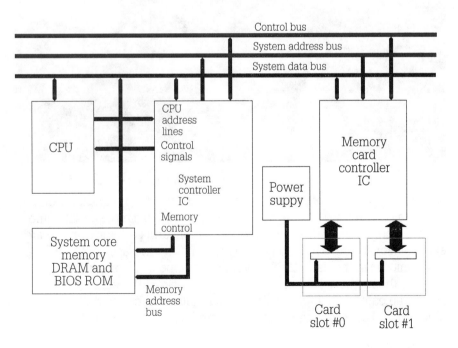

7-26
Block diagram of a complete memory card system.

which processes instructions causing the system controller to address the memory card controller. It is the system controller IC that manages the many redundant processing operations needed to operate the memory card controller IC. In some systems, the memory card controller might be incorporated into the system controller.

Memory card systems are designed to behave in your computer just like magnetic disks. Each card slot is assigned a logical drive specification such as A: or B:. When memory cards are an integral part of your small computer's original design, all of the machine code routines needed to operate the card are contained in BIOS ROM. When your card drive is an add-on device (for desktop systems), you must load one or more device drivers. Your application program accesses the device driver(s) as needed to interact with the card drive. Regardless of whether your card drive is original or after-market equipment, a memory card can be used in many different systems as long as each drive interface is compatible. Figure 2-27 shows how easy it is to transfer cards from drive to drive.

7-27
Swapping memory cards between a desktop and palmtop computer.

Fujitsu Personal Systems, Inc.

An intriguing aspect of memory cards is that the "drive" contains nothing accept a connector. The only mechanical parts are a simple metal frame to align and reinforce the card during insertion, and perhaps a small card ejector lever. There is no circuitry resident in the drive assembly—all the electronics is in the card itself. System interfacing is accomplished through the memory card controller IC on the motherboard. In many cases, the card connector and frame is mounted directly to the motherboard as well. The result is an incredibly small, simple, and shock-resistant mass-storage system. Many palmtops and pen-computers offer one or two built-in memory card slots. Notebook systems are only now beginning to incorporate memory cards.

As with magnetic drives, it is important that memory cards utilize some sort of standard interface at the card connector. A standard interface ensures that a memory card manufactured by one company works properly with a small computer made by any other company. There are four typical memory card interfaces: 34 pin, 60 pin, 68 pin, and 88 pin. This book discusses the PCMCIA (Personal Computer Memory Card Industry Association) standard 68-pin and 88-pin interfaces. The other interfaces are covered in the advanced book, *Troubleshooting and Repairing Notebook, Palmtop, and Pen-Computers: A Technician's Guide* (Windcrest #4427).

Ideally, there should be one standard interface for all types of memory cards regardless of their manufacturers. In practice, it is virtually impossible to design a single interface that can optimize the features of every memory card, but an interface can be made compatible with most cards. The PCMCIA has endorsed the 68-pin memory card interface shown in FIG. 7-28. Mask ROM, OTPROM, EEPROM, SRAM, and flash cards designed to PCMCIA standards should be compatible with the 68-pin interface.

The 68-pin interface

Looking over the interface pinout, notice that there are four signal categories: data lines, address lines, power lines, and control lines. Each signal (except for programming voltages) is fully TTL-compatible, where logic 0 levels are 0.0 to +0.8 Vdc, and logic 1 levels are +2.0 to V_{cc}. In low-voltage systems, V_{cc} might be +3.0 or +3.3 Vdc. V_{cc} is usually +5.0 Vdc in conventional systems.

The 68-pin standard was designed to support a 16-bit bus (D0 to D15). With 26 signal lines allocated for addressing (A0 to A25), the standard interface can address more than 67Mb of memory. Power signals include V_{cc}, which supplies the logic ICs on the card. V_{cc} can be either +5.0 Vdc, +3.0 Vdc, or +3.3 Vdc depending on the design of your particular system. Two programming voltage levels (V_{pp1} and V_{pp2} are used to provide secondary voltages (often +12 Vdc) for EEPROM programming (OTPROM devices are typically not programmed in a small computer). All power supplies are referenced to a common ground (GND).

There are two CARD DETECTION outputs ($\overline{CD1}$ and $\overline{CD2}$), which the memory card controller IC uses to determine whether or not a card is inserted properly. Notice that one card-detect signal is located on each side of the card. If the card is inserted unevenly, one or both card detect

34			1
68			35

1	Ground	35	Ground
2	D3	36	CD1
3	D4	37	D11
4	D5	38	D12
5	D6	39	D13
6	D7	40	D14
7	$\overline{CE1}$	41	D15
8	A10	42	$\overline{CE2}$
9	$\overline{OE}$	43	RFSH
10	A11	44	RFU
11	A9	45	RFU
12	A8	46	A17
13	A13	47	A18
14	A14	48	A19
15	$\overline{WE/PGM}$	49	A20
16	$RDY/\overline{BSY}$	50	A21
17	Vcc	51	Vcc
18	Vppi	52	Vpp1
19	A16	53	A22
20	A15	54	A23
21	A12	55	A24
22	A7	56	A25
23	A6	57	RFU
24	A5	58	Reset
25	A4	59	WAIT
26	A3	60	RFU
27	A2	61	$\overline{REG}$
28	A1	62	BVD2
29	A0	63	BVD1
30	D0	64	D8
31	D1	65	D9
32	D2	66	D10
33	WP	67	$\overline{CD2}$
34	Ground	68	Ground

7-28

Pinout diagram for a 68-pin memory card interface.

signals might be missing. A memory card controller will inhibit operation until the controller detects a properly inserted card. The 68-pin interface standard supports two independent battery output signals (BVD1 and BVD2). Two signals allow the small computer to monitor SRAM or flash cards with one or two backup batteries.

The actual status of a memory card is output with the READY/BUSY (RDY/$\overline{BSY}$) signal. A WRITE PROTECT (WP) output prevents the system from writing new data to a write-protected card. The CARD ENABLE inputs ($\overline{CE1}$ and $\overline{CE2}$), as well as an OUTPUT ENABLE ($\overline{OE}$) and REGISTER SELECTOR ($\overline{REG}$), handle most of the card's overall control. A WRITE ENABLE/PROGRAM (WE/P) input tells the card whether it should be reading (logic 1) or writing/programming (logic 0). A few of the 68 pins are left unused to allow for future expansion.

A memory card standby-mode is invoked anytime the card ENABLE lines are in a logic 1 state. This condition is true regardless of any other control inputs. During standby, a memory card is effectively cut off from the host system and the card draws only a few milliamps from the host. A card in a powered-down system (or removed from a system entirely) is automatically placed in the standby mode, drawing only a few milliamps from its internal batteries. To operate a card, one or both card select lines must be a logic 0.

To read a memory card, the WRITE ENABLE/PROGRAM (WE/P) signal must be logic 1 and the OUTPUT ENABLE (OE) must be logic 0. Data in the memory card that is stored in the address specified by A0 through A25 will appear at the card's data lines (D0 to D15). By bringing WE/P to a logic 0 and OE to a logic 1, any data applied to D0 through D15 is written to the card at the address specified on the card's address lines. Any read operation while OE is also logic 1 will disable the card's data bus. This high-impedance (or disconnected) state prevents the card from being read or written to.

The second memory card interface standard shown in FIG. 7-29 is an 88-pin configuration. The 88-pin standard is generally accepted for DRAM cards where the large number of address lines, data lines, and special

The 88-pin interface

1	Ground	23	CAS0	45	Ground	67	Ground
2	DQ0	24	CAS1	46	DQ18	68	CAS3
3	DQ1	25	Vcc	47	DQ19	69	RAS3
4	DQ2	26	RAS2	48	DQ20	70	WE
5	DQ3	27	Vcc	49	DQ21	71	PD1
6	DQ4	28	PD2	50	DQ22	72	PD3
7	DQ5	29	PD4	51	DQ23	73	Ground
8	DQ6	30	PD6	52	DQ24	74	PD5
9	Vcc	31	nc	53	DQ25	75	PD7
10	DQ7	32	nc	54	DQ26	76	PD8
11	Vcc	33	DQ17	55	nc	77	nc
12	DQ8	34	DQ9	56	Ground	78	nc
13	A0	35	Vcc	57	A1	79	DQ35
14	A2	36	DQ10	58	A3	80	DQ27
15	Vcc	37	Vcc	59	A5	81	DQ28
16	A4	38	DQ11	60	A7	82	DQ29
17	Vcc	39	DQ12	61	A9	83	DQ30
18	A6	40	DQ13	62	A11	84	DQ31
19	A8	41	DQ14	63	Ground	85	DQ32
20	A10	42	DQ15	64	A13	86	DQ33
21	A12	43	DQ16	65	RAS1	87	DQ34
22	RAS0	44	Ground	66	CAS2	88	Ground

7-29
Pinout diagram for an 88-pin memory card interface.

signals quickly swamp the capacity of 68-pin connectors. As with 68-pin memory cards, 88-pin interface signals can be separated into four categories: address lines, data lines, control lines, and power lines.

By multiplexing 14 unique Address lines (A0 to A13), the interface can access a great deal of memory. Most DRAM cards today offer from 4 to 16Mb, but the interface is designed to handle much more. There are 36 data lines (D0 to D35), but the cards can be configured to work with 8-bit, 16-bit, 32-bit, or 36-bit data bus widths.

DRAM card power requirements are simple. Only V_{cc} and ground V_{ss} (ground) lines are used. As you look over the interface pinout, notice that there are multiple V_{cc} and V_{ss} pins interspersed throughout the configuration—this is perfectly normal. V_{cc} levels for conventional DRAM cards is +5.0 Vdc, but many of the newer small computers using low-voltage components may offer a V_{cc} of 3.3 Vdc or +3.0 Vdc. Be careful not to use a low-voltage DRAM card in a conventional voltage (+5.0 Vdc) small computer, and vice versa. Mixing low-voltage and regular voltage components might result in damage to the card, the computer, or both.

All dynamic RAM ICs must be continuously refreshed to maintain the integrity of their contents. If DRAMs are not refreshed, their contents are almost immediately lost. Refreshing is accomplished by firing COLUMN ADDRESS STROBES ($\overline{CAS0}$ to $\overline{CAS3}$) and ROW ADDRESS STROBES ($\overline{RAS0}$ to $\overline{RAS3}$ at desired addresses. Circuitry needed to perform the refresh operations is built into the host system. The only remaining control line is the WRITE ENABLE ($\overline{W}$ or $\overline{WE}$) signal. A logic 1 on the $\overline{W}$ line reads data from the DRAM card, while a logic 0 on the $\overline{W}$ line writes data to the DRAM card. A number of unused interface pins are reserved for future expansion.

Troubleshooting memory card systems

In spite of their small size, memory cards are remarkably complex devices. Mass-storage cards are even more sophisticated. As a result, memory cards are some of the densest and most intricate electronic assemblies that you may encounter. Such demanding circuitry is very unforgiving in the hands of novice troubleshooters, so this book considers memory cards as component parts.

Symptom 1: The SRAM or flash card looses its memory when powered down or removed from the system.   Since flash cards make use of advanced EEPROMs you might wonder why batteries are incorporated. Some flash cards use a small amount of SRAM to speed the transfer of data to or from the card. Batteries are needed to backup the RAM only. If your memory card does not appear to hold its memory, start your investigation by removing the memory card and testing its batteries. Make sure the card's batteries are inserted properly. Use your multimeter to check the battery voltage(s). Replace any memory card batteries that appear marginal or low. You should expect a 2- to 5-year life from your memory card backup batteries. All battery contacts should be clean and bright, and contacts should make firm connections with the battery terminals.

Try a good, working memory card in your system. You can verify a new or good memory card on another computer with a compatible card slot. If another card works properly, your original memory card is probably defective and should be replaced. It is not recommended for you to open or attempt to troubleshoot a memory card without comprehensive experience in SMT device repair and high-quality, surface-mount desoldering equipment.

Symptom 2: You are unable to access the card for reading. You might not be able to write to the card either. Begin troubleshooting by checking memory card compatibility. If a memory card is not compatible with the interface used by your small computer, the interface may not access the card. For example, a PCMCIA-compatible 68-pin card will probably not work in a non-PCMCIA 68-pin card slot, and vice versa. Try a good compatible card in the suspect card slot.

If you are having difficulty writing to an SRAM or flash card, take a moment and inspect the card's write protect switch. A switch left in the protected position prevents new information from being written to the card. Move the switch to the unprotected position and try the memory card again.

The memory card might be inserted incorrectly. Two card-detect signals are needed from the card to ensure proper insertion. If the card is not inserted properly, the host system will inhibit all card activities. Remove the card and reinsert it completely. Make sure the card is straight, even, and fully inserted. Try the memory card again.

If trouble remains, remove the card and inspect the connector on the card and inside the computer. Check for any contacts that might be loose, bent, or broken. It should not be necessary to disassemble the computer in order to inspect its connector. A clear view with a small flashlight will tell you all you need to know. Connections in the computer that are damaged or extremely worn should be replaced. When a memory card connector is worn or damaged, the memory card should be replaced.

If your results are still inconclusive, try a good memory card in the system. Keep in mind that the new card must be fully compatible with the original one. Make sure that there are no valuable or irreplaceable files on the good card before you try it in a suspect system. If a good card works properly, then the old memory card is probably damaged and should be replaced.

If a good card also does not work, the original card is probably working properly. Your final step is to disassemble your small computer and replace the memory card controller IC on the motherboard. A defective controller can prevent all data and control signals from reaching the card. If you do not have the tools or inclination to tackle surface-mount work, you may wish to replace the entire motherboard.

8 Keyboards, trackballs, & pen systems

In simplest terms, *input* is information obtained from the outside world. Your small computer has a voracious need for input (FIG. 8-1). Not only does input allow your computer to react to changes in its environment, but input also allows you to exercise control and work interactively with a computer. This chapter deals with direct input devices—mechanisms that let you control the computer. Topics covered include the construction, operation, and repair of three direct input devices: keyboards, trackballs, and pen digitizers.

Keyboards

The keyboard is the most popular input device. By manipulating a matrix of individual electrical switches, commands and instructions are entered into the computer one character at a time. However, keyboards are not without their drawbacks. While today's keyboard switches are not mechanically complex, there are a number of important moving parts. When you multiply this number of moving parts times the 80 to 100-plus keys on a typical keyboard, you find a substantial number of moving parts. A jam or failure in any one of these parts results in a keyboard problem. Most keyboard failures are not catastrophic, but they are certainly inconvenient. This part of the chapter gives you the information needed to understand and repair small computer keyboards.

8-1
A Compaq notebook computer fitted with a Suncom Technologies ICONtroller input device.

Suncom Technologies

Construction
To understand a keyboard, you must know about the kinds of switches used. There are two types of switches used: mechanical switches and membrane switches. Both switches are used extensively throughout the computer industry, but any single keyboard will use only one type of switch.

A mechanical key switch is shown in FIG. 8-2. Two tempered bronze contacts are separated by a plastic actuator bar, which is pushed up by a

8-2
Diagram of a mechanical key switch.

Keycap

Actuator

Mechanical contacts

Spring

Schematic symbol

spring in the switch base. When the keycap is depressed, the actuator bar slides down, compressing the spring and allowing the gold-plated contacts to touch. Since gold is a soft metal and an excellent conductor, a good, low-resistance electrical contact is developed. When the keycap is released, the compressed spring expands and drives the plastic actuator bar between the contacts once again. The entire stroke of travel on a mechanical switch is little more than 3.56 mm (0.140"), but an electrical contact (a make condition) can be established in as little as 1.78 mm (0.070"). Mechanical key switches are rugged, many rated for 100 million cycles or more.

A diagram of a *membrane* key switch is shown in FIG. 8-3. A plastic actuator rests on top of a soft rubber boot, the inside of which is coated with a conductive silver-carbon compound. Beneath the rubber boot are two open PC board contacts. When the keycap is depressed, the plastic actuator collapses the rubber boot, forcing the conductive material across both PC board contacts to make the contact. When the keycap is released, the compressed rubber boot breaks its contact on the PC board and returns to its original shape. The full travel stroke of a membrane key switch is about 3.56 mm (0.140"), which is roughly the same as a mechanical switch. An electrical contact is established in about 2.29 mm (0.090"). Membrane switches are not as durable as mechanical switches. Most switches are rated for 20 million cycles or less.

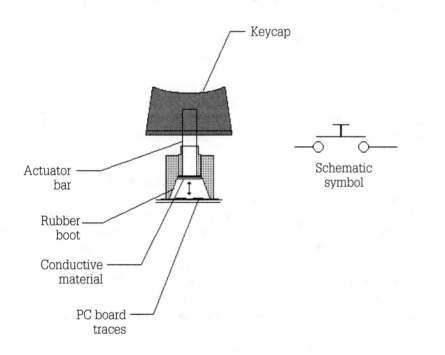

Keycap

Actuator bar

Rubber boot

Conductive material

PC board traces

Schematic symbol

8-3
Diagram of a membrane key switch.

Regardless of what key type is used, the finished assembly appears much like the Fujitsu keyboard shown in FIG. 8-4. The keyboard contains a matrix of keys, and possibly a number of keyboard control ICs on its small PC board. There are one or more connectors on the PC board to connect the keyboard assembly to the motherboard. Keyboard assemblies tend to be very modular and self-contained. It is usually a simple matter to access and repair or replace a small-computer keyboard.

8-4
A notebook computer keyboard assembly.

You can see how a keyboard assembly is mounted into a small computer with the exploded diagram in FIG. 8-5. The keyboard PC board assembly (marked E7-8) is screwed onto an insulated base or chassis. Cables connecting the keyboard and motherboard are routed through the chassis. The finished keyboard (within the dotted line marked E-7) is secured into the computer's bottom housing (not shown) and covered by an upper housing (marked K37). Remember that the diagram of FIG. 8-5 represents only one possible type of assembly. Note the large number of screws holding the keyboard PC board to its chassis. Each of these screws have to be removed before the keyboard PC board itself can be serviced.

The next step in understanding a keyboard is to learn about the *key matrix*. Keys are not interpreted individually; that is, each switch is not wired directly to the motherboard. Instead, keys are arranged in a matrix of rows and columns, shown in FIG. 8-6. When a key is pressed, a unique row (top to bottom) and column (left to right) signal is generated to represent the corresponding key. The great advantage of a matrix approach is that a huge array of keys can be identified using only a few row and column signals. Wiring from keyboard to motherboard is vastly simplified. An 84-key keyboard can be identified using only 12 column signals and 8 row signals. A complete keyboard matrix diagram for a Tandy notebook computer is shown in FIG. 8-7.

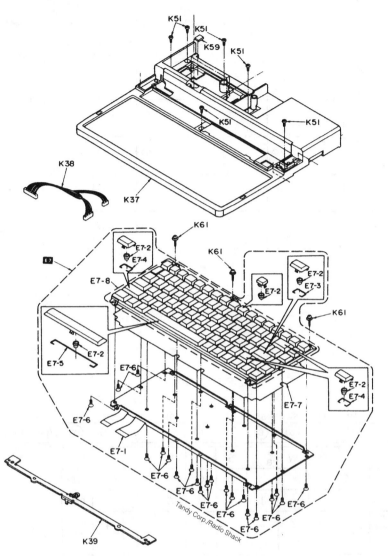

K5I
K5I
K59
K5I
K5I
K5I
K5I

K38

K37

K6I
E7-2
E7-4
E7-8
E7
E7-2
E7-2
K6I
E7-2
E7-3
E7-5
E7-2
E7-6
K6I
E7-2
E7-4
E7-6
E7-7
E7-I
E7-6
E7-6
E7-6
E7-6
E7-6
E7-6
E7-6
E7-6
E7-6

Tandy Corp./Radio Shack

K39

8-5
Exploded diagram of a notebook keyboard assembly.

There is more to a keyboard system than just a matrix of key switches. Row and column signals must be translated into binary character codes that your system controller and CPU can work with. Most keyboards are used in conjunction with a keyboard controller IC, illustrated in the block diagram of FIG. 8-8.

A keyboard controller is an ASIC that converts the TTL-level row and column signals generated from a key matrix into an 8-bit scan code, which is read serially by the system controller. Since the serial transfer of TTL keyboard data takes place synchronously—in sync with the CPU

A keyboard system

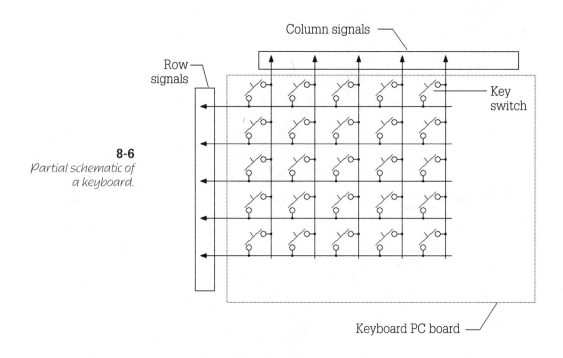

8-6
Partial schematic of a keyboard.

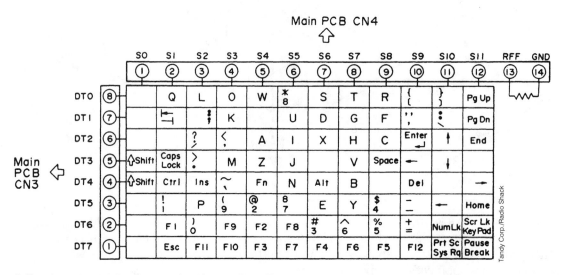

8-7   *Complete keyboard matrix diagram for a Tandy notebook computer.*

clock—a keyboard clock signal is also returned with keyboard data bits. The keyboard controller is usually located on the motherboard for most laptop and notebook systems. A keyboard controller IC is also responsible for handling the keyboard status LEDs (such as Shift Lock, Caps Lock,

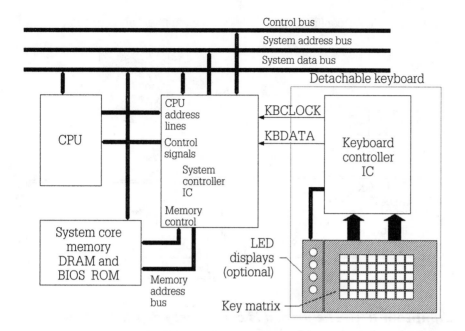

and Num Lock). LEDs might be on the keyboard PC board or on another small PC board elsewhere in the computer.

Notice that the signal path between keyboard and system controllers is marked "Keyboard Interface." For laptops, pentops, and notebooks with detachable keyboards, the keyboard controller IC is incorporated into the keyboard PC board. This means that the cable connecting your external keyboard and computer needs only four wires: the keyboard data, the keyboard clock, +5 Vdc (+3.0 or +3.3 Vdc for low-voltage systems), and ground. For systems with fully-integrated keyboards, all signals travel on the motherboard, so no external cabling is required. Figure 8-9 illustrates the two major connector pinout diagrams for external keyboards.

Keyboards are not terribly difficult to troubleshoot, despite their complicated appearance. This ease is primarily due to the keyboard's modularity—if all else fails, just replace the keyboard. The keyboard's great weakness, however, is its vulnerability to spills, dust, and any other foreign matter that finds its way between the keycaps. These things can easily ruin a keyboard. The keyboard's PC board is also a likely candidate to be damaged by sharp blows or physical abuse. The following procedures address many of the most common keyboard problems. You should have a logic probe and multimeter on hand to use these procedures.

Troubleshooting a keyboard

IBM PC/XT/AT configuration

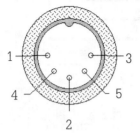

6 pin mini DIN connector

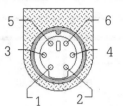

8-9
Connector pinouts for external keyboards.

1	KBCLOCK
2	KBDATA
3	NC
4	Ground
5	+5 Vdc (or +3.0 or +3.3 Vdc)

1	KBDATA
2	NC
3	Ground
4	+5 Vdc (or +3.0 or +3.3 Vdc)
5	KBCLOCK
6	NC

Symptom 1: *The keyboard is completely dead. No keys appear to function at all. All other computer operations are normal.* This symptom assumes that your small computer initializes and boots to its DOS prompt or other operating system as expected, but the keyboard does not respond to use. Keyboard status LEDs might or might not be working properly. Begin your repair by removing power and disassembling the computer to expose the keyboard assembly. Carefully inspect any connector(s) from the keyboard to the motherboard. A loose connector or faulty wiring can easily disable the entire keyboard. Be especially careful if you encounter a keyboard problem right after performing a repair that required you to remove or disconnect the keyboard.

Check to ensure that all connectors are aligned properly and fully inserted into their receptacles. Replace any broken connectors and replace any defective wiring. If you are using a detachable or external keyboard, try a different keyboard in its place. Cables can often fail in external keyboards when pulled and stretched over long time periods. If an alternate keyboard works, check the cable integrity of the original keyboard.

Use your logic probe to test the KBDATA signal between the keyboard controller IC and the system controller. With no keyboard activity, the KBDATA line should read logic 0. When you press a key, you should see a brief pulse indication on the probe as each code bit moves into the system controller. If this pulse burst is too fast to see on your logic probe, try holding the key down for a moment to send a string of characters. You can also use an oscilloscope to track KBDATA. The KBDATA signal is easy to find for detachable or external keyboards (refer to the pinouts in FIG. 8-9). However, you will probably need a schematic to find KBDATA on systems using an integral (built-in) keyboard.

If the KBDATA signal is present when a key is pressed, then the keyboard matrix and keyboard controller IC are probably working. This condition indicates that the system controller IC is partially defective. Try replacing the system controller. A missing KBDATA signal suggests that the keyboard controller IC is defective. Try replacing the keyboard controller. For systems with integral keyboards, the keyboard controller IC and system controller IC both reside on the motherboard. If you do not have the tools or inclination to tackle surface-mount soldering work, replace the entire motherboard. With a detachable or external keyboard, replace the keyboard assembly because the keyboard controller is built into the external keyboard.

Symptom 2: *The keyboard is acting erratically. One or more keys appear to work intermittently, if at all.* The computer operates normally and most keys work just fine, but there seems to be one (or several) keys that do not respond when pressed. Extra force or repeated strikes might be needed to operate the key. This problem can be a minor nuisance or a major headache. The chances are that your key contacts are dirty. Sooner or later, dust and debris works into all key switches. Electrical contacts eventually become coated and fail to make contact reliably. In many cases, you need only vacuum the keyboard and clean the suspect contacts with a good-quality electronic contact cleaner.

Begin by removing all power and disassembling the computer's outer housing to expose the keyboard assembly. Use a static-safe, fine-tipped vacuum to remove any accumulations of dust or debris found on the keyboard PC board. You might wish to vacuum your keyboard regularly as preventive maintenance. Once the keyboard is clean, gently remove the plastic keycap from the offending key(s). The use of a keycap removal tool is highly recommended, but you might also use a modified set of blunt-ended tweezers with their flat ends (just the tips) twisted inward. Grasp the keycap and pull up evenly. You can expect the cap to slide off with little resistance. Do not rip the keycap off because you stand a good chance of marring the cap and causing permanent key switch damage.

Use a can of good-quality, electronics-grade contact cleaner and spray a little bit of cleaner into the switch assembly. When spraying, attach the long narrow tube to the spray tube, as this directs cleaner into the switch.

Work the switch in and out to distribute the cleaner. Repeat once or twice to clean the switch thoroughly. Allow residual cleaner to dry thoroughly before reassembling the computer. Never use harsh cleaners or solvents. Industrial-strength chemicals can easily ruin plastic components and housings. Reapply power and retest the system. If the suspect key(s) respond normally again, install the removed keycaps and return the system to service. As a preventive measure, you might wish to open the computer and clean every key.

Membrane keys must be cleaned somewhat differently from mechanical keys. It is necessary for you to remove the rubber or plastic boot to clean the PC board contacts. Depending on the particular membrane switch, this might not be an easy task. If you are able to see the contact boot, use a pick or tweezers to gently lift the boot. Spray a bit of cleaner under the boot and work the key to distribute the cleaner. If the boot is confined within the individual key, you might have to remove the suspect key before applying the cleaner.

If cleaning does not work, disassemble the keyboard and replace the defective key switch(es). Many key switch designs still utilize through-hole technology, but you should be very careful when desoldering and resoldering. Extra care helps prevent accidental damage to the PC keyboard. You also have the option of replacing the entire keyboard assembly.

Inspect your keyboard PC board carefully to be sure that there are no board cracks or trace fractures that might cause intermittent behavior. You might attempt to repair a PC board problem as outlined in chapter 4, or replace the damaged keyboard entirely. Keep in mind that the components on a damaged keyboard PC board are still usually good. You may save the old PC board and scavenge the key switches or cable assemblies for future repairs.

Symptom 3: The keyboard is acting erratically. One or more keys might be stuck or repeating.   Suspect a shorted or jammed key. Short circuits can be caused by conductive foreign objects (e.g., staples and paper clips) falling into the keyboard and landing across PC board contacts. Remove all power and disassemble the outer housing to expose the keyboard assembly. If you see or hear a foreign object, be careful not to let that object fall into the motherboard or floppy drive where significant damage can result. Once the keyboard is exposed, shake out the foreign object or remove it with a pair of long needlenose pliers or sharp tweezers.

Accumulations of dirt can work into the key actuator shaft and restrict its movement. Apply good-quality, electronics-grade cleaners to the key, and work the key in and out to distribute cleaner evenly. If the key returns to normal, reassemble the computer and return it to service. Keys that remain jammed should be replaced. You might choose to simply replace the entire keyboard assembly. If you elect to replace the keyboard assembly, retain the old assembly for parts.

The biggest complaint about keyboards is that they are a clumsy, time-consuming means of data entry (unless you're a proficient typist). For the everyday computer user who is unfamiliar with normal keyboard layouts, the "hunt-and-peck" process is the only alternative. With the rise of powerful, multilayer menu-driven programs and graphic user interfaces (GUI), a simple and convenient *pointing device* became necessary. A pointing device allows you to navigate through a program's operation by moving a screen cursor to (and selecting) desired program modes or functions without touching the keyboard. The *mouse* has been (and still is) the premier pointing device for desktop systems. Unfortunately, a mouse needs a certain amount of desk space in order to work properly. Trackballs, such as the ones shown in FIG.8-10 and FIG. 8-11, have become popular because they require no additional desk space—an important consideration for mobile-computer users. We focus on trackballs, but you can apply the information to a mouse or any other roller-based pointing devices.

Trackballs

Microsoft Corp.

8-10
A Microsoft Ball Point trackball.

8-11
*A Logitech Trackman
Portable trackball.*

Logitech, Inc.

Construction A trackball uses a remarkably straightforward assembly, as illustrated in
FIG. 8-12. The trackball is an electromechanical device in which a hard
rubber ball rests on a cross of two plastic tracks (thus the term *trackball*).
The ball contacts both metal rollers. Notice how one roller is oriented in
the up-down direction, while the other roller is positioned in the left-right
direction. Each roller is attached to a small optical disk that passes within
an optical sensor (or optoisolator).

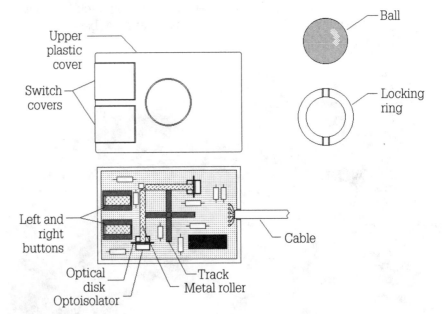

8-12
Disassembled trackball.

The trackball also offers two or three switches designed to emulate the left or right mouse buttons. Buttons allow you to make a selection when the trackball cursor is positioned over something of interest. The trackball's electronics and rollers are assembled onto a single PC board mounted on the lower plastic housing. A thin cable connects the PC board to your computer. An upper plastic housing covers the trackball circuitry. The ball drops into its track through a hole in the upper housing, and is secured in place with a plastic locking ring. Keep in mind that some rubber balls are not removable without removing the upper housing.

When your fingers move the rubber ball, it causes both metal rollers to turn. Just how much each roller turns depends on the angle at which the ball is moved. For example, a ball moved directly up turns only the up/down roller, while a ball moved left turns only the left/right roller. At other angles, both rollers turn to some extent. As rollers turn, the optical disk attached to each roller turns within its corresponding optoisolator. As the disk turns, it creates pulses at the sensor's output. The number of pulses correspond to the amount of ball movement. Signals corresponding to switch conditions and roller pulses are carried on the cable to the computer's serial (or other mouse-compatible) port.

During initialization, the computer loads a short piece of software (called a device driver) designed to read the proper port, interpret signals generated by the trackball, and make switch and roller information available to the programs. Any mouse-compatible program is then capable of accessing trackball data and responding similar to a mouse.

A trackball system

Unlike most other computer devices, the trackball assembly itself constitutes the majority of a trackball system as there are no dedicated controller ICs except for a communication controller IC that works with the serial (or parallel) port. Figure 8-13 is a simple block diagram for a typical trackball system.

The trackball plugs directly into the computer's serial port, but some computers provide a small, dedicated mouse/trackball port that uses a PS/2 connector. Signals generated by ball movement and switch conditions are converted into standard TTL-level logic signals by the serial line receiver IC. A communication controller receives each pulse and accumulates the total number of horizontal (X) and vertical (Y) pulses. The trackball device driver program reads the X and Y data and updates the position of the trackball cursor. The device driver also controls the shape of the cursor.

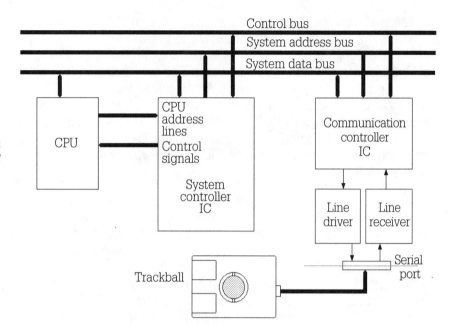

8-13
Block diagram of a typical trackball system.

Control bus

System address bus

System data bus

CPU

CPU address lines

Control signals

System controller IC

Communication controller IC

Line driver

Line receiver

Serial port

Trackball

Troubleshooting a trackball

The weakest link in a trackball system is the peripheral trackball assembly itself. Few peripheral devices are subjected to the wear and tear and abuse that trackballs or mice receive. Trackballs are dropped, yanked, and moved constantly from place to place. Damage to the trackball's PC board or connecting cable is extremely common. Accumulations of dust and debris can easily work into the trackball and create havoc with the rubber ball, tracks, and rollers. This part of the chapter guides you through some simple trackball troubleshooting techniques.

Symptom 1: The trackball cursor appears, but it only moves erratically as the ball moves (if at all). This symptom might occur in either the horizontal or vertical axis, and suggests that there is an intermittent condition somewhere within the trackball assembly. You should not have to disassemble your computer during this procedure. Start your investigation by removing the computer's power. Check the trackball's cable connector at the computer. Make sure the connector is tight and inserted properly. If you are in the habit of continuously plugging and unplugging the trackball, excessive wear can develop in the connectors over time.

A more likely problem is that the trackball's rollers are not turning. In most cases, roller stall is due to a dirty or damaged ball, or an accumulation of dirt blocking one or both optical sensors. Clean the ball and blow out any dust or debris that might have settled into the trackball housing. Many trackballs allow you to remove the ball simply by removing a plastic retainer ring on the upper housing. Wash the ball in a good surfactant (such as ammonia), rinse thoroughly in clean water, and pat dry with a clean, lint-free cloth. Never use harsh solvents or chemicals to clean the ball.

Use a can of electronics-grade compressed air to blow out dust from the trackball assembly. You can obtain cans of compressed air from retail electronics stores. For the purpose of dusting, the air need not be photographic-grade. Be sure to clean within the optical sensors. Check each roller with your finger to make sure the rollers turn freely. If you notice any accumulation of gunk on either roller, remove the gunk completely with a cotton swab dipped in clean isopropyl or ethyl alcohol, or an electronics-grade contact cleaner. As a general rule, always check the owner's manual for your trackball to be sure that there are no warnings or cautions to observe during cleaning.

If cleaning does not correct an intermittent condition, remove the trackball's upper housing to expose the PC board, and use your multimeter to check continuity across each wire in the trackball cable. Since you probably will not know which connector pins correspond to which wires at the trackball PC board, place one meter probe on a trackball wire and "ring-out" each connector pin until you find continuity. Make a wiring chart as you go. Each time you find a wire path, wiggle the cable to stimulate any possible intermittent wiring. Repair any intermittent wiring if possible. If you cannot find continuity or repair faulty wiring, simply replace the trackball.

Symptom 2: One or both trackball keys function erratically (if at all).   Trackball switches are prone to problems from dust accumulation and general contact corrosion. Power down your computer and disconnect the trackball. Remove the ball and upper housing to expose the PC board and switches and spray a small amount of electronics-grade contact cleaner into each switch, working each switch to circulate the cleaner.

If cleaning does not improve intermittent switch contacts, you might wish to check continuity across the trackball cable. With the ball and trackball cover removed, use your multimeter to check continuity across each wire in the trackball cable. Since you probably do not know which connector pins correspond to which wires at the trackball, place one meter lead on a trackball wire and "ring-out" each connector pin until you find continuity. Once found, wiggle the cable to stimulate any possible intermittent wiring. Repair intermittent wiring, if you can, or replace the trackball.

Pen digitizers The most remarkable difference between a pen-based computer and other small computers is the input method. Where laptop, notebook, and palmtop computers utilize keyboards as their primary input device, pen computers use a hand-held stylus to write against a sensitive surface. Many pen computers (especially the larger, more powerful models) do offer support for an external keyboard, but the pen is intended to supply the primary input. A typical pen computer is shown in FIG. 8-14.

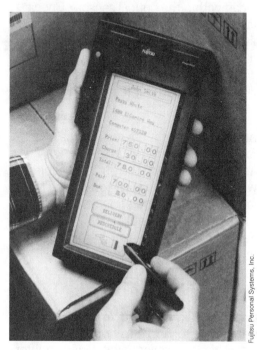

8-14
A Fujitsu pen computer.

Differences go beyond the hardware. The operating system (OS) used with pen computers provides software routines that allow applications software to interact with the pen and display, and to interpret the various pen gestures available for selecting or modifying desired items on the display. The two popular operating systems in use today are Windows for Pen Computing, by Microsoft, and PenPoint, by GO Corporation.

The key to any pen computer is the pen system itself, the *digitizer*, which converts the analog position of a pen on the display into a set of horizontal (X) and vertical (Y) coordinates. The operating system interprets those coordinates and activates pixels on the display that echo the pen's position (called the *ink*). To interpret cursive (handwritten) characters, or gestures drawn with a stylus, the operating system compares the size, direction, and sequence of each stroke to information in a database. When a match occurs, the computer responds accordingly. For instance, the small computer might interpret a crossout pen motion as a delete command, or as an upper- or lowercase "X."

Now I'll describe the technology used in today's pen digitizers, and present a series of troubleshooting procedures for three major digitizer technologies: resistive, capacitive, and electromagnetic.

Resistive digitizers are the simplest and least expensive digitizer. They are applied in most low-end pen-computer systems. You might encounter two varieties of resistive digitizer—single-layer digitizers and two-layer digitizers. The diagram for a single-layer resistive digitizer is shown in FIG. 8-15. A layer of conductive transparent film is applied over a protective glass cover. The film and glass are mounted in position over an LCD module. Notice how the film's four corners are attached to voltage sources switched by the overlay controller IC. In the idle state, all four corners of the film are held at +5 Vdc (low-voltage systems might use +3.0 or +3.3 Vdc).

Resistive digitizers

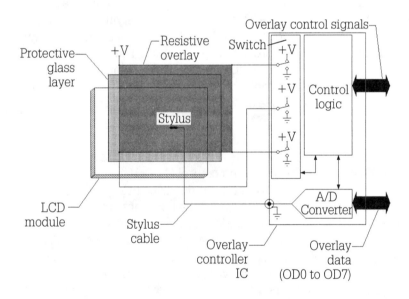

8-15
Diagram of a single-layer resistive digitizer.

X and Y coordinates are read in sequence. The overlay controller IC sets up to measure the Y coordinate by switching controls B and C to the ground position. This configuration keeps the top two corners of the conductive overlay at +V, and places the two lower corners at ground. Since the overlay film has a known resistance (per square area), voltage gradients are set up from top to bottom, as shown in FIG. 8-16. When a

(0,4096)   (4096,4096)

+5V   +5V

Y   Stylus

GND   GND

8-16

Operation of a single-layer resistive overlay.

(0,0)   (4096,0)

A/D converter   Y stylus position data

Overlay controller IC

Measuring the vertical (Y) coordinate

(0,4096)   (4096,4096)

+5V   Stylus   GND

X

+5V   GND

(0,0)   (4096,0)

A/D converter   X stylus position data

Overlay controller IC

Measuring the horizontal (X) coordinate

stylus is applied against the conductive overlay, the stylus cable carries a voltage to an analog-to-digital (A/D) converter. As the stylus nears the overlay top, its terminal voltage nears +V. As the stylus nears the overlay bottom, its terminal voltage approaches 0 V (ground). The A/D converter translates the analog stylus voltage into an 8-, 12-, or 16-bit data word. An 8-bit A/D converter allows the overlay to resolve 256 distinct positions in the vertical (Y) direction, while a 12-bit A/D converter lets the overlay resolve 4096 Y-locations.

Once the Y coordinate is generated, the overlay controller sets up to measure the X coordinate by switching control C to +V and switching controls A and B to ground. This configuration raises the two left corners of the conductive overlay to +V, and places the two right corners at 0 V. Voltage gradients develop from left to right as shown in FIG. 8-16. Assuming the stylus has not been moved since the Y coordinate was just taken, its output voltage now represents the X location. As the stylus nears the left of the overlay, its output voltage to the A/D converter approaches +V. As the stylus nears the right side of the overlay, its voltage nears 0 V.

Two-layer resistive digitizers are just a bit more involved, as illustrated in FIG. 8-17. The upper conductive layer and controller IC are virtually identical to the components already shown, but the transparent conductive film is laminated to a substrate of clear, flexible polyester. The

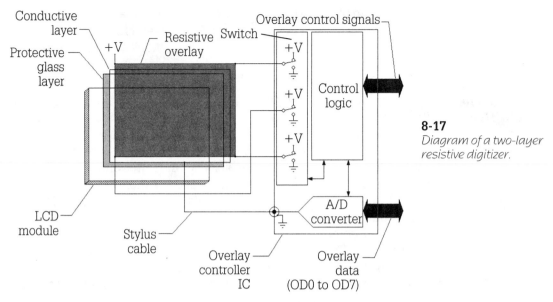

8-17
Diagram of a two-layer resistive digitizer.

Labels in figure:
Conductive layer
Protective glass layer
Resistive overlay
Overlay control signals
Switch
+V
Control logic
+V
+V
LCD module
Stylus cable
Overlay controller IC
Overlay data (OD0 to OD7)
A/D converter

lower conductive layer is highly conductive; that is, virtually zero resistance. The lower layer is bonded to the protective glass. Upper and lower conductive layers are separated by a series of carefully placed flexible spacers.

When a stylus pushes the two layers into contact, it is the lower conductive layer, not the stylus, that conducts the analog position voltage to the A/D converter. Since no cabled stylus is needed, almost any pointing device (including your finger), will work. The basic method of determining X and Y coordinates practically the same for two-layer digitizers as for single-layer digitizers.

Resistive digitizers are not without drawbacks. First, the glass and conductive film(s) placed over the LCD take away from the display's visibility. A single layer can reduce optical transmission by 15%. Two layers can reduce a display's optical transmission by 30% or more. Such substantial reductions in visibility can make LCDs unacceptably dark. Additional backlighting can be used to counter the optical reduction, but only at the cost of shorter battery life or heavier systems.

Also, resistive digitizers only measure position, not contact pressure. Intuitive pen-based systems ideally should leave darker ink when the stylus is pushed hard and should leave lighter ink when a light touch is used. Since a resistive digitizer simply makes contact or doesn't, there is little interest in resistive digitizers for pencentric (character-recognition-oriented) pen systems. Finally, resistive material tends to drift with temperature, humidity, and wear, causing inaccuracies in the digitizer's output.

Capacitive digitizers

A capacitive (electrostatic) digitizer uses a single protective layer of glass with a layer of conductive film bonded underneath, as shown in FIG. 8-18. The digitizer controller IC generates a low-power, high-frequency signal that is sent to the stylus tip. As the stylus nears the glass, the conductive layer bonded underneath the glass picks up this signal and generates a voltage at that point. This overlay voltage is proportional to stylus proximity. The closer the stylus is to the glass, the larger the signal will be on the conductive layer, and vice versa. By comparing signal amplitudes from top to bottom and left to right, the digitizer controller IC extrapolates the stylus' X and Y coordinates as well as its proximity to the glass. Since the pattern of capacitive coupling changes as stylus orientation changes, the digitizer controller IC also detects the stylus tilt and accents the ink feedback to show that tilt.

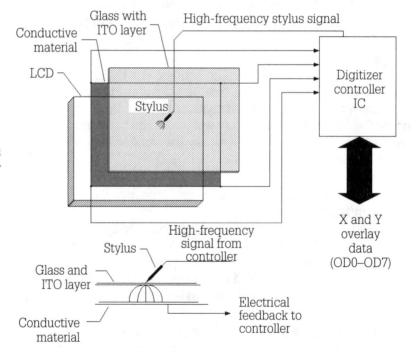

8-18
Diagram of a capacitive (electrostatic) digitizer.

Capacitive digitizers are an improvement over resistive digitizers because the capacitive approach allows the computer to sense pen proximity as well as X and Y position. The front glass used in capacitive digitizers makes the overlay immune to wear. On the down side, the overlay must be positioned in front of the LCD, which reduces the display's visible output by up to 15%. The stylus must be cabled to the system by a wire.

An electromagnetic (RF) digitizer is generally considered to be the top-of-the-line digitizer for pen computers. A thin glass sheet is placed over the top of a standard LCD and backlight assembly as shown in FIG. 8-19. The glass provides a wear-resistant writing surface for a stylus. An RF stylus is designed to produce a very low-power, high-frequency RF signal. The transmitter circuit might be entirely self-contained in a free stylus, or contained in the computer and connected to the stylus by a cable (depending on the designer's particular preference).

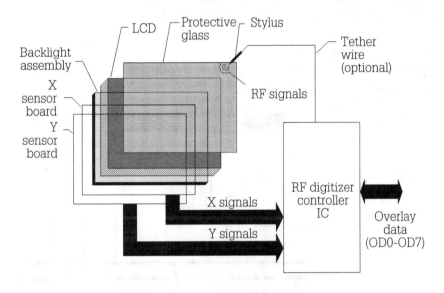

8-19
Diagram of an electromagnetic (RF) digitizer.

The key to an RF digitizer is the sensor PC board. A sensor board is a multilayer PC board providing two closely-spaced but separate layers. One layer provides sensing coils for the X orientation and another layer places sensing coils in the Y orientation. Each coil is wired into a controller circuit that rapidly scans through each coil to measure stylus signal levels. The controller circuit measures the RF level on each X and Y coil and extracts the stylus position accordingly. Stylus position is then converted into digital data and made available to the computer. Due to the presence of RF, the motherboard must be well-shielded to prevent circuit interference.

RF digitizers are appealing because they can use an untethered stylus, they do not reduce the LCD's optical output, are immune to wear, and can sense stylus proximity. Unfortunately, RF sensing and control circuitry is rather expensive to use, and careful EMI shielding is needed to prevent RF interference from upsetting the motherboard's operation.

Now that you have a basic understanding of the major pen digitizer techniques, you should see how the digitizer fits into the overall computer system.

Pen systems   Figure 8-20 shows a block diagram of how a digitizer is interfaced to a computer's main busses (address, data, and control). The figure is generic, so it generally holds true for any of the three pen technologies. A pen system is basically composed of three major parts: the overlay assembly, an overlay controller IC, and a bus interface ASIC. The entire system can be implemented with an overlay and two ICs.

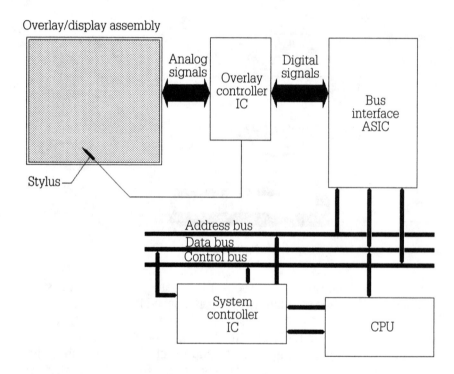

8-20
Block diagram of a pen system.

You have already been introduced to the resistive, capacitive, and electromagnetic overlay assemblies, so we will not repeat them here. The entire purpose of an overlay (regardless of its technology) is to supply an analog voltage that corresponds to the X and Y coordinates of a stylus. As the stylus moves, the X and Y analog voltages change in real time.

However, your small computer is unable to work with analog voltages: analog voltages must be converted into digital voltages for any processing to be performed. An overlay controller IC serves two major purposes. First, it switches the overlay assembly between X and Y measurement modes. Second, the overlay controller uses a built-in A/D converter to translate measured analog signals into digital data words. Data words can be 8 bits long, but are usually 12 or 16 bits.

Even though the overlay controller IC performs analog to digital conversion, its digital output is not suitable for the computer's data bus. A custom gate array is used to interface the overlay controller to the system data bus. The bus interface ASIC acts as an addressable bidirectional buffer. Commands can be sent from the bus to the bus interface, to be held until the overlay controller is ready to read them. Similarly, the overlay controller can write coordinate data to the bus interface. Data remains in the interface until the CPU is ready to access it. This process of buffering is very important in computer systems. In actual practice, the bus interface ASIC usually handles other operations in addition to the overlay controller (such as an interface for solid-state memory cards).

The biggest advantage to pen systems is modularity (FIG. 8-21). There are really only four components in a digitizer: the overlay, the stylus, the overlay controller, and the bus interface. When trouble occurs, the problem is almost always located in at least one of these four operating areas. Since most of the wear and tear in a pen digitizer takes place in the stylus and overlay (especially for resistive digitizers), you will probably find that most problems occur there. The following symptoms will give you some additional insight.

Troubleshooting pen systems

8-21
A pen digitizer integrated into a notebook computer.

Symptom 1: The stylus seems to operate intermittently as it moves along the overlay. When you slide a stylus across the overlay, some portions of the stroke might not be visible as ink feedback on the LCD. In other cases, entire strokes might be missing while other strokes are fully visible. Fortunately, the ink that does appear shows up in the right places. This problem can be maddening, especially when you attempt to write cursive characters. Resistive digitizers are extremely sensitive to stylus contact. Be certain to hold the stylus gently but firmly in contact. A careless touch might allow bad contact between the overlay and stylus.

This symptom is almost always the result of a faulty stylus cable. Remove your stylus from its input jack, open the stylus body and jack (if possible), and use your multimeter to check the continuity along each cable wire. Once your multimeter is connected, wiggle the cable to stimulate any intermittents. If your stylus cable is hard-wired into the computer, remove the pen-computer's outer housing to expose the cable wiring. If you find a faulty stylus, repair or replace the defective wiring, or replace the entire stylus altogether.

If your stylus checks out properly (or is not cabled to begin with), suspect a faulty resistive overlay. Both single-layer and double-layer resistive overlays are extremely prone to wear. As the stylus wears out, overlay resistance and surface features might become irregular. Your stylus might not make proper contact at all points of a worn overlay. Try replacing the resistive overlay. Some small computer manufacturers sell overlay assemblies as component parts. Use extreme caution when replacing an overlay to avoid accidental damage to the LCD or backlight assemblies.

Symptom 2: The stylus or overlay does not appear to respond at all. Other pen-computer functions seem normal. The external keyboard adaptor (if available) works properly. Before checking anything else, make sure that the stylus is properly plugged into the computer. Also make sure that the stylus tip is in good contact with the overlay. Good contact is critical for resistive digitizers. A careless touch might allow bad contact between an overlay and stylus, especially when the overlay is worn.

An open stylus wire can easily disable your pen input. Remove the stylus from its input jack, open the stylus body and jack (if possible), and use your multimeter to measure continuity along each cable wire. Once your multimeter is connected, wiggle the cable to stimulate any possible intermittents. Repair or replace any faulty wiring, or replace the defective stylus. If the stylus cable is hard-wired into the computer, remove the computer's housing to expose the cable wires.

If the digitizer still does not function, you should suspect the overlay controller IC. Disassemble the pen-computer to expose the motherboard and use a logic probe to measure the overlay controller output data bits. You will probably need a schematic or detailed block diagram to locate the overlay controller data lines. Move the stylus across the overlay while measuring each data bit. If the controller is working, you should see a pulse signal or rapid shift between logic 1 and logic 0 levels. Remember that higher (more significant) bits change more slowly than lower bits. If one or more data bits remain at a constant logic level, the overlay controller might be defective. Try replacing the overlay controller IC. If you lack the tools or inclination to perform surface-mount work, try replacing the entire motherboard.

If each data bit from the overlay controller IC appears to be active as you move the stylus, the overlay controller is probably good, but the bus interface might be defective. The bus interface ASIC is also responsible for other operations in a small computer, so you might also encounter problems with memory card slots or other devices. Try replacing the bus interface ASIC or the entire motherboard.

Symptom 3: Ink appears on the LCD as the stylus moves, but ink is not exactly under the stylus.   This symptom is much more of a nuisance than an actual defect in resistive digitizers. You might assume that the stylus is working adequately. The trouble is most likely in the resistive overlay material. Resistance is a characteristic that is extremely dependent on temperature and humidity. Variations in an overlay's temperature or humidity can introduce small analog voltage errors when a stylus passes over the resistive surface. The net result is a small shift in the visual feedback that appears on the LCD.

There is little you can do with temperature or humidity problems except to keep the overlay in a stable, consistent room-temperature environment. If the overlay is damp for any reason, be certain to dry its surface very carefully.

Problems can also occur when the overlay is extremely worn. As resistive material becomes thinner, its resistance at the thinner areas becomes greater. Worn areas can upset the overall resistance of the overlay and result in erroneous voltage signals at the stylus. Again, such errors are digitized and appear somewhere in the display. Your best course of action with a worn resistive overlay is simply to replace it. Use extreme caution when replacing an overlay to avoid accidental damage to the LCD or backlight.

9 *Main logic boards*

I have covered most sections of your small computer in previous chapters (FIG. 9-1). This chapter shows you the motherboard—the processing engine that ties everything together. At the end of this chapter, you will find a set of additional troubleshooting procedures that concentrate specifically on main logic problems.

9-1
Sharp PC-6781 notebook computer.

Reprinted with permission of Sharp Electronics Corp.

The use of a main logic board is nothing new in computer designs. Most computer systems (even before IBM's PC/XT) incorporated a single primary PC board to support its core processing components (i.e., CPU, memory, or peripheral interface adaptors). Your small computer also uses a single PC board to hold its core ICs. Fortunately, today's small computer takes full advantage of highly integrated ASICs, gate arrays, and the latest SMT components. These advances not only simplify the PC board, but reduce the IC count to only 10-or-so ICs. The newest, low-end small-computer designs use a single-chip IC that actually offers all the major computer functions directly on one sophisticated IC.

The motherboard shown in FIG. 9-2 is an excellent example of a typical motherboard assembly. As you look over the figure, notice that almost every IC, especially the controllers, are high-density, SMT devices. The only major IC that is not surface-mounted is the BIOS ROM. The ROM IC is a conventional DIP inserted into a socket for easy replacement whenever the BIOS program is updated in the future. Most of the resistors, capacitors, and transistors on the motherboard are also surface-mounted (although FIG. 9-2 might not show that as clearly).

Physical characteristics & assembly

A selection of connectors (marked CN1, CN2, CN3, etc.) are used to interconnect the motherboard to other areas of the computer, such as the keyboard, LCD, or floppy drive. Notice the buzzer (marked BZ1) included to provide computer sound. Since piezoelectric buzzers are generally capable of providing only a single tone, they are much more limited than normal speakers.

The physical mounting of a motherboard is different from machine to machine depending on the particular model, manufacturer, and system complexity, but there are some general design approaches that you should be familiar with. Knowing what kind of assembly to expect will help you access the motherboard much more easily.

A bottom-up motherboard assembly is an older, more classic design approach. The bottom-up technique basically places the motherboard at the bottom or base of the computer (usually somewhere in the lower housing) and packs the rest of the computer on top of the motherboard. Figure 9-3 shows the bottom-up assembly of a Tandy notebook computer. As you examine the diagram, notice the small computer's many intricacies. The main logic board is roughly in the lower center surrounded by a dotted line marked E1. Just below the motherboard is a thin plastic insulator (K41). Insulators protect the motherboard from

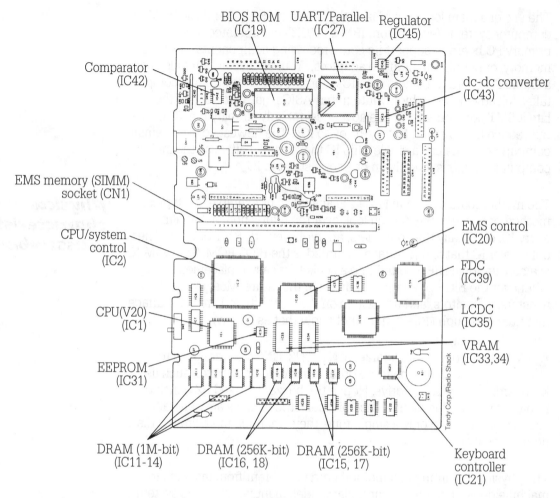

BIOS ROM
(IC19)

UART/Parallel
(IC27)

Regulator
(IC45)

Comparator
(IC42)

dc-dc converter
(IC43)

EMS memory (SIMM)
socket (CN1)

EMS control
(IC20)

CPU/system
control
(IC2)

FDC
(IC39)

CPU(V20)
(IC1)

LCDC
(IC35)

EEPROM
(IC31)

VRAM
(IC33,34)

Tandy Corp./Radio Shack

DRAM (1M-bit)
(IC11-14)

DRAM (256K-bit)
(IC16, 18)

DRAM (256K-bit)
(IC15, 17)

Keyboard
controller
(IC21)

9-2   *Component layout of a Tandy notebook motherboard.*

metallized surfaces on the lower housing assembly. The lower housing is in the lower left corner within the dotted line marked K45.

Once the motherboard and insulator are mounted to the lower housing, a floppy drive (E8) and hard drive (E9) are bolted in place. A keyboard assembly is in the lower right corner within the dotted line marked E7. The keyboard is mounted over the motherboard. After the LCD components are fully assembled, the display is attached to the upper housing, marked K37. The finished LCD/upper housing assembly then sits directly over the lower housing to form a finished system.

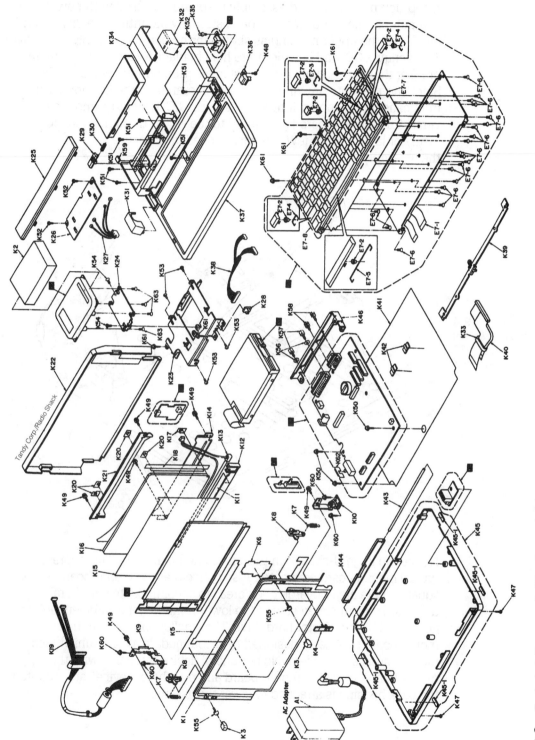

Tandy Corp./Radio Shack

A top-down motherboard assembly is sometimes used with newer pen computers. The top-down approach starts by mounting the display and overlay in the upper housing as shown in the partial assembly in FIG. 9-4. An overlay, LCD, and backlight are held in place by a perforated metal bracket that serves double-duty as an electromagnetic noise shield. Shielding prevents unwanted signals generated by the motherboard from causing unwanted interference in the LCD circuitry, and vice versa. The motherboard is mounted to the shield through a plastic insulator layer. Only a few screws are needed to secure the assembly.

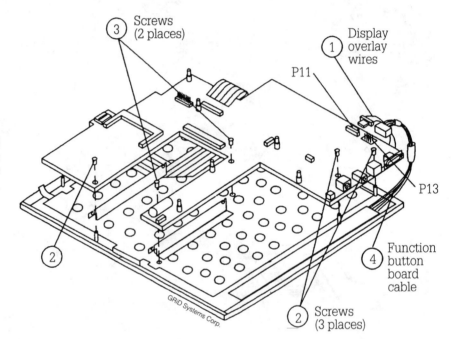

9-4
Partial assembly diagram of a GRiDPAD motherboard.

Notice the large U-shaped in the left motherboard area. That represents a typical memory card connector. Also notice that the motherboard is not square. There are two large open areas to accommodate peripheral devices. The large open area in the lower right corner is large enough to accept a 2.5" form factor hard drive. The smaller open area in the motherboard's center is designed to accommodate a communications module, such as a modem. No peripheral device interferes with the motherboard. Once the motherboard and peripheral devices are mounted, the back housing is attached to cover the assembly.

A motherboard's *architecture* is defined by the parts it contains, and how each component is interconnected to make a working system. Notebook, palmtop, and pen-computer systems each offer their own unique architectures.

Laptop and notebook systems are the largest and most powerful of the small computers. Notebooks are typically large enough to hold an 8.89 cm (3.5") floppy drive, a hard drive, a full-sized keypad, a large LCD or gas plasma display, and a full suite of standard external connections for a mouse, parallel port, serial port, external monitor, etc. Notebooks generally use the most advanced microprocessors (such as Intel's 80486) with 4Mb or more of RAM to tackle the most demanding program requirements. In many cases, notebook computers rival desktop systems in computing power and performance. The very newest notebook computers incorporate removable solid-state memory cards instead floppy drives.

The block diagram of a high-performance notebook computer is given in FIG. 9-5. As you study the figure, you might notice quite a few similarities to the block diagram of the Tandy 1500HD, shown in FIG. 1-7. A CPU forms the foundation of every computer system. For FIG. 9-5, the CPU is an Intel 80486SX operating at 25 MHz. The CPU could also be replaced directly with an advanced Intel 80486DX operating at 33 MHz. The DX suffix indicates that the microprocessor contains all the elements for a math coprocessor already built-in, so an external math coprocessor (MCP) is not required. A clock oscillator drives the CPU.

Notice that the CPU directly addresses the system controller IC. The CPU's 32-bit data bus connects to the system's core DRAM, and is available at a memory expansion module. With a full memory expansion module, the system can address 20Mb of DRAM. Note the system controller's many functions. It provides the RAS and CAS timing signals needed to refresh the core DRAM, as well as the DRAM address signals. The system controller also provides three system busses: a 20-bit system address bus, a 16-bit system data bus, and an additional 7 bits of address information for use by an expansion module or ISA-compatible plug-in board. The latest system controllers are large ICs, typically with 100 to 240 pins.

A single 128K×8-bit BIOS ROM IC connects directly to the system address and data busses. The many small software routines contained in BIOS are used for such things as power-on and self-test, keyboard access, hard disk I/O, floppy disk I/O, serial and parallel communication, RTC support, and video output. BIOS tells the computer how to perform all of its mundane, hardware-level functions.

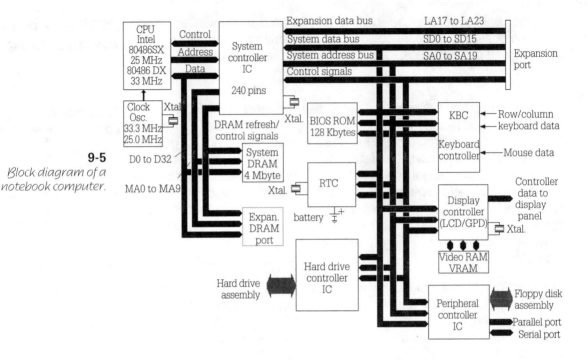

9-5

Block diagram of a notebook computer.

An advanced keyboard controller supports input from three places: a mouse, an internal keyboard, and an external keyboard. All three input ports accept information in a serial form that is converted to parallel data words, stored in the controller, and read onto the system data bus as required. A different address is used depending on whether the system controller is reading the mouse, internal keyboard, or external keyboard.

A secondary system controller IC (more appropriately called a system interface controller) is attached to the system address and data busses. The system interface controller provides two serial ports: one modem port and another generic serial port for printers or a serial mouse. The interface controller also operates an electromagnetic speaker. Using a real speaker allows the computer to generate a wide variety of sounds or music. An internal 8.89 cm (3.5") floppy drive is connected to the interface controller's floppy drive interface port. The interface controller also provides a dual-purpose parallel port. In the printer mode, the parallel port supports any standard Centronics-type printer, while the floppy disk mode allows the parallel port to operate a second (external) floppy drive.

The real-time controller (RTC) IC is responsible for maintaining the computer's current time and date. Most RTCs record time as hours (in GMT), minutes, seconds, and sometimes milliseconds, while the date is maintained as years (and leap years), months, days, and day of the week. BIOS routines allow the date and time to be read from or written to the RTC. To ensure the greatest possible timekeeping accuracy, the RTC is driven by its own precision crystal oscillator. When power is removed from the RTC, it continues to operate from small lithium backup batteries.

A hard drive interface controller IC connects the system busses to the hard drive assembly. The hard drive controller is also a sophisticated IC that converts data and control bytes from the system into data and discrete control signals needed by the particular drive, and vice versa. Most hard drive controller ICs are designed to work with IDE drives, but growing numbers of systems are supporting SCSI hard drives. Notebook hard drives can generally hold up to 280Mb.

The display control system is composed of several powerful ICs. A display controller IC is usually the most important component of the display system. The controller accesses display information contained in video RAM (VRAM). With VGA displays, 1Mb of VRAM is needed to contain all the video data. The controller also provides a special digital output port to drive an external TTL monitor.

Data from the display controller IC is passed along to a color graphics system (CGS) IC. A CGS IC adapts the color palette for color or monochrome displays. By manipulating color data in advance depending on the display panel, it is possible to attach a gas plasma, monochrome LCD, or color TFT panel to the same motherboard without any modifications to the motherboard.

Pen computers are a diverse group of sub-notebook systems characterized by a pen digitizer as the primary input device instead of a keyboard. The term *sub-notebook* indicates that the computer is physically smaller and lighter than most typical notebook computers. Pen computers also cover a wide range of computing power. Small, simple pen-computers might serve as basic data-collection devices, while more powerful pen systems might serve as more full-featured computers. Regardless of their particular strengths and weaknesses, most pen computers share a great many things in common.

Pen-computer systems

A block diagram for the GRiDPAD pen computer is shown in FIG. 9-6. An NEC V20 CPU performs system processing. The V20 is a 10 MHz equivalent to the older Intel 8088 microprocessor. While a simpler microprocessor results in slower operation, it also consumes less power than an Intel 80386 or 486, so battery life for pen computers can be

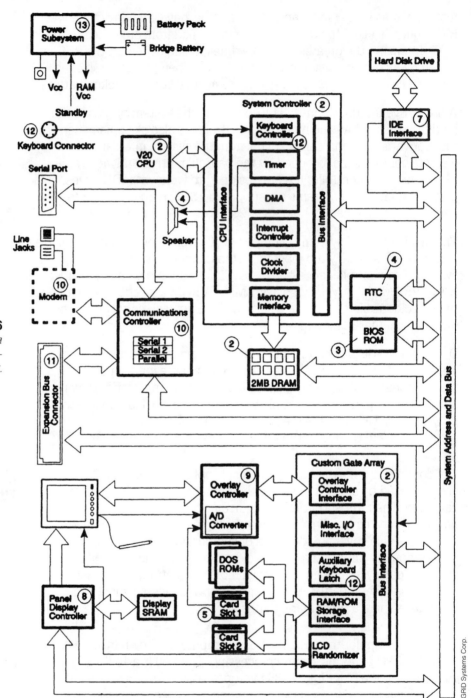

9-6
Block diagram of a GRiD Systems pen-computer.

GRiD Systems Corp.

extended significantly. Also, most of today's pen systems are not intended to run the calculation or graphics-intensive software now running on many notebook or desktop systems. Some pen systems, however, utilize advanced microprocessors and large amounts of memory to tackle DOS and Windows applications.

A highly integrated system controller IC is connected directly to the CPU, which communicates with the system controller. It is the system controller that is responsible for supporting most of the computer's major work. The system controller provides the RAS and CAS refresh signals to the computer's 2Mb of core DRAM. An external keyboard connector is available to supply serial ASCII characters to the system controller. Notice that there is no specific keyboard controller IC. Since the keyboard is external, it is assumed to have an appropriate built-in IBM PC/XT- or PC/AT-compatible keyboard controller IC. A timer circuit is used to drive a small speaker or piezoelectric buzzer. Perhaps the most important function of the system controller is its bus interface, which provides system address and data busses to the entire computer.

An IDE hard drive controller IC is connected directly to the system busses. IDE drives are plentiful and relatively inexpensive devices. A standard physical interface allows the hard drive to be replaced easily or moved to another system. The real-time controller IC is used to track the current date and time. A BIOS ROM provides many of the basic service routines needed to operate the computer.

A pen computer's communication controller IC provides two serial ports and a parallel port. One serial port is available to operate an optional modem module, and another generic serial port is intended for printer operation or mouse input. The parallel port is available through an expansion bus connector. The communication controller works directly through the system address and data busses.

The secondary system controller IC is actually a complex custom gate array. System address and data bus signals interface directly to the custom gate array. The gate array also handles interfacing between the overlay controller IC and system busses. The system DOS can be supplied on ROM instead of being stored in the hard drive. When DOS ROMs are installed in the system, the custom gate array also supports ROM interfacing to the system busses.

An overlay controller IC not only controls the digitizer overlay's scanning operations, but converts raw stylus feedback into digital data that represent the current stylus position. When the system reads the stylus, X and Y digital position information is passed through the gate array to the system. Commands or control bytes written from the system bus are passed through the gate array and written to the overlay controller.

Video data sent over the system busses are processed through the panel display controller IC. Information is decoded and stored in VRAM. Each location in VRAM corresponds to a pixel on the LCD. The display controller periodically reads through all VRAM locations and manipulates LCD pixels accordingly to update the display. When cursive writing is being interpreted, stylus movement data is also sent to the display controller, which echoes pen movements on the LCD. The displayed pen movements is the ink.

Palmtop computer systems

Palmtop computers are typically the smallest and simplest computers. Intended to fit easily into a briefcase or a shirt pocket, palmtops lack the physical size to house high-performance components. Even the display and keyboard are tiny. While some palmtops are DOS-compatible, most current palmtops are sophisticated pocket organizers.

A simple palmtop computer is illustrated in FIG. 9-7. As you see, there is not very much to the design when compared to a larger system. At the heart of a palmtop computer is a microprocessor. DOS-compatible palmtops generally use recognized CPUs, but many organizer-type palmtops make use of proprietary microprocessors. Custom CPUs often incorporate some additional controller functions that notebooks and pen systems have long since relegated to highly integrated system controller ICs. The large amount of processing overhead makes the palmtop slow—its CPU clock runs at only 3.072 MHz. This does not mean that all palmtops are underpowered. Some systems, such as the Poquet PC (manufactured by Fujitsu) or the Zeos PC use mainstream CPUs at more reasonable clock speeds.

An RTC is used to maintain the system's date and time, but notice that the palmtop directly accesses the RTC. The piezoelectric buzzer can be triggered either by an alarm signal from the RTC or a signal from the CPU. The keyboard assembly also interfaces directly to the CPU. Custom CPU circuitry converts keyboard row and column signals into scan codes.

The liquid crystal display is a simple, low-resolution 240×64 device. Since the display is reflective, no backlighting is used. Data is delivered to two

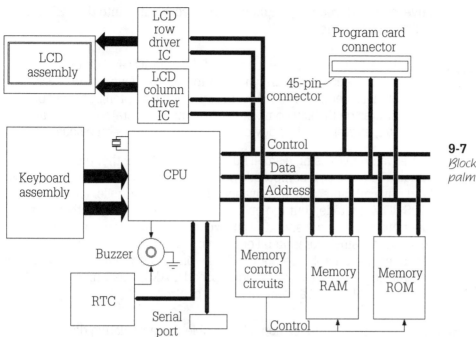

9-7
Block diagram of a palmtop computer.

simple LCD driver ICs using control signals generated by both the CPU and memory control circuitry. One LCD driver controls the display's rows, while the other driver controls the display's columns.

Palmtop memory is often rather limited. While more powerful palmtop systems might offer up to up to 1Mb of memory, many simpler palmtops supply only 64K to 128K of SRAM. Using SRAM eliminates the need for refresh circuitry. A ROM IC contains the routines needed to initialize and operate the palmtop. There are few similarities between a palmtop ROM and a notebook BIOS ROM. The palmtop in FIG. 9-7 also provides a 45-pin connector for special program cards, although more powerful palmtops supply one or two PCMCIA-compatible 68-pin memory card slots.

Since palmtops are typically used to supplement desktop systems, many palmtops supply a serial interface connector to allow attachment to a host computer. However, palmtop serial ports rarely use standard connectors, so a special cable is needed to connect the palmtop to its host, where a host interface lets a desktop system read or write files to the palmtop. The serial port is also important because it is often the only way to get files in or out of basic machines, as palmtops do not offer floppy drives, and desktop systems are seldom fitted with card drives. As yet, no palmtops offer hard drives yet, but Hewlett-Packard's Kitty Hawk drive (and its decedents) might soon be incorporated into their HP95LX palmtop computers.

Core functions A motherboard contains the majority of different ICs and other components needed to operate the computer. You have already seen some of these controller ICs at work in previous chapters. This chapter concentrates on the key components common (or core) to the overall computer, as well as a few devices that have not yet been discussed.

The advantage to using a small number of core ICs is that they can remain the same as a computer's peripherals change. For example, a new hard drive might require an advanced hard drive controller (and perhaps a BIOS ROM upgrade), but the microprocessor, memory, and other core functions remain unchanged. Visualize the core functions as the engine that drives a small computer. For our purposes, there are six core functions: the microprocessor (CPU), the primary system controller IC, the central memory array (usually high-speed DRAM), a real-time clock (RTC), a speaker, and a communication controller IC.

Microprocessor (CPU) A CPU is a programmable logic IC capable of manipulating data as directed by a set of instructions (the program). The CPU can perform mathematical operations, logical comparisons or decision making, and data transfers. Math operations include addition, subtraction, multiplication, and division. There are an assortment of logical comparisons, such as greater-than, less-than, or equal-to. The CPU can use the results of these comparisons to make conditional "If/Then" decisions. Data manipulations include reading or writing to or from specific locations in memory or I/O locations. Data can also be manipulated in the CPU's stacks and internal registers. All together, there might be more than 200 unique operations possible depending on the particular CPU being used.

Older CPUs offer fewer, simpler operations than the newer, more powerful processors. The microprocessor is directly responsible for executing every program instruction. As a result, a CPU has ultimate control over the entire computer system. You can refer to any of the many fine books available on microprocessor architecture for more detailed information.

The program that operates a CPU is initially taken from BIOS ROM during the computer's power-up, self-test, and initialization. With so many operations possible for different CPUs, BIOS is often CPU-specific; that is, the BIOS written for an NEC V20 or V30 CPU will not work for an Intel 80486, and vice versa. BIOS is also responsible for directing the CPU to load its operating system (OS). Since most operating systems involve the use of disk drives, the term disk operating system (DOS) is typically used. It is the software "set-up" through BIOS that allows so many microprocessors to run DOS. For example, Microsoft's MS-DOS 5.0 will run on computers with Intel's 80286, 80386, or 80486 CPU.

DOS is a program that is loaded into core memory. DOS files are typically stored on a floppy drive, hard drive, or solid-state memory card. You know DOS is ready when you see the DOS prompt (typically C:\>) on your display. Once DOS is loaded, it runs in the background as long as your computer is on. You can then use your input device to enter DOS commands such as Format, Dir, or Copy. Your computer's DOS User's Guide can supply more instruction on DOS capabilities. You can also order DOS to load and execute almost any application program. The CPU is responsible for executing every program instruction within that running program, as well as running any DOS routine or BIOS service call that the application program might require. When the application program is ended, you return to DOS.

As you might imagine, the advantage of a microprocessor is not in its internal circuitry. In fact, the generic, general-purpose construction of a CPU makes it rather inefficient. It is the software that gives a small computer its power and flexibility. A computer can be used to perform a mind-boggling array of tasks simply by executing different pieces of software.

A microprocessor uses three major sets of signals in order to operate, as shown in FIG. 9-8: address lines, data lines, and control lines. Power and ground signals are also required. Microprocessors can offer 8, 16, or 32 data lines depending on the particular CPU. Each data line corresponds to one binary digit (or bit). Older CPUs used an 8-bit data bus, while newer devices typically use 16- or 32-bit data busses. The data carried over a data bus can represent just about anything, such as program instructions, destination addresses, and variable values.

Every data word in the computer, regardless of its size, is held in a unique memory location, or address. Most CPUs provide more than 20 address lines. When a CPU reads or writes data, the CPU must first provide the address where the desired information is (or should be) placed. Do not be fooled by the number of address lines. Today's CPUs use sophisticated addressing techniques to access much more memory than the direct 2^n capacity of its address lines might suggest.

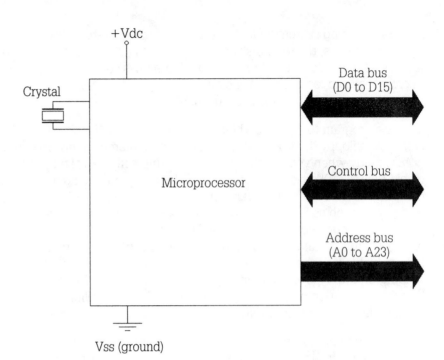

+Vdc

Crystal

9-8
*Simplified diagram of a
microprocessor.*

Microprocessor

Data bus
(D0 to D15)

Control bus

Address bus
(A0 to A23)

Vss (ground)

Control lines serve two purposes. First, controls inform the CPU of system conditions and emergencies that require immediate attention. Second, controls inform the system of the CPU's actions. This bidirectional action requires both input and output control lines. The exact number of control signals available will depend on the particular CPU. Newer microprocessors usually provide more control signals than older devices.

System controller   Microprocessors require substantial amounts of external circuitry in order to operate a small computer. Keyboard interfacing, hard drive and floppy drive access, dynamic RAM control, and video support are only a few of the tasks that must be directed by a CPU. In the early days of desktop computers, the circuitry to perform each task was implemented using discrete logic such as the 7400 series TTL ICs. Motherboards on the older IBM PC/XT desktop computers used almost 200 ICs, resulting in a large, power-hungry system. The add-on boards for video control, drives, other peripherals were equally cumbersome.

Fortunately, the many advances in solid-state IC design have allowed designers to integrate a tremendous amount of discrete logic onto a single IC. A system controller is one such highly integrated device. Instead of building huge PC boards with many simple ICs, the system controller incorporates much of a computer's logic onto a single piece of silicon. A typical system controller, as shown in FIG. 9-9, might offer a keyboard controller, timer circuit, direct memory access (DMA) circuit, interrupt controller, core memory interface, and several external address and data bus interfaces in the same IC. The CPU works through the system controller. System controllers are generally large ICs with 120 or more pins. Some system controllers have more than 240 pins. The exact number of pins depends on the CPU and the number of functions integrated into the controller.

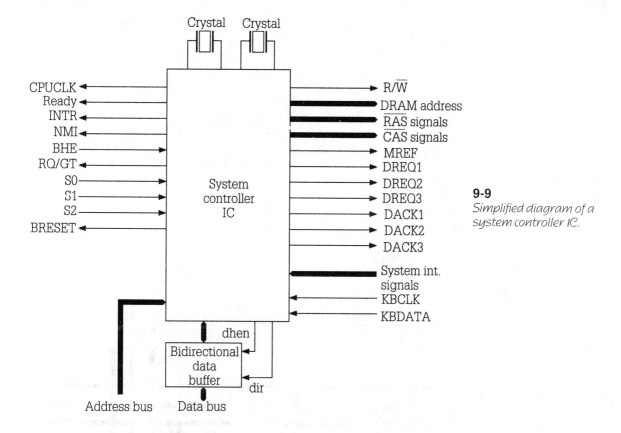

9-9
Simplified diagram of a system controller IC.

There are advantages and disadvantages to using highly integrated devices such as system controllers. Advantages include substantial reductions in overall circuit size and power requirements, critical considerations for a small computer. System controllers can also be optimized for fast, efficient operation. On the down side, you cannot experiment or tinker with system controllers as you could with older, discrete circuits. The finished system controllers are proprietary devices specifically designed and manufactured for particular computers.

Proprietary devices are sometimes difficult to obtain. You usually must contact the computer manufacturer for proprietary replacement parts.

Core memory

Memory is just as important to a computer system as a CPU. The computer uses small amounts of memory to store system setup information, BIOS routines, and video display data, but the vast majority of a computer's memory is devoted to holding loaded program instructions or related data. Since this memory is under direct control of the system controller (or the CPU in very rare cases), DRAM is central, or core, to small computer operation. Computers use two types of memory: ROM and RAM. Programs to initialize and operate basic functions are normally a permanent part of the system's ROM, while application programs are loaded into DRAM from a hard drive, floppy drive, or memory card. Some palmtops use SRAM instead of DRAM.

The amount of available memory can vary tremendously depending on the computer's age and processing power. Palmtop computers offer anywhere from 64K to 1Mb or more of core memory, pen computers supply 2 to 4Mb of DRAM, and off-the-shelf notebook computers usually start at 2 or 4Mb and are expandable to 20Mb of DRAM with SIMMs or DRAM cards.

Like CPUs, memory ICs provide three sets of signals, as shown in FIG. 9-10: data lines, address lines, and control lines. Power and ground signals

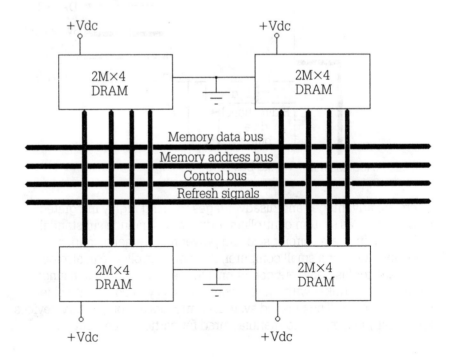

9-10
Simplified diagram of a core memory bank.

Main logic boards

are also required. Memory ICs typically provide 1, 4, 8, or 16 data bits, depending on the particular ICs chosen for the computer. The data lines from multiple memory ICs can be joined together to form a complete bus. For example, suppose a small computer provides 1 million address locations to a CPU with a 16-bit data bus. Using 1 Mbit×1 bit ICs, 16 individual ICs would be needed (one IC to handle each bit of the data bus). If 1 Mbit×4 bit ICs were used, only 4 ICs would be needed because each IC provides 4 bits. If a 1 Mbit×16 bit IC is used, it is the only IC needed since it supplies enough data bits to handle the entire bus. Additional banks of memory can be added to extend the computer's memory as desired.

Address lines specify the precise bit(s) to be read or written. The number of available addresses is 2^n where n is the number of address lines. For example, a memory IC with 1,048,576 memory locations requires 20 address lines (2^{20}). Keep in mind that memory ICs are logic devices, so they are operated with Boolean logic. Not all available address lines must be connected directly to memory ICs. Some high-order address lines can be used to select banks of memory. As an example, suppose you find memory ICs with 8 address lines (A0 to A7). With 8 address lines, the IC can access 2^8 or 256 locations. You are not concerned with how many bits are available at each location. Suppose you need more than 256 locations. Higher address lines can be decoded to select from multiple banks of memory. If two banks of 256 location memory are needed, the next higher address line (such as A8) from the available address bus can operate a simple decoding circuit to each set of memory chip select inputs. When A8 is logic 0, the first memory bank of locations 0 to 255 will be active, and the other bank(s) will be deactivated. When A8 is logic 1, the second memory bank of locations 256 to 511 will be active, and the other bank(s) will be deactivated.

So what if you want 16 banks of 265 locations? The upper four address lines (A8, A9, A10, and A11) can be decoded to provide a unique chip-select signal to each of 16 memory banks. For example, if A8 through A11 read 0101 (decimal 5), then the fifth bank would be active, while all other memory banks would be deactivated, and so on.

The memory addressing scheme described above is merely a simple example, but it is the same fundamental approach used to access core memory since solid-state computers were first introduced. While this bank addressing scheme is still in use, it is being used less and less as DRAM ICs continue to pack more locations into the same IC. Today, 2Mb and 4Mb DRAMs are commonplace, 16Mb DRAMs will soon be available to computer designers, and 64Mb DRAMs are on the drawing board.

DRAMs need only a few control signals: RAS signals, CAS signals, a read/write signal, and a chip select (CS) or output enable (OE) signal. As mentioned earlier, DRAM contents must be refreshed every few milliseconds to maintain data integrity. Refresh is needed because of the DRAM's internal memory cell structure. If refresh signals are not provided, the DRAM will loose its contents in a matter of milliseconds. Row refresh (RAS) and column refresh (CAS) signals are provided as needed by the system controller IC. A R/W is also supplied by the system controller to determine whether data on the data bus is being read or written to the DRAM. Chip select (CS) or output enable (OE) signals might be provided by the system controller, or generated by some other motherboard circuitry governing the selection of DRAM banks. As long as the select line is logic 0, the DRAM reads or writes as instructed. If the select line is logic 1, the DRAM is effectively disconnected from the system.

Real-time clock (RTC)

A real-time clock (RTC) is little more than an oscillator, as shown in FIG. 9-11. It provides a fairly accurate time base for the computer's clock and calendar. During power-up, the computer obtains the current time from registers within the RTC. Once your small computer is initialized and running, new date and time information can be written to the RTC through BIOS routines called by DOS or an application program.

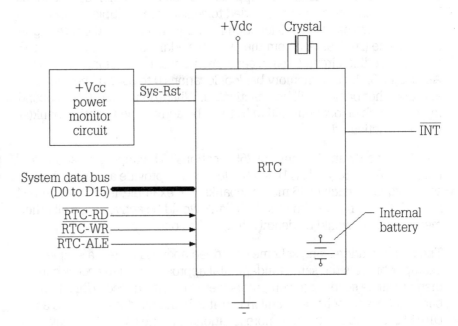

9-11
Simplified diagram of a real-time clock (RTC).

An RTC is especially useful because it tracks date and time whether the computer is on or off. The RTC must receive power at all times or its date and time information will be lost. When the computer is off, the RTC receives power from a small lithium battery. Some RTCs use a discrete coin cell assembled on the motherboard, while other RTCs utilize built-in batteries. When battery voltage drops below a preset limit, the RTC becomes write-protected and will not accept changes to its registers during a low-voltage condition. However, it still continues to keep time until the battery fails. If the computer is on, the RTC receives its power from the computer.

Speaker

Just about every small computer is capable of producing sound. The sound devices found in most systems are either the typical 8 ohm electromagnetic cone speaker, or a tiny piezoelectric tone element. Sound might be variable to allow the computer to produce frequencies across the audio spectrum, or sound might be fixed at one particular frequency.

In most small computer designs, a speaker is handled through the system controller IC. Sound is generated using a series of two gated square wave oscillators. One oscillator is fixed at a certain system frequency, and the other is set by a digital value written to the computer's oscillator port. By writing different values to the system controller's tone oscillator port, the speaker can be set almost anywhere within the audio range for any length of time.

Communication controller

Small computers generally communicate with printers, modems, or pointing devices. These peripheral devices, however, are never attached directly to a computer's system busses. With so many variations in computer designs, it would be almost impossible for peripheral manufacturers to create a single bus-compatible device. Instead, peripherals and small computers communicate over either a serial or parallel communication link. The interface between a peripheral and the system busses is established using a highly integrated communication controller IC.

The communication architecture of a typical small computer is shown in the block diagram of FIG. 9-12. Notice how the controller IC is attached to the main system busses much like the other controller devices shown in this book. The communication controller supports Centronics parallel and RS232 serial communication ports. Both communication techniques will be detailed a bit later.

9-12
Simplified diagram of a communication controller.

When your computer writes to a communication port, the system addresses its communication controller IC. There are various possible addresses in the controller to handle different ports. For example, an ASCII character to be sent over the serial port is written to a particular address in the controller, which breaks the character into individual bits, inserts control bits, and sends one bit at a time (serially) over the transmit data line (Tx). As bits are received serially over the receive data line (Rx), the controller strips away any control bits and reconverts the serial data bits into a parallel word. When the received character is complete, the controller sends an interrupt signal to the system controller (or sometimes directly to the CPU). An interrupt causes the CPU to read the completed word from the communication controller. The other serial signals (RTS, DTR, CTS, DSR, and DCD) are *handshaking* signals used to coordinate data transfer to or from the computer. Not all handshaking signals are needed for every serial application.

Notice the two small ICs between the controller and the serial connector. These are the line control ICs. Serial communication does not use TTL voltage levels. Instead, bipolar signals are transmitted between computers and serial peripherals. A line driver IC converts TTL logic levels from a communication controller into positive or negative voltages (±5 to ±15 Vdc) for the serial link. Similarly, a line receiver converts the bipolar signals from a serial link into corresponding TTL levels that a communication controller can recognize.

The process of sending or receiving a serial data word is not terribly complex, but you should have a clear understanding of serial data characteristics. A typical serial data word is illustrated in FIG. 9-13. The word looks identical whether it is sent from computer to peripheral, or vice versa. Serial data exists in two logic states. A mark state is logic 1 that is represented by a negative voltage. A space state is logic 0 that is generated with a positive voltage. Notice that the word is made up of four sections: a start bit, 7 or 8 data bits, a parity bit, and 1 or 2 stop bits. Each bit is critical in serial port operation since the peripheral and small computer must be set to exactly the same parameters.

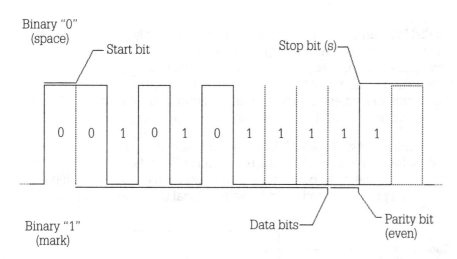

9-13
A typical serial word.

When the serial signal line is idle, it rests in the mark state. The first bit received must be a start bit. Start bits are always the first space (logic 0) to be received. The 7 or 8 bits immediately following the start bit are the data bits. Data bits might be either marks or spaces as required. A parity bit follows the last data bit. Parity is a simple means of checking a serial data stream for single-bit errors. You might encounter even and odd parity. The word is finished with one or two stop bits. Stop bits are always marks (logic 1s). The communication controller adds start, parity, and stop bits to the data bits, and removes those extra bits from received data words. Finally, bits must be sent at a constant rate, known as *baud* rate. All serial parameters can be set through DOS, or through applications software. Figure 9-14 illustrates the pinout for a standard small computer serial port.

Parallel communication is quite a bit different than serial communication. Where a serial link carries one bit at a time over a single signal wire, a

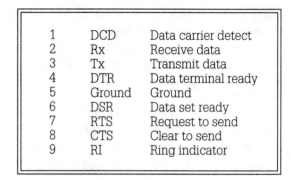

9-14
Pinout of a 9-pin serial port.

1	DCD	Data carrier detect
2	Rx	Receive data
3	Tx	Transmit data
4	DTR	Data terminal ready
5	Ground	Ground
6	DSR	Data set ready
7	RTS	Request to send
8	CTS	Clear to send
9	RI	Ring indicator

parallel link carries an entire 8-bit word simultaneously over 8 individual signal lines. Just about every laptop or notebook computer offers a Centronics-type parallel port. A Centronics parallel port provides unidirectional output that was only intended to drive printers. By writing data words to a different address in the communication controller IC, the entire byte appears and latches to the waiting printer.

The entire process of parallel data transfer is shown in FIG. 9-15. In order for data transfer to take place, the printer must be in its on-line mode and connected to the small computer's parallel port. An on-line condition causes the printer to send a logic 1 Select signal to the computer. A

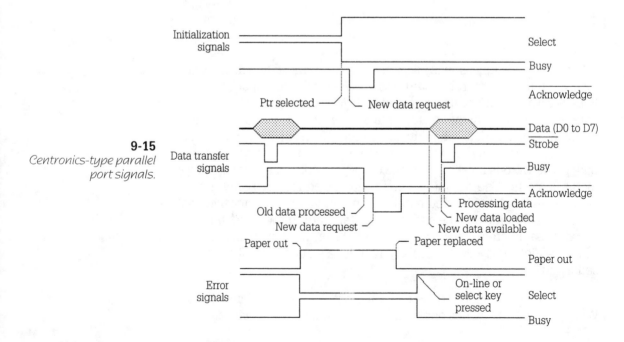

9-15
Centronics-type parallel port signals.

printer follows immediately by dropping the Busy line to a logic 0. Data transfer is now ready to begin. The communication controller can place its data in parallel data lines D0 to D7 and pulse the Strobe line to a logic 0 level. The printer responds by raising its Busy line to a logic 1 until the written byte is stored in the printer's buffer. Once the printer is ready for a new byte, Busy returns to a logic 0, and the Acknowledge line pulses low to request new data whenever the computer is ready. With a parallel port, a computer sends data as fast as the printer can accept it. All signals in the parallel port are TTL-compatible. Figure 9-16 shows the corresponding pinout for a Centronics-type port.

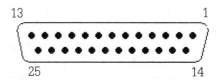

1	Strobe	14	Auto feed
2	Data bit D0	15	n/u
3	Data bit D1	16	Signal ground
4	Data bit D2	17	Chassis ground
5	Data bit D3	18	Data ground 0
6	Data bit D4	19	Data ground 1
7	Data bit D5	20	Data ground 2
8	Data bit D6	21	Data ground 3
9	Data bit D7	22	Data ground 4
10	Acknowledge	23	Data ground 5
11	Busy	24	Data ground 6
12	Paper out	25	Data ground 7
13	Select		

9-16
Pinout of a 25-pin parallel port.

When trouble arises in a core function, the effects can usually be seen throughout the computer. Trouble can manifest itself in many ways depending on the location and degree of the problem. A faulty system speaker might only be a minor inconvenience, while a defective CPU can stop a computer in its tracks. Where many of the problems detailed elsewhere in this book might be caused by relatively simple defects such as faulty wiring or connectors, core function problems are almost always IC related.

Troubleshooting the core functions

Another concern when working with motherboards is IC replacement. Most ICs used in small computers are low-profile, high-density SMT devices that have been assembled onto intricate PC boards. Surface-mount ICs might also be located on both sides of the motherboard. If you do not have the tools necessary to tackle surface-mount desoldering and resoldering jobs, you can replace the entire motherboard. Replacing a motherboard is certainly not the least expensive repair option, but the amount of anxiety and frustration that can be prevented is often worth the price. Make sure to have your multimeter and logic probe (and oscilloscope if available) on hand before starting your repair.

Symptom 1: The computer does not start when power is turned on. This is perhaps one of the most perplexing problems found in small computer repair. Nothing happens when you press the power button. It is often difficult to determine which part of the motherboard to start with since there are no tones, displays, or disk activity to indicate what the computer is doing. Begin by checking the computer's power indicator. If the power indicator is dark, check the system's ac adaptor or battery pack. The computer cannot run without power. Replace or recharge the battery pack, or use a power supply (either internal or external). Make sure all power connectors are inserted correctly.

If the power indicator remains off under ac power, remove all power, disassemble the power supply or ac adaptor, and check any power fuses. When power supplies are built into the computer, you will have to disassemble your system to access the supply. Fuses that are intact (or fuses that fail as soon as you replace them) suggest a serious defect in your ac supply. Troubleshoot the power supply or ac adaptor with the procedures in chapter 5.

Your small computer should also be powered by a battery pack. If the power indicator remains out while under battery power, the battery pack might be faulty. The battery protection or regulating circuit might also be faulty. Refer to chapter 5 for battery system troubleshooting. If the power indicator does light, use your multimeter to check proper dc voltage levels at the motherboard. You will probably have to remove the upper or lower outer housing to access the motherboard. If one or more voltages reads low or absent, refer to chapter 5 for power system troubleshooting.

Once adequate power is applied to the main logic board, the system CPU should initialize the computer through the system controller and BIOS ROM. Even a minor failure in either of these three components can disable the computer. The CPU and system controller are tightly coupled devices. In many cases, the system controller is tailored to the particular CPU being used. Some system controllers require a power confirmation signal from the power supply or dc-dc converter(s) before the CPU is allowed to start. Use your logic probe to examine any power confirmation signal(s). You will probably need a schematic or detailed block diagram to find power confirmation signals. Missing or erroneous signals suggest a problem in your power supply logic. If power confirmation signals are correct, replace your system controller IC.

Check clock signals at the CPU and system controller next. Some small computer designs provide separate clock oscillators for the CPU and system controller, while other systems derive the CPU clock from one system controller oscillator. Again, you will probably need a schematic or detailed block diagram to determine just what clock signals are actually available. Use your logic probe to check the CPU clock as well as the system controller clock. Both clock signals should read as high-frequency pulse indications on a logic probe. If the CPU clock is missing from the system controller IC, the system controller is probably defective. If the missing CPU clock is being produced by a local crystal oscillator, replace the crystal. When a new crystal fails to restore the CPU clock, replace the CPU. If the system controller clock signal is missing, replace the crystal for the system controller clock. When a new crystal fails to restore the system controller clock, replace the system controller IC.

Should you find adequate power and clock signals, turn your attention to the BIOS ROM IC. Since a BIOS ROM contains all the program instructions and data needed to start and support a computer, a defective ROM can cause the CPU (and the entire system) to halt. Use your logic probe to check the chip select ($\overline{CS}$) signal at the ROM. During normal initialization, a $\overline{CS}$ signal should read as a high-frequency pulse as the CPU loads and processes BIOS instructions. A missing $\overline{CS}$ signal suggests a problem at the system controller. Try replacing the system controller IC.

If the chip select appears as expected, use your logic probe to check each address and data line during initialization. All address and data lines should appear as high-frequency pulse signals. Check address and data lines from CPU to system controller. Faulty address lines suggest a problem in the CPU. Faulty data signals suggest trouble in either the system controller or CPU. Try replacing the CPU first. If a new CPU does not restore normal operation, replace the system controller IC. Check each data and address signal from the system controller to the rest of the system. If any address or data line appears faulty, you should probably replace the entire motherboard. The system controller is probably defective, but any other controller or bus interface IC can pull down the questionable signal line. It simply is not economical for you to pull each bus IC off the motherboard until you find the one causing the problem. If your test results are inconclusive and your back is to the wall, go ahead and replace the motherboard.

Symptom 2: You see a memory error warning on your display during initialization and system operation halts.

When your small computer begins to initialize, one of its first operations is to test and clear the core memory (DRAM). You see the memory test being conducted on the display. The computer tests memory by writing a known bit pattern to every address, then reads each bit pattern back again. If the pattern read matches the pattern written, that particular address is assumed to be intact. If a match does not occur, the computer flags and displays a memory error warning, as well as the address (or block of addresses) where the error occurred. Since your system controller IC is typically in direct control of DRAM addressing, data handling, and control, the objective of this procedure is to determine whether the DRAM or system controller is at fault. You should have a schematic or detailed system diagram before attempting this procedure.

Start by using your logic probe to check the DRAM refresh signals ($\overline{RAS}$ and $\overline{CAS}$) being provided by the system controller. There might be multiple RAS or CAS signals depending on the amount and architecture of the system DRAM. During initialization and normal operation, each refresh signal should appear as a pulse reading. If any refresh signal is missing, the system controller IC is probably defective. Try replacing the system controller IC. The system controller also provides an R/$\overline{W}$ signal to core DRAM. During initialization, the R/$\overline{W}$ line should appear as a pulse signal. If the R/$\overline{W}$ line does not pulse, the system controller is defective and should be replaced. Keep in mind that simple palmtop systems might use SRAM addressed directly by the CPU.

Next, use your logic probe to check the address and data bus lines between your system controller and DRAM IC(s). The system controller usually provides separate busses for DRAM use. Older system controllers might only provide a DRAM address bus where data signals are supplied by the CPU. Palmtops might address SRAM components directly from the CPU. During initialization, memory address lines should read as pulse signals on your logic probe. If any address lines do not pulse, the system controller is probably defective and should be replaced. Repeat your check for each data line. During initialization, each data line should appear as a pulse signal. If you find one or more DRAM data lines that do not pulse, try replacing the system controller. If data lines are supplied by the CPU, check any bus interface ICs between the CPU and memory.

If a new system controller or bus interface does not rectify the problem, replace the offending memory component(s). The memory warning shown during initialization should match with one or more DRAMs on the motherboard. If you cannot locate the defective DRAM(s), you can replace all the DRAM ICs on the motherboard. If your warning indicates a failure in expanded memory, you might simply wish to replace the suspect SIMM or memory card. As a final step, you could replace the entire motherboard.

Symptom 3: There is no sound output. The speaker or buzzer does not work, and all other operations appear normal.

This is actually one of the more straightforward symptoms to deal with in a small computer. Your first step in tracking down this problem is to check settings of your application program. Remember that a speaker or buzzer is operated by writing a word to a particular address that is usually in the system controller IC. If one program generates sound properly and another program does not, it is very likely that the program (not the computer) is at fault. Check any setup options offered in the program making sure that the sound or music option is not switched off or set to a selection other than PC Internal Speaker. If it is, change the selection to the PC speaker and try the program again.

If the speaker or buzzer does not work at all regardless of what software is running on your small computer, remove all power and disassemble the computer enough to expose the sound element. The sound element is attached either directly to the motherboard, or on the upper or lower housing. Remotely mounted sound elements must be connected to the motherboard using a small, two-wire cable. Check to see that the wiring and connector are intact and inserted properly. Replace any faulty wiring.

A sound element (either a speaker or a buzzer) is typically driven by TTL-level square waves generated at the system controller. There is usually one or more simple logic gates to buffer the signal. Use your logic probe to check for sound signals at the sound element's terminals. One of the element's two terminals will be ground. Try to produce sound using software that you know produces clear sound from a PC speaker or buzzer. If you find a signal with no sound being produced, replace the defective speaker or buzzer.

If you do not find a sound signal when you expect to, trace the sound signal back through any glue logic to the system controller. You will probably need a schematic or detailed block diagram of the system to trace sound signals. The point at which the sound signal disappears is the point of failure. If there is no sound signal from the system controller, replace the defective system controller or the motherboard.

Symptom 4: The computer does not retain date and time information after computer power is turned off. Fortunately, there are only three elements to an RTC system: the RTC IC, a crystal for the RTC's time base oscillator, and a battery backup to keep the RTC running when power is off. If the RTC loses its contents when computer power is turned off, suspect the battery backup that supports the RTC. In most systems, a small lithium coin cell on the motherboard is used for RTC backup. However, newer RTC designs encapsulate the IC time base crystal and backup battery into a single oversized DIP package. If your RTC uses a discrete battery, use your multimeter to check battery voltage. A lithium cell produces about +3.0 Vdc when fully charged, so voltage around or below +2.0 Vdc suggests a dead battery. Try replacing the battery. If the RTC is a single, integral unit, replace the entire RTC package. The RTC package can be replaced simply and easily.

If the RTC battery measures within an acceptable range, or if the RTC will not keep date and time information at all, use your logic probe to measure clock signals at the RTC's time base oscillator crystal. You should measure a fast pulse signal on each clock pin. If the clock signal is missing, replace the time base crystal. If a new crystal does not restore the clock (or if the RTC is a single, integrated unit), replace the RTC package.

Symptom 5: The parallel port is erratic or inoperative. As with any examination of a peripheral port, your first step should be to check the cable and connectors between the peripheral device and computer. In this case, you should check the printer cable and printer. Make sure the cable is inserted properly at both ends and ensure the printer is turned on and in its on-line mode. Run the printer's self-test to be certain that the printer is operating correctly. As another check, use your computer with another printer that is configured similarly to your original printer. If that printer also behaves badly with your small computer, continue with the examination of your parallel port. If the printer works properly, your parallel port is working correctly. Concentrate your effort on the questionable printer. Refer to the book *Troubleshooting and Repairing Computer Printers* (Windcrest #3923) for in-depth printer repair techniques.

You need a logic probe to measure the parallel port's TTL-level signals. You also need easy access to the cable wires. Insert a 25-pin breakout box between the computer and cable, or disassemble the computer to access the connector's pins on the motherboard. Instruct the computer to output to the parallel port, which is easily done with any application program such as a word processor or painting package. In many cases, the parallel communication port is called LPT1:. Once a print is initiated, use your logic probe to check the Strobe signal leaving the computer. Conventional parallel ports provide the Strobe signal on connector pin 1. During data transfer, the Strobe line should appear as a pulse signal. If the Strobe pulse is missing, data is not being transferred to the computer. Try replacing the communication controller IC.

The Busy and Acknowledge lines are two other important handshaking lines sent back from the printer. Busy (connector pin 11) becomes a logic 1 when the printer has received a byte. When the printer is ready to acquire a new byte, Busy returns to a logic 0 and Acknowledge (connector pin 10) generates a logic 0 pulse to request a new byte. Both of these signals appear as pulse signals during normal data transfer. If either Busy or Acknowledge is missing, data transfer does not take place.

Next, check the data lines. Parallel ports offer 8 data lines (D0 to D7 on connector pins 2 through 9). During data transfer, these lines appear as random pulses on your logic probe. You might see the probe indications shifting between fast and slow pulses since data is unpredictable. If any data line is locked at one logic level, the data bytes might be corrupted, resulting in erratic or faulty data. Replace the communication controller IC. Examine the soldering at each connector pin on the motherboard. Wrenching the connector can result in lead pull-through. Resolder any questionable connections.

As you might see, the communication controller is usually responsible for most of the problems encountered in a parallel port. However, if you do not have the tools or inclination to attempt surface-mount work, replace the entire motherboard.

Symptom 6: The serial port is erratic or inoperative.
Whenever you troubleshoot a peripheral port, your first step should be to check the cable and connections between the peripheral device and computer. Inspect the serial cable and peripheral. Make sure that the cable is inserted and secured properly at both ends, and ensure that your peripheral is on and ready. As another check, try your small computer on another similarly configured peripheral that is known to be good. If that peripheral also behaves badly with your computer, continue checking the serial port. If the peripheral works properly with your computer, the serial

port is probably working correctly, and you should concentrate on the questionable peripheral.

Disassemble your small computer to expose your motherboard and locate the serial port connector. Chances are that the serial port connector is a D-type 9-pin male connector (DB-9M). Attach a serial port breakout box between your port and cable. A breakout box is little more than an adaptor with LEDs to display the conditions of transmitted and received data, as well as the conditions of major handshaking signals, but it is a handy tool for its ability to provide a convenient overview of serial port activity. Figure 9-17 illustrates a simple LED breakout box, which is also designed to handle the wide range of bipolar signal voltages found in serial ports. High bipolar voltages can damage your logic probe. You can find LED breakout boxes in just about any electronics retail store.

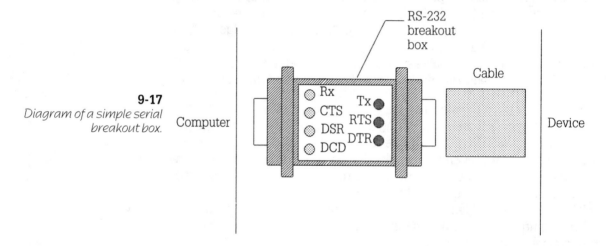

9-17
Diagram of a simple serial breakout box.

Initiate a data transfer over your serial port using any convenient software package, depending on what peripheral you are using. For example, you can drive a serial printer using any standard word processor. The one thing to remember is that your serial port is typically COM1:, and the serial configuration must be set properly for the computer and peripheral device. If communication parameters are not the same, a serial communication link will not work. During normal data transfer, both the Tx and Rx LEDs should illuminate dimly or give some indication of activity. You will also see activity on many of the port's handshaking lines.

If the Tx signal is inactive, your system is not transmitting data. Use your logic probe to check the TTL-level Tx signal entering the line driver IC. You might need a schematic or a detailed block diagram to locate the appropriate IC and pins. If TTL Tx data enters the line driver but does not exit as a bipolar signal, the line driver IC is probably defective and should be replaced. Check the TTL Rx data from the line receiver. If the Rx line is active but no TTL data is leaving the line receiver IC, then replace the defective line receiver. If Rx is inactive at the serial connector, you are not receiving data from the peripheral device, but this might not represent a problem.

Check your handshaking signals next using the same procedure as outlined above. Make sure that any bipolar signal activity on your LED breakout box has corresponding TTL activity at either the line driver or line receiver (depending on whether the handshaking signal is being sent or received). If sent handshaking signals are available as TTL levels at your line driver but are not appearing as bipolar signals at your breakout box, replace the defective line driver IC. If bipolar handshaking signals are received at the serial connector, but are not available as TTL-level signals from the line receiver IC, the line receiver IC should be replaced. You might need a schematic or detailed block diagram of your system to locate and trace each handshaking signal.

If outgoing TTL-level signals, such as Tx, are missing or incoming TTL-level signals are available as expected, you should suspect the communication controller IC. Use your logic probe to check the communication controller clock at the time base crystal. If the clock is missing, replace the time base crystal. If a new crystal fails to restore the clock, replace the communication controller IC. Some systems provide the time base clock from the system controller. If the system controller clock is absent, replace the system controller IC. If the system controller clock is present, replace the defective communication controller.

Your system controller provides a number of interrupt or control lines used to coordinate the communication controller IC. Just what signals are available depends upon your specific small computer, but a schematic or detailed block diagram can usually identify such control signals. Measure each control line with your logic probe. During data transfer, those control lines should each appear as pulse signals. If serial control lines being output by your system controller are missing, replace the system controller IC. If serial control lines being output by your communication controller are missing, replace the communication controller IC.

If your measurements are inconclusive, or if you lack the tools or inclination to perform surface-mount work yourself, you can replace the entire motherboard.

Index of computer, tool, and materials vendors

Legend of vendor codes:

(C) = Computer vendor/manufacturer
(P) = Parts manufacturer/vendor/distributor
(D) = Service/technical data
(T) = Tools and/or test equipment

(P) Active Electronics (national chain)
11 Cummings Park
Woburn, MA 01801
800-677-8899, 617-932-4616

(P) Allied Electronics (national chain)
7410 Pebble Drive
Ft. Worth, TX 76118
800-433-5700, 817-595-3500

(C) Altec Technology Corp.
18555 E. Gale Avenue
Industry, CA 91748
800-255-9971, 818-912-8688

(C) Aquiline, Inc.
449 Main Street
Bennington, VT 05201
800-370-3322, 800-442-1526

(C) AST Research, Inc.
16215 Alton Parkway
P.O. Box 19658
Irvine, CA 92713
800-876-4278, 714-727-4141

(C) Atari Corp.
1196 Borregas Avenue
Sunnyvale, CA 94088
408-745-2031

(C) Austin Computer Systems, Inc.
10300 Metric Boulevard
Austin, TX 78758
800-752-1577, 512-339-3500

(C) BCC
1610 Crane Ct.
San Jose, CA 95112
800-827-4222, 408-944-9000

(C) Blackship Computer Systems, Inc.
2031 O'Toole Avenue
San Jose, CA 95131
800-531-7447, 408-432-7500

(C) Blue Star Computers, Inc.
2312 Central Avenue NE
Minneapolis, MN 55418
800-950-8884, 612-788-5000

(C) Bondwell Industrial Co., Inc.
47485 Seabridge Drive
Fremont, CA 94538
510-490-4300

(C) Casio, Inc.
570 Mt. Pleasant Avenue
P.O. Box 7000
Dover, NJ 07801
201-361-5400

(C) CompuAdd Express
12306 Technology Boulevard
Austin, TX 78727
800-925-3000, 512-219-1800

(C) Compudyne Products
15151 Surveyor Boulevard
Addison, TX 75244
800-932-2667, 214-702-5600

(C) Cumulus Corp.
23500 Mercantile Road
Cleveland, OH 44122
216-464-2211

(C) Dauphin Technology, Inc.
450 Eisenhower Lane
N. Lombard, IL 60148
800-782-7922

(C) Dell Computer Corp.
9505 Arboretum Boulevard
Austin, TX 78759
800-289-3355, 512-338-4400

(P) Digi-Key Corp.
701 Brooks Ave. South
Box 677
Thief River Falls, MN 56701-0677
800-344-4539

(C) Digital Equipment Corp.
146 Main Street
Maynard, MA 01754
800-722-9332

(C) Epson America, Inc.
20770 Madrona Avenue
Torrance, CA 90503
800-922-8911, 310-782-0770

(C) Everex Systems, Inc.
48431 Milmont Drive
Fremont, CA 94538
800-992-3839, 510-498-1111

(C) Fora, Inc.
3096 Orchard Drive
San Jose, CA 95134
800-367-3672, 408-944-0393

(C) Fujitsu Personal Computers, Inc. (Poquet Computer)
650 N. Mary Avenue
Sunnyvale, CA 94086
408-982-9500

(C) Gateway 2000
610 Gateway Drive
P.O. Box 2000
N. Sioux City, SC 57049-2000
800-523-2000, 605-232-2000

(C) GRiDSystems Corp.
47211 Lakeview Boulevard
Fremont, CA 94637
510-656-4700

(C) Hewlett-Packard Co.
1000 NE Circle Boulevard
Corvallis, OR 97330
800-443-1254

(D) Howard W. Sams & Co.
2647 Waterfront Parkway East Drive
Indianapolis, IN 46214
800-428-7267, 317-299-0952

(C) IBM Corp.
1133 Westchester Avenue
White Plains, NY 10604
800-772-2227

(C) Identity Systems Technology, Inc.
1347 Exchange Drive
Richardson, TX 75081
800-723-8258, 214-235-3330

(C) Insight Computers
1912 W. Fourth Street
Tempe, AZ 85281
800-755-9628, 602-350-1176

(C) Intelec Corp.
6075 NW 82nd Avenue
Miami, FL 33166
800-683-0969, 305-594-0001

(C) KRIS Technologies
260 E. Grand Avenue
S. San Francisco, CA 94080
800-282-5747, 415-877-8048

(C) Librex Computer Systems, Inc.
1731 Technology Drive, #700
San Jose, CA 95110
408-441-8500

(C) Master Computer, Inc.
10742 Fifth Avenue NE
Seattle, WA 98125
206-365-1156

(C) Matrix Digital
1811 N. Keystone Street
Burbank, CA 91504
800-227-5723, 818-566-8567

(C) Maxtron
1825A Durfee Avenue S.
El Monte, CA 91733
818-350-5707

(C) Micro Express
1801 Carnegie Avenue
Santa Ana, CA 92705
800-989-9900, 714-852-1400

(C) Micronics Computers, Inc.
232 E. Warren Avenue
Fremont, CA 94539
800-659-5901, 510-651-2308

(C) MicroStar Computers, Inc.
35 Cotters Lane, Building C1
E. Brunswick, NJ 08816
908-651-8686

(C) Micro Telesis, Inc.
17891 Skypark Circle #E
Irvine, CA 92714
714-557-2003

(C) Mitsuba Corp.
1925 Wright Avenue
LaVerne, CA 91750
800-648-7822, 714-392-2000

(C) Momenta Corp.
295 N. Bernardo Avenue
Mountain View, CA 94043
800-666-3682

(C) NBCC USA Corp.
216 Technology Drive, Suite E
Irvine, CA 92718
714-753-8866

(C) National Micro Systems, Inc.
2979-B Pacific Drive
Norcross, GA 30071
800-642-7649

(C) NCR Corp.
1700 S. Patterson Boulevard
Dayton, OH 45479
800-225-5627, 513-445-5000

(C) NEC Technologies, Inc.
1414 Massachusetts Avenue
Foxboro, MA 01719
800-388-8888, 508-264-8000

(P) NTE Electronics, Inc.
44 Farrand Street
Bloomfield, NJ 07003
201-748-5089

(C) OEM Limited, Inc.
70 Flagship Drive
N. Andover, MA 01845
800-878-6427, 508-686-4441

(C) Olivetti ISC Bunker Ramo
22425 E. Apple Way Avenue
Spokane, WA 99019
800-633-9909, 509-927-5600

(C) Packard Bell Electronics, Inc.
9425 Canoga Avenue
Chatsworth, CA 91311
818-886-4600

(C) Phillips Consumer Electronics, Co.
One Phillips Drive
Knoxville, TN 37914-1810
800-835-3504

(P) Phillips ECG Co.
1025 Westminster Drive
Williamsport, PA 17701
717-323-4691

(C) Polywell Computers, Inc.
61-C Airport Boulevard
S. San Francisco, CA 94080
800-999-1278, 415-583-7222

(P) Print Products International
8931 Brookville Road
Silver Spring, MD 20901
800-638-2020, 301-587-7824

(C) Psion Inc.
118 Echo Lake Road
Watertown, CT 06795
203-274-7521

(P) Robec Distributors
425 Privet Road
Horsham, PA 19044
800-223-7087, 215-957-0800

(C) Sanyo Business Systems Corp.
51 Joseph Street
Moonachie, NJ 07074
800-524-0047, 201-440-9300

(C) Sharp Electronics Corp.
P.O. Box 650, Sharp Plaza
Mahwah, NJ 07430
800-237-4277, 201-529-9593

(C) Standard Computer Corp.
12803 Schabarum Avenue
Irwindale, CA 91706
800-662-6111, 818-337-7711

(C) Swan Technologies, Inc.
3075 Research Drive
State College, PA 16804-9959
800-468-9044, 814-238-1820

(C) Tandy Corp.
1800 One Tandy Center
Ft. Worth, TX 76102
817-390-3011

(C) Tangent Computer, Inc.
197 Airport Boulevard
Burlingame, CA 94010
800-223-6677, 415-342-9388

(C) Tartan Computers
44 W. Ferris Street
E. Brunswick, NJ 08816
908-390-1900

(C) Tenex Computer Express
56800 Magnetic Drive
Mishawaka, IN 46545-7481
800-776-6781, 219-259-7051

(C) Texas Instruments, Inc.
P.O. Box 202230
Austin, TX 78720-2230
800-527-3500, 214-995-2011

(C) Toshiba America Information Systems, Inc.
9740 Irvine Boulevard
Irvine, CA 927181
800-334-3445, 714-583-3000

(C) Transource Computers
2033 W. North Lane, #18
Phoenix, AZ 85021
602-997-8101

(C) USA Flex, Inc.
135 N. Brandon Drive
Glendale Heights, IL 60139
708-351-7334

(C) Zenith Data Systems
2150 E. Lake Cook Road
Buffalo Grove, IL 60089
800-553-0331

Summary of troubleshooting charts

Chapter 5
Batteries and power systems
Troubleshooting battery charging circuits

The battery pack does not charge	Check battery pack insertion and connections
	Check/trace the charging voltage
	Replace the battery pack
	Replace the power supply
The system does not run from battery power, but runs from main power alright	Check battery charge and charger
	Check battery pack insertion and connections
	Check bypass diode(s) and limiting diode(s)
	Replace battery pack
Short battery life	Check battery pack insertion and connections
	Check the computer's power saver configuration settings
	Check limiting diode(s)
	Replace battery pack

Troubleshooting linear power supplies

Power supply is completely dead	Check ac input voltage
	Check power switch
	Check main fuse
	Check connectors and wiring
	Check PC board
	Trace supply
Power supply is intermittent; charge lamp may flip on and off.	Check ac input voltage
	Check PC board
	Check for thermal failures
Computer operation erratic; charge lamp may flip on and off.	Check ac input voltage
	Check wiring and connectors
	Trace supply

Troubleshooting inverter supplies

Backlight is inoperative; LCD appears washed out or invisible in low light	Check dc source voltage
	Check ac inverter output
	Check/replace backlight panel or CCFT(s)
	Check/replace inverter board

Troubleshooting dc-dc converters

The computer is dead or acting erratically. Both the ac-powered supply and battery pack check OK.	Check dc source voltage
	Check dc output voltage
	Check/replace limiting diode(s)
	Check/replace dc-dc converter IC
	Check/replace output filter capacitor(s)
	Check replace regulator IC(s)

Chapter 6
Display systems
Troubleshooting flat-panel displays

One or more pixels defective. Pixel(s)may be black, white or a fixed color.	Replace the display assembly
	Replace video RAM IC(s)
Poor LCD visibility. Display easily washed out by ambient light.	Check contrast control and voltage
	Check backlight voltage and inverter power supply

	Check/replace backlight CCFT(s) or EL panel
Poor plasma visibility. Low display brightness.	Check brightness control and voltage level(s) Check plasma drive voltage(s)
Display is dark. No visible activity. The computer seems to boot normally.	Check all connectors and wiring Check display supply voltage(s) Check/replace the display controller IC Replace the display assembly

The display is erratic. Shows disassociated characters and garbage.	Check all connectors and wiring
	Check/replace the display controller IC
	  and/or: Replace video RAM IC(s)
	  or: Replace the main logic PC board.
	Replace the display assembly

Chapter 7
Hard, floppy, & card drives
Troubleshooting floppy drive systems

Drive is dead. Disk does not initialize when inserted.	Check diskette and disk insertion Check all connectors and wiring Check drive power Replace floppy drive Replace the floppy controller IC
Drive does not seek. All other operations appear OK.	Inspect the mechanical assembly Check drive power Check physical interface for floppy controller/drive failure
Drive does not spin. All other operations appear OK.	Inspect the mechanical assembly Check drive power Check physical interface for floppy controller/drive failure
Disk not being read/written. All other operations appear OK.	Check/replace the diskette Gently clean the read/write heads Check physical interface for floppy controller/drive failure

Troubleshooting hard drive systems

Hard drive does not function properly
(if it all). Check computer setup configuration
All other functions appear OK. Check all connectors and wiring
Check drive power
Check/replace hard drive
Replace hard drive controller IC

Troubleshooting memory card systems

SRAM or flash card loses its memory Check/replace any backup batteries
when powered down or removed from . Replace the memory card
the system cannot access the card for reading Verify card compatibility
(or writing) Check the write-protect switch
Check the card's insertion
Inspect card connector(s)
Replace the memory card
Replace memory card controller IC

Chapter 8
Keyboards, trackballs, & pen systems
Troubleshooting a keyboard

Keyboard is completely dead. No keys Check keyboard connectors
function at all. Check keyboard data for fault in keyboard controller or
system controller IC

Keyboard acting erratically. One or more Clean the keyboard assembly
keys intermittent or inoperative. Clean suspect key contacts
Replace defective key switches
Check keyboard PC board
Replace the keyboard assembly

Keyboard acting erratically. One or more Check for short circuits from foreign objects
keys stuck or repeating. Clean suspect key contacts
Replace defective key switches
Replace the keyboard assembly

Troubleshooting a trackball

The trackball cursor appears but moves erractically (if at all) as ball moves.	Check the trackball connector Clean the trackball Check trackball cable integrity Replace the trackball unit
One or both trackball keys function erratically (if at all).	Clean trackball switches Check trackball cable integrity Replace the trackball unit

Troubleshooting pen systems

Stylus works intermittently.	Check stylus wiring and connection Replace the stylus Check/replace resistive overlay
Stylus totally inoperative.	Check stylus contact on overlay Check stylus wiring and connection Replace the stylus Check/replace overlay controller Check/replace bus interface
Ink does not appear directly under stylus.	Check/replace the digitizer overlay

Chapter 9
Main logic boards
Troubleshooting core functions

The computer does not start.	Check power or batteries Check power confirmation signal at system controller IC Check clock signal at CPU and system controller IC Check chip select at BIOS ROM Examine address and data lines Replace the motherboard
You see a memory error.	Check refresh signals from system controller IC Check R/W signal from system controller IC Check DRAM address lines from system controller IC Check DRAM data lines from system controller IC or CPU

	Replace faulty DRAM ICs or expansion module
	Replace the motherboard
Speaker/buzzer does not work.	Check application program
	Check connector and wiring
	Check sound signal to system controller IC
	Replace speaker or buzzer
Will not keep date or time	Check RTC backup battery
	Check RTC clock signal
	Replace RTC IC or module
Parallel port erratic or inoperative.	Check printer cable and connectors
	Check Strobe signal
	Check Busy and Acknowledge signals
	Check data lines
	Replace the communication controller IC
	Replace the motherboard
Serial port erratic or inoperative.	Check peripheral cable and connectors
	Check Tx and Rx lines
	Check handshaking signals
	Check controller clock signals
	Check communication controller interrupt or select signals from system controller IC
	Replace the motherboard

Glossary

address   A unique set of numbers that identifies a particular location in computer memory.

anode   The positive electrode of a two-terminal semiconductor device.

ANSI   American National Standards Institute. An organization that sets standards for languages, database management, etc.

architecture   Describes how a system is constructed and how its components are put together. An open architecture refers to a nonproprietary system design that allows other manufacturers to design products that work with the system.

ASCII   American Standard Code for Information Interchange. A set of standard codes defining characters and symbols used by computers.

asynchronous   Circuit operation in which signals can arrive at any point in time. A coordinating clock is not required.

attribute memory   PCMCIA cards provide fixed memory space to hold basic card information and configuration data.

base   One of the three leads of a bipolar transistor.

batch file   An ASCII file that combines several DOS commands into a single file.

baud   The rate at which bits are transferred between devices.

bezel   A metal or plastic frame fitting over the LCD glass that holds part of the display system together.

BIOS   Basic input/output system. A series of programs that handle the computer's low-level functions.

bit   Binary digit. The basic unit of digital information written as a 0 or a 1.

block   A fixed-length sequence of bytes on a memory card. A structure similar to sectors on a magnetic disk.

boot   The process of initializing a computer and loading a disk operating system (DOS).

boot device   A drive containing the files and information for a disk operating system.

boot sector   A section of a hard disk that holds information defining the physical characteristics and partitioning of the drive, as well as a short program that begins the DOS loading process.

bpi   Bits per inch. The number of bits placed in a linear inch of disk space.

buffer   A temporary storage place for data.

byte   A set of eight bits. A byte is approximately equivalent to a character.

C   A symbol representing the normal charge capacity of a battery.

cache memory   Simply called "cache." Part of a computer's RAM operating as a buffer between the system RAM and CPU. Recently used data or instructions are stored in cache. RAM is accessed quickly, so data called for again is available right away, improving overall system performance.

capacitance   The measure of a device's ability to store an electric charge. The unit of capacitance is the farad.

capacitor   An electronic device used to store energy in the form of an electric charge.

cathode   The negative electrode of a two-terminal semiconductor device.

CCFT   Cold-cathode fluorescent tube. The light source used in edgelighting liquid crystal displays so that the display is visible in low light or darkness.

cell   Also known as a battery. An electromechanical device capable of storing an electrical charge.

cell gap   The space between two pieces of glass that contains the fluid liquid crystal.

CGA   Color graphics adaptor. A low-resolution graphics mode featuring 320×200 resolution four-color or 640×200 resolution two-color operation; commonly found in pen computers and older laptop systems.

chip carrier   A rectangular or square package with I/O connections on all four sides.

cluster   The smallest unit of disk storage defined as one or more contiguous sectors.

CMOS   Complementary metal-oxide semiconductor. A type of MOS transistor commonly used in digital integrated circuits for high-speed, low-power operation.

collector   One of the three leads of a bipolar transistor.

configuration   The components that make up a computer's hardware setup.

contiguous   All together, or one right after another. Usually refers to files that are not fragmented or on separate sectors of a hard disk. Contiguous files can be accessed more quickly than fragmented or noncontiguous files.

contrast ratio   The difference in luminance between a selected (ON) pixel and an unselected (OFF) pixel.

control characters   ASCII characters that do not print out but are used to control communication.

CPU   Central processing unit. The primary functioning unit of a computer system. Also called a microprocessor.

cyclical redundancy check   An error-checking technique for data recording typically used by systems that perform hardware error checking.

cylinder   A collection of tracks located one above the other on the platters of a hard drive.

dichroic host   Also known as guest host. A type of liquid crystal fluid in which color dye is added.

DMA   Direct memory access. A fast method of moving data from a storage device directly to RAM.

DOS   Disk operating system. A program or set of programs that directs the operations of a disk-based computing system.

DOS extender   Software that uses the capabilities of advanced microprocessors running under DOS to access more than 640K of RAM.

dot   Also called a pixel. A single picture element of a flat-panel display. Pixels are typically rectangular.

drain   One of the three leads of a field-effect transistor.

EGA   Enhanced graphics adaptor. A medium-resolution graphics mode featuring up to 640×350 resolution, 16 color operation; commonly available in older notebook systems.

EIA   Electronics Industry Association. A standards organization in the USA that develops specifications for interface equipment.

EIAJ   A Japanese standards organization that is the equivalent of the US Joint Electronic Device Engineering Council (JEDEC).

EL   Electroluminescent. Material that glows when voltage is applied across it. Many monochrome LCDs use a sheet of EL material as a backlight so the LCD can be seen in darkness.

electrolyte   A chemical compound that allows ions to flow between the electrodes of a battery in order to create a potential difference.

emitter   One of the three leads of a bipolar transistor.

EMS   Extended memory system. A highly-integrated IC controller used to access extra RAM.

ESD   Electrostatic discharge. The sudden, accidental release of electrons accumulated in the body or inanimate objects. Static charges are destructive to MOS ICs and other semiconductors.

ESDI   Enhanced small device interface. A popular physical interface for large-capacity hard drives that replaced the ST-506 interface. ESDI can transfer data up to 10Mb per second.

FAT   File allocation table. A table recorded on disk that keeps track of which clusters and sectors are available, which have been used by files, and which are defective.

file   A collection of related information that is stored together on disk.

file attributes   The DOS identification that denotes the characteristics of a file: copy-protected, read-only, or archival.

flatpack   One of the oldest surface-mount packages with 14 to 50 ribbon leads on both sides of its body.

form factor   A reference to the general size class of a system or device such as a hard drive.

fragmentation   The state of a hard disk on which files are stored in two or more small pieces across a disk rather than contiguously.

FSTN   Film-compensated STN. A modified version of super-twist nematic liquid crystal material.

gate   One of the three leads of a field-effect transistor.

ghosting   A phenomenon where voltage from an energized element leaks to an adjacent OFF element, which seems to turn the OFF element partially on. An effect typically found in passive matrix LCDs.

GUI   Graphic user interface. Software that allows a user to interact with a program.

head   A device consisting of tiny wire coils that moves across the surface of floppy or hard disks. Heads are used to read or write information to disks.

head actuator   The mechanism that moves a read/write head radially across the surface of a hard or floppy disk.

high memory   The RAM locations residing between 640K and 1Mb.

hot insertion/removal   The ability to insert or remove a memory card from a system with the system power turned on.

ICMA   International Card Manufacturers Association.

IDE   Integrated Drive Electronics. A physical interface standard commonly used in medium to large hard drives. IDE control electronics are housed in the drive itself instead of an external control board.

inductance   The measure of a device's ability to store a magnetic charge. The unit of inductance is the henry (H).

inductor   An electronic device used to store energy in the form of a magnetic charge.

ink   In pen computing, ink is the term used for the display pixels that mark where the pen has traveled against its digitizer.

ISO   International Standards Organization.

JEDEC   Joint Electronic Device Engineering Council. The U.S. standards organization that handles packaging standards.

JEIDA   Japanese Electronics Industry Development Association.

LCD   Liquid crystal display. A display technology using a thin layer of liquid crystal sandwiched between two electrodes. An electric field across the liquid crystal causes the crystals to rotate and appear opaque.

LIF   Low insertion force. A term used to describe sockets that require only a minimum force to insert or extract an IC.

logic analyzer   An instrument used to monitor signals of an integrated circuit or system.

MCP   Math coprocessor. A sophisticated processing IC intended to enhance the processing of a computer by performing floating point math operations instead of the CPU.

MFM   Modified frequency modulation. The most widely used method of encoding binary data on a disk.

motherboard   In a small computer, the major PC board containing the CPU, core memory, and most of the system's controller ICs. Also called the main logic board.

operating system   The interface between the hardware and software running on your PC.

page   A reference to a block of memory in a computer.

parallel port   A physical connection on a computer used to connect output devices. Data is transmitted as multiple bits sent together over separate wires.

Typically used to connect a printer.

parity   A means of error checking using an extra bit added to each transmitted character.

PCMCIA   Personal Computer Memory Card Industry Association.

permeable   The ability of a material to be magnetized.

pitch   The center-to-center dimension between adjacent pixels.

pixel   Pixel element. A single dot element of a computer display. See **dot**.

platter   An actual disk inside a hard disk drive that carries the magnetic recording material.

polarizers   Sheet material made of polymer acetate incorporated with iodide molecules. The molecules allow scattered light to enter in one plane only. TN LCDs require two polarizers, one in front and one in back.

POST   Power on self-test. A program in BIOS that handles the computer's initialization and self-test before loading DOS.

primary battery   A battery that is useful for only a single discharge.

printer driver   A data file describing the attributes of a particular printer. The data is used by application programs.

QWERTY   The term for a standard typewriter-style keyboard. The first row of letters begin: Q, W, E, R, T, Y, U, I, etc.

resistance   The measure of a device's opposition to the flow of current. The unit of resistance is the ohm (Ω).

resistor   A device used to limit the flow of current in an electronic circuit.

RLL   Run length limited. A technique for encoding binary data on a hard disk that can pack up to 50% more data than MFM recording.

RS-232   A standard for transmitting serial data.

SCSI   Small Computer System Interface. A physical interface standard for large to huge (up to 3Gb) hard drives.

secondary battery   A battery that can be recharged and discharged through multiple cycles.

sector   The smallest unit of storage on the surface of a floppy or hard disk.

serial port   A physical connection on a computer used to connect output devices. Data is transmitted as individual bits sent one at a time over a single wire. Typically used to connect a modem or mouse.

SIMM   Single in-line memory module. A quantity of extra RAM mounted onto a PC board terminated with a single, convenient connector.

SMT   Surface-mount technology.

source   One of the three leads of a field-effect transistor.

spindle   The part of a hard or floppy drive that rotates the disks.

spindown   The process of removing power and decelerating a hard drive to a halt.

spinup   The process of applying power and accelerating a hard drive to running speed.

ST   Super twist. An improved liquid crystal material that is more stable and provides much better contrast than regular twisted nematic liquid crystal. Also called STN for super twisted nematic.

ST-506   The oldest physical interface standard for small hard drives (under 40Mb) with a data transfer rate of only 5 Mbits per second.

synchronous   Circuit operation where signals are coordinated through the use of a master clock.

TFT   Thin film transistor. A fabrication technology used in flat-panel displays where transistors that operate each pixel are fabricated right onto flat-panel displays.

TN   Twisted nematic. A type of liquid crystal material.

track   The circular path traced across the surface of a spinning disk by a read/write head. A track consists of one or more clusters.

transfer rate   The speed at which a hard or floppy drive can transfer information between its media and the CPU, typically measured in Mbits per second.

TSR   Terminate and stay resident. A program residing in memory that can be invoked from other application programs.

TST   Triple super twist. An improved liquid crystal material that provides better contrast than regular super twist liquid crystal.

TTL   Transistor transistor logic. Digital logic ICs using bipolar transistors.

viewing angle   A conceptual cone perpendicular to the LCD where the display can be seen clearly.

VGA   Video graphics array. A high-resolution graphics mode featuring 640×480 16-color and 320×200 256-color resolutions; widely available in pen computers and notebook systems.

Bibliography

Alting-Mees, Adrian. 1991. *The Hard Drive Encyclopedia*. San Diego, Ca.: Annabooks.

Anonymous. 1992. "Card Related Terms and Abbreviations," *Memory Card Systems & Design*. 2 (1): 38–40.

Arrow Electronics Corporation. 1992. *1992 Arrow Systems Product Guide*. Melville, NY.

Bigelow, Stephen J. 1990. "Designing Power Supply Circuits," *Popular electronics*. 7 (2): 35–41, 102.

_____. 1990. "All About Batteries," *Popular electronics*. 7 (88): 57–63, 99.

Bond, John. 1992. "Testing Flat-panel Displays," *Test and Measurement World*. May: 61–62.

Barr, Christopher. 1992. "Pen PCs," *PC Magazine*. November 10: 175–203.

GRiD Systems Corporation. 1991. *Computer Technical Reference Manual*. Fremont, Ca.

_____. 1991. *GRiDPAD-HD/GRiDPAD-RC Computer Service Manual*. Fremont, Ca.

Gupta, Sandeep. 1992. *Low-power Design Issues Regarding Flat Panels*. San Jose, Ca.: S-MOS Systems, Inc.

Hall, V. Douglas. 1980. *Microprocessors and Digital Systems*. New York, NY: McGraw-Hill.

Howard, Bill. 1992. "High-end Notebook PCs," *PC Magazine*. April 14: 113–143.

Integral Peripherals, Inc. *Product Manual for the Stingray*. Boulder, Co.

Margolis, Art. 1991. *Troubleshooting and Repairing Personal Computers, 2nd ed.* Blue Ridge Summit, Pa.: Windcrest/McGraw-Hill.

Matzkin, Howard. 1991. "Palmtop PCs: Power by the Ounce." *PC Magazine*. July: 197–226.

Osborne, Adam. 1980. *An Introduction to Microcomputers*. V1, 2nd ed. Berkely, Ca.: Osborne/McGraw-Hill.

Prosise, Jeff. 1992. "Tutor" [monthly column]. *PC Magazine*. April 28: 359–362.

Quantum Corporation. 1989. *ProDrive 40S/80S Product Manual*. Milpitas, Ca.

Rosch, Winn L. 1991" Choosing and using hard disks," *PC Magazine*. December 31: 313–331.

Seiko Instruments USA. 1992. *Liquid Crystal Display Modules*. Torrance, Ca.

Sharp Corporation, Information Systems Division. 1990. *Sharp Service Manual OZ/IQ-8000 & OZ/IQ-8200*. Yamatokoriyama, Nara (Japan).

Tandy Corporation. 1990. *Service Manual: Tandy 1500HD Laptop Computer*. Ft. Worth, Tx.

Tillinghase, Charles. 1992. "IC DRAM Technology and Usage," *Memory Card Systems & Design*. 2 (1): 28–31.

Toshiba America Information Systems. 1992. *Color LCD Technology in Toshiba Portable Computers*. Irvine, Ca.

_____. 1988. *T5100 Maintenance Manual*. Irvine, Ca.

_____. 1992. *T6400 Maintenance Manual*. Irvine, Ca.

Index